Richard Matlick

Metaphoresis

*Do We Know
What We Are
Talking About?*

Erica House

BALTIMORE   AMSTERDAM   SALAMANCA

Copyright 1998 by Richard Mat

First printing

ISBN: 1-893162-01-X

PUBLISHED BY ERICA HOUSE BOOK PUBLISHERS
www.ericahouse.com
Baltimore   Amsterdam   Salamanca

Printed in the United States of America

DEDICATION

*This
book
is
for
my wife Martha
who
has
kept
the
faith*

*and shares my gratitude to Kathy Moore, the first reader beyond
the walls of our own house, and to Susan Myers, the librarian
who somehow always managed to find the books I needed.*

Foreword

THIS book is about the mental models that humans employ in their daily contests with some of the more intractable problems of existence. More precisely, it is about how their metaphorical language can reveal those models, can allow them to be pulled up from the murky depths of the unconscious for examination. It is, therefore, an effort to explain, to myself, the persistence of certain problems—or, rather, our failure to solve them—in terms of the mental models that constitute understanding and thus shape attempted solutions. It is, more precisely, the artifact of my personal search for understanding of myself and others of this strange species. If I've got a problem, what am I thinking and saying, and subsequently doing, that is wrong? That is, what is wrong with my mental models?

It is neither wildly conjectural, as lawyers and other gored oxen will contend, nor cruelly prescriptive, as the moralists will cry, but predominantly descriptive, and the part that is not descriptive is personal commentary within the bounds of informed civility. I have gathered—and continue to gather—hundreds of actual human utterances that occurred within a certain context of interest and then examined them to discover metaphors; I have examined—and continue to examine—those metaphors to discover the models that guided the utterances and, presumably, the accompanying actions. I have also employed the inferred models in an attempt to explain a few strange individual and institutional behaviors. It is in that sense science. I have also at least pointed in the direction of alternative models, and it is in that sense philosophy. To the extent that the commentary transgresses the bounds of science, philosophy, and informed civility, it is satire.

It is *not* to be regarded as formal scholarship within any of the academic disciplines on which I have drawn: literature, psychology, archeology, anthropology, linguistics, philosophy, religion; and I am not certain that this is an exhaustive list. I have at times made assertions lawful to my own academic discipline, literature, but even here I confess that my old professors of times long past would most likely have frowned and sent me off to the library again. Perhaps I should say that this book does not represent scholarship but rather the use of it; scholars and scientists produce knowledge to increase the human estate, while I, on the other hand, use knowledge the way ordinary folk should: to increase my size by consuming it, to solve problems, to answer questions because they are there and thus affirm that I am different from my dog, lovable chap though he is.

As for the notion of scholarship, I plead that I am not yet sure of the difference between a *school* and a *scheme* and that if ever I am I may—even though I detest standing in lines—perform an act of contrition. But for now, even as I write, I struggle with the certain knowledge that I do not know what I am talking about, and as I read—as I must to avoid being alone in this black hole—that the greatest of intellects also do not know. They—we—are always more uncertain than they have any way of knowing because their principal instrument of knowing, the human mind, is—to an extent we do not know—unknown, and let no one remind me that this sort of remark is commonplace, even trite. I know that it is; I have seen and heard the empirical evidence of many such remarks: "It is better to light one candle than to..." And as for the notion of discipline, as generally understood and which one would expect to guide and restrain scholarship, I freely admit that I have gone wherever my bloodhound's nose has led me. Neither fence, nor wall, nor door has deterred me, and I hold myself guiltless of any and all transgressions. I have merely done the bidding of the hunter behind me, and let no one suggest that I am that hunter. I could not obey yet another model.

Why the title, metaphoresis?[1] This book, I say again, is *not* a *formal* treatise. It is, rather, a much more fleshy attempt to understand my fellow humans—especially those who are members of my immediate civilization and whose fates are thus linked to my own—in terms of their utterances, the pointed and deliberate, of course, but more importantly the visceral and unconscious.[2] Put it this way: You can discover much about a human by examining his urine; I hold that you can also discover much by examining the language that comes from him. In both urine and language there is evidence of hidden processes and events that can explain at least some of the problems.[3] You will, of course, be quick to point out that many brilliant scholars have spent their lives working within the *formal disciplines* that examine both urine and language. And I will be quick to agree— and to assert that I have made my appeals. Most of my life I have done what the lay person should do in seeking understanding, but finally I have come to the realization that none of us know what we are talking about.

Nevertheless, I have in my hands these strange seeds that I have found, and I intend to plant them, just to see what might grow. Standing here on this primordial bank, the flood having receded, I see that the ground has been well prepared. Carl Jung, I believe, did the plowing though he did not clear the trees. Many others before him, including such ancient ones as Socrates and Plato and Aristotle, did that. Thousands of laborers in these fields have harrowed and raked. Of these lesser tillers after Jung, I feel compelled to mention S. G. F. Brandon, Noam Chomsky, Walter A. Shelburne, and Paul M. Churchland, certainly not because they are all famous, nor because they are all indispensable to the chain of knowledge, but rather because they were the most important lights along my way.

An iconoclast I am not. I love icons and would never break one, not even in a paroxysm of high dudgeon. An icon, after all, is but a tip rising above the surface of a mystery, and I also love a mystery. Nor would I put an ice pack on a swollen appendix; the relief is momentary and the denial deadly.

Finally, in making my apology, I must acknowledge my debt to Plato, Aristophanes, and Jonathan Swift. Some will suggest that my debt includes abject apology.

1

An Introductory Dialog

Persons of the dialog:
PROTAGORAS: an ancient Greek philosopher, sophist, and progenitor of all lawyers. His ungracious demeanor may be explained by his having been called from his grave to participate.

AUTHOR: an amateur cynic.

THE CHORUS: consisting of various pundits, sages, inquisitors, and ducks.

THE SCENE: A duck pond.

PROTAGORAS: Tell me, Author, what is that you are throwing about?

AUTHOR: It is corn. I am feeding the ducks.

PROTAGORAS: I was summoned here to watch you feed ducks?

AUTHOR: No. You were summoned here to disprove my argument. If you can do that, I can give up this madness and return to my usual occupation.

PROTAGORAS: Which is?

AUTHOR: Flying.

PROTAGORAS: Flying? You mean like these ducks? When they are not eating your corn?

AUTHOR: Yes. Like these ducks.

PROTAGORAS: Why would you want to do that? They do fly well but they land so ungracefully. And what do they know of virtue or of right living?

CHORUS: Are we being offended?

AUTHOR: You see, I do tell the truth. What you see is what you get.

PROTAGORAS: Wonderful! And only a sophomore!

CHORUS: Tell us, learned gentlemen, which quacking are we to attend to? There is so much of that on this little pond, and we

8

have not been told what we are to do. Are we to dance and sing? Moralize? What?

PROTAGORAS: I will tell you, dissonants, that I did not come from my grave to be desecrated. I have come to refute this aged sophomore's argument, and when I have done that I will return to my doom and be done with your taunts.

CHORUS: Wonderful! Let us hear the argument.

PROTAGORAS: Come, Author, stop feeding your ducks and tell us, what is the proposition of this argument I am to disprove?

AUTHOR: That our system of justice is hopelessly, fatally flawed and has always been so.

PROTAGORAS: What! You taunt me too! I shall take my leave!

AUTHOR: No, I do not taunt you. I bear the burden of believing that this is true.

PROTAGORAS: Tell me, my dear duck, how did you come upon this wondrous belief?

AUTHOR: Just by listening and watching and reading.

PROTAGORAS: Just by listening and watching and reading! In what schools were you taught? Have you never learned to reason? Have you no logic? No virtue?

AUTHOR: I have never attended very well to school.

PROTAGORAS: What! You brought me here to listen to you and you never went to school!

AUTHOR: I went to many schools but never attended very well.

PROTAGORAS: You cannot have it both ways. How can you say you went to school if you did not attend?

CHORUS: Please! Please! Stop embarrassing the ducks and get on with the argument!

AUTHOR: I was there but did not heed.

PROTAGORAS: You did not pay attention?

AUTHOR: I paid tuition. I got inattention.

PROTAGORAS: You did not each day feel that you were better than the day before? You did not increase in virtue, in wisdom, and in love of justice? You were not told the truth?

AUTHOR: What is truth?

PROTAGORAS: Great Zeus! Why have you sent me here? Have I not been tormented enough?

9

CHORUS: What of our torment? Can we hear the argument?

AUTHOR: I certainly became better at debauchery, at cynicism, and at defiance of the Authority I detested. But of virtue I did not partake because of the examples that were set for me, and I saw at once that wit was more to be desired than wisdom. I thought learning would be a wonderful revelation, but the more was revealed to me the more I wondered.

PROTAGORAS: You did not wonder, you questioned—and did not get the answers you expected. All sophomores have the same problem. You will outgrow it.

AUTHOR: I did learn to endure. Until this latest revelation.

PROTAGORAS: And again you are tormented. But why me? Why have I been chosen for this?

CHORUS: You two know nothing of torment! Let us hear the argument!

AUTHOR: No doubt because of your reputation. It is said that you are the greatest of twisters, that you can get anyone to believe—or at least say—almost anything.

PROTAGORAS: And you want me to persuade you that your proposition is not true?

AUTHOR: Yes. If you can. And if I should become a sophist in the meantime, so much the better. I have read Plato and am thus well prepared for your teachings.

PROTAGORAS: If what you say is true, then of course I can. I will simply teach you to listen, watch, and read differently.

CHORUS: Something has gone awry here.

AUTHOR: As you shall hear, something has been awry, since long before this great philosopher argued in the assembly.

PROTAGORAS: Let us hear. And we shall weigh.

AUTHOR: Yes! Yes! Socrates said that you are indeed a skillful weigher, and I want to know much more about that.

PROTAGORAS: Yes! Yes! Yes! Let us hear the argument.

CHORUS: Yes! Yes! Yes! Yes! Let us hear the argument.

AUTHOR: Very well. I begin. Just for the sake of argument, let us say that you are concerned about crime.

PROTAGORAS: Yes, I am. And my concern is growing by the moment.

CHORUS: Let us have more corn. Our hunger is growing by the moment.

AUTHOR: Let us say that you have noticed that violent crime is rampant, that everywhere in our society murder, assault, robbery, rape, and other forms of criminal violence grow ever more common. Speaking figuratively, you say that we are losing our streets, though what you mean, whether consciously or not, is that we are losing our civilization, just as the ancient Romans lost theirs. You have seen that our criminal courts are overwhelmed and often give up even a pretense of the administration of justice. More and more frequently, you note as you watch the evening news, persons arrested for violent crimes are found to be free on bail while awaiting trial for previous violent crimes. But, you are appalled to discover, as prisons fill to capacity, sentences are reduced—as a means of creating more space—to absurdly short periods of time, and you must conclude that our prisons have become mere temporary holding pens for an ever smaller fraction of an ever growing population of criminals, that at any moment perhaps one dangerous criminal in twenty is restrained through imprisonment while the other nineteen have free access to their victims. What is sanctimoniously called the criminal justice system seems to you to be only another failed institution. You have listened to endless commentary and you know that the people in general blame the courts, the government, and perhaps even the police, that sociologists blame social conditions and all social policy for which they are not directly responsible, that lawyers blame a lack of courts and prison space, that politicians blame the lack of tax revenues with which to build more prisons, and that demographers blame relative increases in the crime-prone segment of the population. And perhaps you have noticed that only law itself and its underlying concepts seem to have escaped blame.

PROTAGORAS: May I remind you that this is your civilization, not mine? In my day we knew what to do with criminals.

AUTHOR: So I understand - by the words of Plato. You would deter the criminal by teaching him to be virtuous.

PROTAGORAS: That is not true! I meant that this was Athenian justification for the punishment of criminals, that punishment teaches virtue. I myself would favor exile or death for those who could not learn it. To be ignorant of carpentry is merely to be unskilled but to be without virtue is to be uncivilized. The barbarian may build well his house but if he cannot bring virtue to it he cannot be civilized.

CHORUS: Please, Protagoras, let us hear Author's tedious argument.

AUTHOR: If these are your thoughts, then listen to this tedious argument. It may disturb you, amuse you, bore you, or even offend you as preposterous, but there is a chance—just a chance— that it will startle you, as it did me, into a new way of looking at the problem of crime.

These factors that we all point to—lack of prisons, too few police officers, inundated courts, incompetent government, social conditions, and on and on—certainly do influence the amount of crime we endure, but we have focused on them for many years without success. We have built more prisons, hired more police officers, established more courts. We have enacted more stringent laws, taken sentencing discretion from judges, and in some cases removed the possibility of parole. These are steps that we have taken in good faith and at considerable expense, but crime continues unabated and the criminals, to employ a metaphor we may have to take more seriously, seem to be winning. And our protests avail us nothing. All that we common folk perceive to be wrong with the administration of justice the lawyers tell us is absolutely necessary for the protection of the rights of the accused, and without these rights, we have come to believe, we would all be in danger. Perhaps, but this view was certainly more credible fifty or a hundred years ago, before the threat of violent crime became so grave. Now, the abject failure of our system of criminal justice must be apparent to us all, and all of the postulates and tenets of that system must be held suspect. We should begin to understand that this claim the lawyers make— that the failed system must continue to be what it is, though perhaps with minor adjustments here and there—begs the question of how we should deal with violently antisocial behavior. Their argument seems to go something like this: the system that results in criminals going free to continue their crimes must not be altered for fear that the innocent will become victims of the system. If that is indeed their argument, perhaps we could conclude that we may choose between being victims of criminals or victims of the criminal justice system. Perhaps we could conclude that there is nothing to choose, that we are all simply victims of the criminal justice system. Since the present system is presumably the invention of the legal establishment, perhaps we could go one step further and conclude that we are simply the victims of lawyers. You may recall that the common people of some past civilizations were the victims of a priesthood devoted entirely to its own welfare and the security of its masters.

PROTAGORAS: Marvelous! Do you, these days, actually listen to what lawyers say?

CHORUS: Please, Protagoras, don't interrupt!

AUTHOR: After so much hard experience with the failure of this most crucial institution of civilization, perhaps we should consider the possibility that we have missed something important, perhaps something fundamental. Before we humans could begin to exercise the power of modern science, we had to drastically alter our understanding of the universe we beheld. Against the overwhelming urging of intuition, we had, for example, to give up our belief that the ground on which we stood was the center of the universe. Likewise with medicine. Before we could begin to conquer disease, we had to discard ancient beliefs about the human body, about the nature of living things. Perhaps now our understanding of the regulation of human behavior is due for such a fundamental revision, and perhaps this revision is a necessary condition for the survival of civilization.

PROTAGORAS: The universe *is* what you behold!

CHORUS: Please!

AUTHOR: In recent years we have read and heard much about crime. Because it has struck at so many of us, it has become one of our principal concerns. But all that we have read and heard has rested on ages-old ways of beholding crime and the criminal, ways that we do not examine because they are for the most part unconscious. Listen to us as we talk about crime:[1]

A man in the street, responding to a question about a particular crime, says of the accused: "He must pay for this crime."

A murderer who has been criticized for serving a ludicrously brief sentence says, "I have paid my debt to society."

In a report on the pending release of a serial rapist, the reporter says, "He claims that he has paid his debt to society and should be released."

A news report on a street demonstration protesting the release of a serial rapist showed a sign carried by a demonstrator. It read: "Make all criminals pay their debt to society."

During a news report, a prosecutor who helped convict John Wayne Gacy for the murder of thirty-three young men said, "John Wayne Gacy got an easier death than he deserved, but the important thing is that he paid for his crime with his life."

During a news report on proposed changes to the parole system, the reporter said, "... people are tired of criminals getting a discount on their debt to society."

Talking about the problem of crime, a politician says, "We must increase the criminal's cost of doing business."

Commenting on the causes for the increases in crime in recent years, a researcher says, "Society does not charge a high enough price for crime."

During a televised report on the controversial acquittal of murder charges against a celebrity athlete, a law professor says, "In our system the scales are heavily weighted in favor of the innocent."

This, you may have noticed for the first time, is the language of the marketplace, of buying and selling, of business, of exchange. It most decidedly is not the language of desperate struggle against the darkness of human nature. But it is merely metaphorical language, you will argue; we do not mean that crime *is* exchange in the marketplace, only that crime seems somewhat like business or exchange in that, for example, if you give me this basket of grain—blow to the head— then I will give you this fine fish—ax to your neck. That is, with a willing suspension of logic, with full knowledge of our deliberate falsehood, we say that two things are the same so that, in some sense, the hidden will be revealed, so that, at least tentatively, the unknown will be known.

PROTAGORAS: I ask you, Author, to stop putting words in my mouth. I find them distasteful.

AUTHOR: Feeding you this way is simply a rhetorical device, but did I not think that I might have taken these very words from your own mouth I would not have put them back. I might have learned this from you had I had the good fortune to be your student.

PROTAGORAS: You presume to tell Protagoras about rhetoric! Had you been my student you should have learned some virtue, and I should have been a man of his word!

AUTHOR: Upon my word, I meant no disrespect. I have only proceeded as I thought you might. But to get back to your argument. You should add that the earliest of humans seem to have extended their linguistic grasp of their world in this way but that they had no need to suspend logic for they had not yet invented it. For them the river as god—that is, as a great human—posed no problems, but for civilized humans, especially those of enormously complex advanced civilizations, there is a problem: logic must at some time be brought back to remind us of the tentativeness, and deliberate falsehood, of our conceptions. Else we must think and act irrationally, without regard for demonstrable reality.

In resorting to this metaphor, you go on, we use certain terms from the marketplace that clearly do not *literally* apply to crime; we cannot rationally claim that crime *is* commerce or exchange, that a murderer, for example, can simply exchange something of value for the life of his victim. Rather, we must conclude that we use them *figuratively*, that is, imaginatively or fancifully, to help us comprehend and deal with crime, much in the way that an infant might call the sun a ball. And that use, in itself, is not a problem, you will point out; the problem is that with the passage of time, and apparently a great deal of time, the situation that gave us the figurative terms has been forgotten—perhaps we should say submerged in the unconscious, shut away from any possible test of logic—and we have come to behave as though the terms were literal. We say that John Doe has paid seven years of his life for the killing of Mary Smith, and such language seems altogether appropriate to us, even if we do think the price may be too low. Is this similar to what happens when we pay twenty-five dollars for a license to kill a deer? No? Why not? It seems consistent with the practices of the marketplace. The state, taking into account the salaries of wardens and other costs of wild life, reckons a deer to be worth twenty-five dollars and charges you accordingly. No, you will argue, *paying for* a crime is a different kind of paying. How is it different? Is it different because you cannot pay in advance for the killing of another human. Is this *paying for* a crime essentially what we mean when we talk about atonement for sin? Do we make amends, and are we redeemed, when we are locked up in a cage for a few months or years?

PROTAGORAS: These are your words, not mine, and I spit them out!

AUTHOR: Indeed you do! And marvelously!

PROTAGORAS: A word to the wise, Author!

CHORUS: If we could eat your words we should grow fat.

AUTHOR: Thank you. Now if you propose to argue that John Doe, in a literal sense, *pays*—exchanges—seven years of his freedom for the life of Mary Smith, which freedom has very real—even monetary—value, then I would argue that you have justified human slavery. If John Doe can exchange a few years of his freedom for the life of another human, why cannot I buy the freedom of another human for a few thousand dollars? If Mary Smith's life can thus be bought, then is it not consistent to regard Mary Smith, or any human, simply as property or commodity?

PROTAGORAS: Both sides he argues! He might have been my student after all.

AUTHOR: Again I thank you.

CHORUS: Do you not thank us? It is we who would eat your words had they substance enough.

AUTHOR: Yes, I thank you too. I should certainly not want to eat them. There is an ancient image frequently associated with the administration of justice: a majestic but blindfolded woman with a sword in one hand and a balance in the other. The blindfold of course represents the attitude of impartiality while the sword is the instrument of punishment, seemingly appropriate symbolism so far. The balance scales, however, the scales of justice, apparently the central symbol of this image and the one that most directly stands for jurisdiction, does not seem so appropriate. Are not the literal balance scales an instrument of business, of exchange? So much corn in exchange for so much gold? If you put Mary Smith's life and seven[2] years of John Doe's life into the figurative scales of justice will the scales then balance? Will they balance if you put in twenty years, or one hundred years, or even John Doe's life?

PROTAGORAS: Most troublesome. Is this his argument or mine?

AUTHOR: If you find these questions troublesome, Protagoras, consider for a moment that our fundamental ways of thinking and talking and acting in regard to crime truly are *fundamentally* in error, not just inappropriate in a *merely* metaphorical sense but rather wrong conceptually, in the way that early philosophers were often wrong because they lacked not only knowledge but also the instruments, such as the telescope, through which concepts are tested and knowledge acquired. That is, our model, our fundamental guide or pattern—which is what this marketplace metaphor actually is—cannot lead us to the solution we so fervently desire, for it has nothing whatever to do with the problem we desire to solve. It is as though we humans in our effort and longing to fly, to be carried aloft, had chosen as our model the wagon rather than the duck. It is not that a metaphorical grasping for an understanding of crime, or of any phenomenon, is wrong or inappropriate— indeed, the metaphor appears to be the sole means by which the human mind takes its first tentative steps into any unknown realm; rather, the essence of this error is that it is the result not of mistakes of that human faculty we call logic, an invention of you early Greeks, but of uncertain leaps of that human faculty we call language and of one of its principal organs, metaphor, both inventions of the earliest humans.

But you may still wish to argue that the choice of a metaphor is not dictated by logic but by the need to understand and communicate, that the test of a metaphor is neither logic nor appropriateness but rather usefulness. That is, you might insist, a metaphor is a reaching beyond logic for truth and may properly be arbitrary, even whimsical or capricious. Everyone will understand that we are speaking metaphorically and no harm will be done. I would argue that this marketplace metaphor is not one of those common figures of speech that we all constantly reach for as we strive to make our utterances carry our meaning. It is *not* such a figure as "He is a mule," which calls up an amusing image that both speaker and listener know well and that never for a moment deceives either; the falsehood is on the surface and is winked at by both. It is, rather, one that we all seem to share at an unconscious level, the falsehood hidden, and we adhere to it reflexively, without any need to examine it, as we might examine, for example, an article of faith that conflicts with desire. It is one, furthermore, that we humans seem to have been misguided by for thousands of years. And great harm has been done.

PROTAGORAS: At this point I do not know which side of this argument I am on, but I do hope I have command of a few facts. I commend the same to you.

AUTHOR: I have facts; the word is fact. I do not propose to sift either the literal sands of archeology or the figurative sands of history to make my point, although clearly this can be done. The conceptual—and seemingly linguistic—error that has put our civilization at risk is fully open to examination by these disciplines. Rather, I hold that the evidence of our language, the most important artifact of all, is sufficient. If we pay attention, if we listen to ourselves, if we look closely at what we have written, it is adequately revealing. If you think, as apparently most do, that crime is what lawyers say it is in the laws that they write, then

18

seek the origin of the very word *crime*. This word is ancient, and at its primitive roots it means *scream*. Before there were laws or lawyers to write them, there were screams and lamentations to indict the criminal.

Consider other metaphors that aid us as we think and talk about the administration of criminal justice. There is, for example, the *revolving door*. We obviously got this one very recently since there were no actual revolving doors until very recently. Someone, perhaps a newspaper reporter, while standing near the portal of a courthouse with such a door, possibly noticed that those accused of crimes were arriving and departing in almost the same instant, as a child does when he attempts to make a merry-go-round of a revolving door. This metaphor does not seem either inappropriate or dangerous, though I must admit that a criminal might take a different position. He might take such talk about his ways of dealing with the law as an effort to increase his cost of doing business.

How many times have you heard this expression: The wheels of justice turn slowly. So now justice is a machine, cranking along mindlessly, taking something in at this end and putting it out at the other. Surely we must ask who designed it and what it was meant to do.

There is also the metaphor of the contest or game as applied to the description of the relationship between opposing lawyers in a trial. This, too, may be a recent acquisition, perhaps as recent as our present preoccupation with spectator games, but since the ancient Romans also devoted much of their time and energy to such games perhaps they too drew on them to describe their administration of law. Thus when we watch televised reports of the notable trials of our period, we are told that this lawyer or that scored the most points. We are told of a game or a contest as opposed to an explicit search for truth. If we were seriously questioned, most of us would certainly say that a criminal trial is a test of the guilt, or innocence, of a person accused of a crime, but what we are often made to see is actually a test of the skill of the lawyers, including the judge, in playing the game that they alone contrived. The truth of the guilt or innocence of the accused may thus be obscured by the drama—another metaphor, of course—and the jury, transformed into a panel of critics, may fix its attention on the stars rather than the drab defendant and the tedious facts. Being too much under the control of this latter metaphor could lead us to believe that the law, as we know it, is a drama played out by lawyers for their own amusement and their own benefit. They, after all, write the script—the laws—and they are the only players; the rest of us are mere spectators, like those in a real theater, or mere objects, like those of a real chessboard.

It is clear that much of what we say and do about crime was borrowed from the principles and practices of the marketplace. To argue otherwise could do great violence to our understanding of our language, and there has already been enough violence. But this borrowing should not surprise us. Early civilizations apparently developed out of the human organization required for the efficient cultivation and distribution of grain and other foods. Surely, then, the earliest efforts at a formal jurisdiction would focus on the central objects and activities of civilization: property and labor for the production of food and exchange as the mechanism of distribution. Although crime, and violent crime in particular, may often have been dealt with outside the purview of formal law, when it did come to court it would certainly have employed the language, and the concepts, and the images, and the symbols that already prevailed. How to treat crime and criminals would have been regarded, perhaps unconsciously, as a problem already solved. In proportion to his debt—crime—so shall the forfeit —punishment—be imposed. So many blows for this, so many for that, death for this, dismemberment for that, as the balance scales shall require.

But, I can hear you arguing, is that not natural and inevitable? Would you have disproportionate punishment? Death for a parking violation, for example? I could answer that I would not have punishment at all. Punishment has a poor standing in behavioral science[3], since apparent harmful effects seem to be more significant than questionable benefits, and as employed in our society, particularly in response to crime, a very poor record, as should be apparent to everyone. An eye for an eye and a tooth for a tooth and so on and on and on to infinity. If you do something bad, we as a society say to the individual, then we as a society will do something equally bad to you, and, as you well know, bad is forbidden. But as bad as punishment sounds in principle, it is even worse in practice, for it is not applied with conviction as to its efficacy. Instead, we plead that we are doing whatever we do for the criminal's own good; we are *correcting* him. Even when the system rises to the grand absurdity of multiple life terms—the criminal has but one life to give and is thus required to give it several times—this fiction is maintained. And when the punishment is death, the criminal justice system is piteously unable to conjure any confidence at all. Prince Hamlet himself, in the company of the hordes of lawyers who accompany the condemned to the gallows, stands out as supremely confident, even bold and reckless.

How then would I deter criminals? I would answer that the clear, daily evidence that television, and newspapers, and direct experience force on all of us shows that punishment as employed by our society does not deter criminals or alter their behavior, and I am not aware of anything, short of death, that does. But, of course, the dead do not fear, and deterrence—that long discredited shibboleth of the lawyers—is not the issue. Nor is punishment the issue. The issue is this: how can we understand and deal with criminal behavior so that we do not live in fear of it and are not destroyed by it? What metaphorical models are appropriate, logical, effectual? How can we speak of crime so that speaking itself does not lead us astray? When, for example, we ask a jury to *deliberate*, we ask it, in the sense of the Latin word for scales—*libra*—, to weigh, to metaphorically engage in an act of commerce. Of course we want a jury to be thoughtful and careful, but we do not want it to be illogical. What metaphorical model could we put before a jury that would not lead it to ask what a human life is worth?

But you are not persuaded. If the established way of viewing crime and of dealing with it is inappropriate or even erroneous, you might ask, then why has it persisted for thousands of years and permeated the laws of all great societies and the works of all great jurists? Is it possible that the enormous and august edifice of the law is so much in error? I would answer that what Galileo saw through his telescope destroyed views of the universe that had persisted for thousands of years and had permeated the works of great men. I could also answer that these linguistic borrowings from the marketplace are what some call *dead metaphors* because their sources have been forgotten, that they are unconscious and almost certainly have been for thousands of years, that they may even be part of what Carl Jung called the collective unconscious, common cultural possessions of commoners and jurists alike. That is, this particular way of dealing with crime could be innate in nearly all humans, inherited as an archetype from the remote past, from the time when we made the transition from simple, wandering food gatherers to sophisticated builders of cities. Alternatively, it could arise from prototypes in the neural networks of our brains, created there by the incessant training exercises imposed by the culture into which we are all born—a culture that contains language, tools, established ways of doing things, and an abundance of instructive artifacts and images, all of which we may regard as inheritance from the past. But however we account for the making of this model within us—this model that guides our approach to the problem of crime and that becomes apparent to us through our metaphors—its presence cannot be doubted; as I intend to show, the evidence is abundant.

You could argue, Protagoras, that while some of our utterances concerning crime may indeed be inappropriate metaphors, our actual beliefs and our behavior are quite different and altogether appropriate. I would argue that what we believe about crime and, particularly, what we do about crime are altogether consistent with the marketplace metaphor, simply because we have no other model for what we think and do. And it furthermore seems quite possible that we have never had a different model, at least not in the five thousand years or so that mankind has had formal law. Even that most ancient of rules—an eye for an eye and a tooth for a tooth—is true to the marketplace metaphor. And no matter how hard we press that metaphor, it seems to hold up as the explanation of what goes on in our criminal justice system. Consider, for example, our frequent insistence that only the crime with which a person is charged is of relevance to a trial. Often a jury does not know that a defendant has committed many other crimes; it must limit its deliberations to the particulars of the charges being tried. That is, the accused is charged one crime or exchange transaction at a time; in the marketplace each item has its own price, and the price of one item purchased usually has no bearing on the price of another. Consider also the *weighing* of punishment against the crime, an activity that seems to go on in the minds of criminals as well as judges and legislators. Consider especially the sentencing guidelines created in recent years to make the criminal justice system more fair. Let's see, just what is a human life worth? Twenty years of a murderer's life spent in prison? Discounted, of course, if the felon doesn't insist on a lot of extras, that is, if he behaves well. So the net cost would be about seven years, a little less if we run short of space.

Nonsense, I can hear you saying. Sentences are based on what is good for the criminal and thus ultimately on what is good for our society. Sentences—punishments —must exist on a scale from mild to severe—from cheap to expensive—else the system would be considered unfair, just as a market that charges high prices for cheap goods is considered unfair. I would respond that the balance scales approach to crime leads inevitably and obviously to absurdity. The highest *price* a criminal can *pay* for a crime is his own life—in our society nothing but murder has this price tag, not even treason—and if that is the price actually charged—it almost never is—then that price must be considered payment in full, even if he has been charged with a dozen murders or more. Thus, the penalties—prices—for all other crimes, no matter how much pain or loss they cause, must be less than this and are, in fact, usually much less. And as you ponder prices consider the practice of releasing on bail bond those accused of crimes but not yet tried, a practice with revered standing in the courts for hundreds of years yet one which is clearly rooted in the marketplace and not in any concern for public safety. In current practice, the price of the crime is discounted by ninety percent, and any accused person so released who can pay the balance—literally, in money—is free to commit more crimes. But, you will scoff, the accused may actually be innocent and should not have to spend time in jail, let alone spend money to get himself out of jail. I would respond that the accused is likely to regard his crime as a commercial transaction—he has, after all, been told by a judge what it is worth in money—and may even consider the fraction he pays to the bail bondsman as payment in full. It is because of this shameless commerce, more than any other reason, that I say that our system of justice is hopelessly flawed.

PROTAGORAS: You also said that it is *fatally* flawed. Why did you say *fatally*?

AUTHOR: It can be argued, Protagoras, that in the national capitol of this my land murder is frequent, casual, and easy, not because the criminal justice system poses only a small threat to the criminal, but because the criminal justice system, with its balance scales approach to violent crime, has made life very, very cheap. For within this prevailing view of crime, at least within the mind of the criminal, a life is worth what it costs to take one, and on average it now costs very little. Both life and property are rapidly losing their value within this system and, at the present rate, will soon be worthless. For many of my compatriots, this system of justice has been *fatal*.

PROTAGORAS: But why *hopelessly*? Surely change is possible.

AUTHOR: I would like to believe so, Protagoras, but I cannot— simply because I have no model for such change. All such flawed edifices of the past—monarchy, aristocracy, feudalism, colonialism—all have simply been destroyed and buried. I cannot believe that it will be otherwise with this one.

PROTAGORAS: A few metaphors have gone awry! If mistaken metaphor is the agent of destruction, we surely all are doomed!

CHORUS: Surely what you say does not apply to ducks. You very clearly said *doomed*, not *dead ducks*.

AUTHOR: This edifice is riddled by unfit metaphor. It is as though it had been built of eggs instead of bricks. Consider the status of the accused in our courts. What we call the presumption of innocence, a fiction and often a transparent falsehood that we endure as an article of faith, is often forced to extremes that shake even the most faithful. Judges may tell prosecutors that their evidence is *tainted* and therefore may not be given to the jury, meaning that it is like the spoiled meat in the literal marketplace that has perhaps not been slaughtered and offered for sale according to the rules, not that it is necessarily unfit or untrue, and thus is a condition imposed on legal evidence that is imposed on no other search for truth. If the seeing is not in accordance with the rules, then that which was seen becomes invisible. Judges have told juries that prosecutors must prove guilt *beyond a shadow of a doubt,* even though the most rigorous of our sciences, by their own assertions, never prove anything to be true beyond doubt, even though the shadow-of-a-doubt metaphor itself is as inappropriate as that of the marketplace. If the doubt is substantial enough to cast a shadow, I might say, then the guilt must lie beyond that shadow or the accused goes free. But, I reply, doubt—insubstantial stuff that it is—must be ponderous indeed to cast a shadow, and since my doubt is nowhere near so ponderous, the accused must go to the gallows. If this shadow-of-a-doubt instruction is given in the interest of fairness—that is, in an effort to make the scales read true—then it is no worse than useless, but if it is simply another instance of the criminal justice system tilting—tipping the scales—in favor of the accused, as many have complained, then we are cheated as though by rigged scales in the literal marketplace. Many have also complained that in our courts the accused is often treated better than the victim. Perhaps, in this metaphorical marketplace, the accused is seen as the customer, the client, with all the perquisites that distinction implies, while the victim is regarded as little more than an item of evidence, perhaps even as an urchin with nothing to spend. What lawyer, after all, does the victim pay?

Finally, consider our reluctance to hold the immature, the insane, or the mentally impaired accountable for their crimes—responsible for making payments. It does not matter, in our current view, that a violent crime committed by a person in any of these states of relative incompetence is, so far as the victim is concerned, the exact equivalent of the same crime committed by a fully qualified criminal; we insist that only those who fully understand what they have done be held responsible. Note that a very similar attitude prevails in the marketplace; a buyer or seller must understand the fundamentals of exchange, the balance scales among them, in order to be considered qualified. Otherwise, a transaction could be regarded as unfair—not according to the balance scales, the ancient witness that this value is equal to that. A small child may, of course, be allowed to buy a nickel piece of candy, offering a dollar bill in exchange, but notice how carefully we watch to make sure that the child receives the correct change, and notice how careful the seller is to make sure that onlookers understand that the child has received the correct change.

I am sure that you are aware, Protagoras, that in some societies both buyer and seller are expected to engage in vigorous oral deliberation of the price of an item, and the price thus arrived at can no doubt be regarded by both buyer and seller as scrupulously fair. In our own society, it is apparently sufficient if the price of an item, three dollars and ninety-eight cents, for example, *appears* to be the product of such deliberation; such an odd price may be perceived as eminently fair while a more approximate, even, price may seem too arbitrary. Thus, we are satisfied with the fairness of a sentence that includes such fine adjustments as reductions for time served while awaiting trial, probation as a substitute for incarceration, monetary fines precisely arrived at, and work done in the service of humanity. But the immature, the insane, and the mentally impaired do not comprehend the workings of the metaphorical balance scales and cannot therefore be held responsible for the debts they incur. If you wish to argue that the real test applied to such persons is whether they know the difference between right and wrong, I will argue that all any of us is expected to know is that *right* incurs no debt while *wrong* does.

Civilization developed through a slow accretion of solutions to the problems of settled life. Civilization *is*, I suggest, no more than a set of institutionalized solutions to the problems of settled life. The problems that beset the first humans to attempt a settled existence may not have been articulated in the precise and businesslike language of today, may not even have been conscious, but they would surely be familiar to us now: How shall we provide for the production of food? How shall we regulate the behavior of individuals within our society? How shall we protect ourselves from outsiders who would kill or enslave us and take our riches? How shall we provide for our survival in times of drought, plague, and pestilence? Once satisfactory solutions to these most urgent problems were developed, they were institutionalized, and civilized mankind was then free to move on to other problems. But some solutions, institutionalized or not, often did not prove out.

One needs little knowledge of history to recall, for example, that early civilizations fared poorly against the hordes of nomadic humans who still lived in the manner of earlier wandering food gatherers and from time to time became merciless plunderers. The institutionalized solution to this problem—the army—was often inadequate, and early civilizations were regularly destroyed, not because they were threats to competing civilizations or nomadic cultures, but simply because they were bright baubles in the sun to be wantonly crushed by what was little more than a natural force. And even in recent times the institution called the army has provided no guarantees that civilization as we understand it can be preserved. Barely more than seven hundred years ago the Mongol hordes of Genghis Khan conquered Asia and came within a throw of the dice of destroying Western civilization. Some might say that even now such a natural force threatens civilization. But only for the most powerful of civilizations has this solution been a satisfactory one, and even for them it has only been temporary.

Witness the Romans. It is not so surprising, then, that the institution of criminal justice is now, and has perhaps always been, ineffective as a means of dealing with the destructive or dangerous members of society. What is surprising is that the evidence of our language should reveal a fundamental flaw of such great age. Little wonder, in an age of vast overpopulation and free movement of enormous numbers of humans, that our cities should again become the dangerous places they were at the dawn of civilization. Well, Protagoras, that is my argument. What do you think?

PROTAGORAS: Abominable rhetoric.

AUTHOR: No, no! My argument is finished. Please refute it.

PROTAGORAS: Oh, no, my dear novice, that is not all of your argument. You have left out much. I have no knowledge of certain concepts on which your argument rests, and you must explain these before I can justly weigh your argument. You seem to have found some meaning in the word metaphor that I was never aware of. And what is this collective unconscious of which you speak? Or alternatively, as you say, what in the name of the Olympian gods are the neural networks of our brains? And why do you make so much of weighing? What is wrong with metaphorical weighing as a way of thinking, of judging?

AUTHOR: As for weighing, you shall judge for yourself when I have finished. I intend to show that this metaphorical weighing is essentially magical, that the archetype from which it came is wholly magical.

PROTAGORAS: Marvelous! But do go on. What do you moderns mean by archetype? What do you mean when you say that you are in danger of losing your civilization because of unsafe streets? If you don't have safe streets, you don't have civilization. Surely you are aware of this contradiction. You will elucidate?

AUTHOR: Yes, gladly. But I have no experts to call. I can only tell you what I have read and heard.

PROTAGORAS: Oh, my! Socrates babbled much about experts. Because I had no skill in sculpture or painting or carpentry, he thought I had no virtue. I will not miss the experts. What you have read and heard will do quite well. It is your reality that we are to weigh.

CHORUS: Must we stay for this? May we have more corn?

2

Metaphor

PROTAGORAS: When I asked you to elucidate, I did not mean that I wanted you to make a light. I meant that I wanted you to make clear, to let me see. You see, I also know something about metaphor. Why did you light that candle?

AUTHOR: To make a point.

PROTAGORAS: The sun has not yet set so there is not much of a point.

AUTHOR: Imagine, Protagoras, that it is many thousands of years ago and that I am not yet quite human.

CHORUS: Granted.

AUTHOR: The sun has set and the dark has fallen down upon us.

PROTAGORAS: Not yet but I am sure it will before I get back to Hades.

AUTHOR: I watch one of my fellows make this light. How wonderful! How overwhelmingly, stunningly wonderful! He made this light, a fellow just a little greater than myself, not the great one who throws down the thunderbolt and lights the trees. We shall never again be the same. We shall never again be in darkness when the sun has set. I feel so different, here, inside. It is as though my soul has torn itself open and taken in the light.

CHORUS: It has certainly taken in something.

PROTAGORAS: Yes, yes. We had a story like this in Greece, you know. But do we yet know what the point is?

CHORUS: Dilemmas have points, we have feathers, Author has a candle. Can we get on with this?

AUTHOR: It seems to me, Protagoras, that Aristotle may have done us all some harm in describing metaphor as he did. Both because of his intellectual stature and his fortuitous place in the development of our culture, most current explanations of the metaphorical aspect of language appeal to Aristotle's view in some way and none that I know of ignore it. But that view, like nearly all that have followed—again, so far as I know—erred in a critical way. Aristotle treated metaphor as a primarily conscious and creative use of language while it is almost certainly the reverse, primarily unconscious and involuntary. A metaphor, "good" or otherwise, implies not "...an eye for resemblances...", as Aristotle wrote[1], but rather an unconscious and compelling model, what Carl Jung described as an archetype of the collective unconscious[2], what we might now think of as a prototype created in our neural networks by the content of our culture.[3] This is not to suggest there are not many conscious and creative uses of metaphor. Obviously there are, just as obviously as there are many not-so-creative and perhaps only semi-conscious uses, as one suspects in hearing the jarring and contrived metaphors of, say, politicians: "The Democrats should get on board and stop putting up roadblocks." But to suggest that creative, literary use of metaphor is primary and that ordinary use secondary would be just as erroneous. Long ago poets discovered the metaphorical nature of language and got themselves great status by artfully exploiting their discovery. Makers, they were called, makers of words, but even Aristotle had difficulty saying just what words the poets made.[4] And even if they did make words, they did not make the underlying, unconscious psychic content—archetypes or prototypes, take which you choose—that the words called forth. No, poets do not make words or emotions or ideas; they evoke through their magical incantations the ghostly memories that are in us all. Metaphor is the instructing genius of the common language, not just the literary. I have said, I think, that I am talking about how metaphorical language can reveal the mental models that govern our speech and actions, but I need to add that metaphorical language is not, as often regarded, a special occurrence. It may not be unreasonable to say that language is almost wholly metaphorical—at least in the sense in which I choose to use the term—in that language constantly refers to, is supported by, rests on models that are not language. Since we talking about what you would call figurative language, call these models figures if you wish. To support this contention that language is almost wholly metaphorical I call as witness one Weller Embler, noted linguist and scholar of metaphor, who said as much, or very nearly so.[5] And these mental models, figures if you wish, while they are perhaps abundant enough for our needs, are neither infinite in number nor wholly appropriate when they are invoked. Rather they are like the words in our dictionaries in that they only imperfectly guide us in our actions and in our efforts to be intelligible in speech. And like our words they are surely capable of being put into a book along with descriptive information so that we could more consciously and deliberately bring them into use.[6]

PROTAGORAS: I knew it! He is mad!

CHORUS: Would one of you look up corn? Wonderful model and good to eat, too.

AUTHOR: Actually, we already have such a book, or at least the beginnings of one. I am thinking of Egyptian hieroglyphic signs, those little pictures of things of significance to early civilized man. There are—or should I say were—not a great many of them, perhaps a thousand, plus or minus a few hundred. One can peruse the list given by one notable scholar of the Egyptian language[7] and conclude, furthermore, that the essence of human life upon this planet at that early time is given by far fewer than that number. And if we should extend that list to include all fundamental experiences of man from that day to this, we should certainly no more than double it.

PROTAGORAS: Some time ago you said that you wanted to make a point. What point are you making now?

CHORUS: The point is that corn is the essence of life. May we have some?

AUTHOR: My point is—if I have not already said so—that metaphor is not a matter of suggesting a certain kind of likeness between two different things but rather of calling forth— consciously or unconsciously but most often unconsciously—a fundamental model of human experience. We may call this model an archetype, as Carl Jung[8] did, or a prototype, which term may be more appropriate given the knowledge we now have of the neural networks that are the basic structures of these precious brains of ours.[9] We fit the data of our new or unfamiliar experience to this model and thus comprehend and communicate that experience.

PROTAGORAS: The entirety, then, of all human life is summed in a few thousand models? You surely don't mean that. What happens then to the enormous complexity of the human mind? What happens to poetry, to philosophy, to science?

AUTHOR: Yes, I think I do mean that, but what do I know? I don't know what I am talking about any more than you do. That is, I do not know what models come forth from moment to moment to guide my thoughts and my speech. Of course, the balance scales and the marketplace startled me into this inquiry but more of that latter. Much more. As for the human mind and poetry and philosophy and science—these golden ideas of our species—what can I say? If they reduce to archetypes of the collective unconscious or, perhaps more disillusioning, prototypes of our neural networks, what does that matter? They are still what they are. Explaining something by discovering its simpler elements changes only perception not substance. Ho! Did you hear what I said without even thinking? Of course the substance does not change! The substance is that which *stands under*, the very elements of which I have been speaking.

Allow me, Protagoras, to now introduce a couple of crucial words of your language, *logos* and *mythos*. Do not think that I intend either in any literal sense, though I am aware that in your language either could be used to mean *speech*. Allow me to say, in simple words—as befits me, since I have no philosophical robes—and without summoning a host of authorities, that logos is reality, or perhaps rather the pervading principle that orders reality, and mythos is mind, whatever we shall eventually discover that to be. This is the only dualism I can accept, and I believe that Jung, who thus made his first cut across the web of being, thought likewise, though he did tiptoe around the topic.[10] I believe also that you yourself held such a conception. What else

32

could you have meant when you said, "Man is the measure of all things"?

PROTAGORAS: Did I say that?

AUTHOR: So your admirers have said.

PROTAGORAS: I don't recall.

CHORUS: Of course not. That would be like trying to give significance to every quack of a duck, as some would do.

AUTHOR: I think you meant that we apprehend nothing except by means of what we are, that is, what mankind is, and what we are includes all that we have been since the very beginning of life. This is the substance of everything I think and say and do, but it is quite beyond me. Of logos I know nothing and of mythos very little. Could you question, then, my assertion that we do not know what we are talking about?

PROTAGORAS: This is sheer sophistry!

AUTHOR: You should know! You invented it!

CHORUS: Please! We will not listen to the quarreling of school boys!

AUTHOR: As I was saying, the substance cannot be ignored. The idea of a literal use of a word, for example, as opposed to a metaphorical use, seems to me to be highly suspect. By *literal*, linguists and others seem to mean that a word or larger utterance has an explicit meaning—strictly limited, no more and no less than the letters or sounds that are there—that we have consciously arrived at, such as, in the case of the word *rose* used as a noun, a prickly plant with five-petalled red, pink, yellow, white, or other flowers and an appealing fragrance. But we cannot restrict out the substance.[11] Most speakers of the English language, when asked what a rose is, would *not* say that a rose is a prickly plant with five-petalled red, pink, yellow, white, or other flowers and an appealing fragrance. They would, rather, try to describe an image, an olfactory memory, or perhaps even a feeling or an experience for which the rose has become a personal symbol, for all of that is, for them, the very substance on which all understanding must stand. And no such descriptions could be taken as the explicit—restricted, definite, all obscurity

33

removed—meaning of the word rose that linguists wish for. My point here, if it needs further elaboration, is that if a word or utterance has a literal meaning then there should be something like a literal, limited response to, or understanding of, it. But I know that I cannot limit my response to the word rose to anything like an explicit, dictionary-given meaning, and I of course believe that other humans also cannot. Rather, even when there are no conscious metaphorical intentions, the word for me evokes an image, and that image evokes another, and that another, until the word itself seems no more than a distant and irrelevant sound. Yes, the rose—itself—by any other name would smell as sweet, but it is the name that calls back the fragrance when there is no rose. I will agree, Protagoras, even before you make words of that frown, that few words bear such a burden as rose does.

PROTAGORAS: What! Rose is now a beast of burden?

AUTHOR: Very good, Protagoras, very good! My defense is that I have already told you that I do not know what I am talking about, but now that I am conscious I will say that few words gush the way rose does.

PROTAGORAS: And now it bleeds?

AUTHOR: No, it weeps.

CHORUS: No, it spouts oil that befouls our pond! Must we go so far afield?

PROTAGORAS: Yes, yes. We are not hunting. He must come back to the point.

AUTHOR: Yes, yes, yes. Now for the next point.

CHORUS: We must now study geometry? You are going to connect points and finally make some sense of this?

AUTHOR: No, I want to tell you of a scholar who has dealt with this matter in a most interesting fashion.

PROTAGORAS: Who cares what he was wearing? What did he do?

CHORUS: We thought better of you, Protagoras.

AUTHOR: I have said that our mental models—figures, archetypes, prototypes—only imperfectly guide us in our actions and in our efforts to be intelligible in speech. For at least one writer on the subject of metaphor, this imperfection of the model is no less than the principal criterion.[12] He would not—could not—accept my views, but he does nevertheless provide some support for them. Imagine two columns.

CHORUS: We are in a temple?

AUTHOR: No, two columns of writing. In the first column we list the features of that which we want to comprehend and communicate. In the second column we list the features of that which we intend to use to describe the first thing. We might use such terms as *human* or *not human*, *male* or *female*, *common* or *uncommon*, and *dead* or *alive*. Any such terms will do so long as they are mutually exclusive, that is, do not overlap. You cannot of course be both dead and alive.

PROTAGORAS: Of course not.

AUTHOR: Now, once we have written our two lists we examine them carefully. If there is exact correspondence between them, then what we have is not metaphor. What we have is in fact what most would call a literal statement, though as I have said there could be an almost limitless stream of associations evoked by that statement. And, quite possibly, we will have described a model— an archetype, a prototype, a figure, that which lurks within our brain to guide us in our attempts to comprehend and communicate. If there is no incompatibility—no imperfection— between the two lists then there is no metaphor. We look at a person, a prince, let's say, and we want to comprehend him. We know the essential facts. In the first column we write *human*, *male*, *uncommon*, and *alive*. In the second we write *human*, *male*, *uncommon*, and *alive*. The two lists are identical. There is no incompatibility—no imperfection—and this is not metaphor; we must be looking at the son of a king. Of course, we cannot help but color him according to the prince model we already had when we saw him, a very wonderful model that we got perhaps from a fairy tale told to us when we were children, even though he may be a dissolute scoundrel, but we must agree that he is a literal, actual prince. Let's say that we had actually looked at someone else and in the first column had written human, male, *common*,

35

and alive. Ah, now we have metaphor—because *common* is incompatible with *uncommon*. The prince model is imperfect, for this person, wonderful though he is, is the son of a plumber, and thus when I say "He is a prince" I am speaking metaphorically.

PROTAGORAS: I am troubled by your rejection of literal statements. Surely I can say "He is a prince" and mean only that he is the son of king, without any unintended extensions of his attributes.

AUTHOR: You may well not intend any such extensions of his attributes, but if you are speaking to me your intentions will be for naught. If you say he is a prince, I will have great expectations of him, whether or not he is the son of a king. I cannot do otherwise, no matter how hard I might try. And why would I try? If I try to suppress the model that rises up from the depths of my unconscious, I have already acknowledged it.

PROTAGORAS: But you would make science and philosophy impossible! In my own time, I only made them exceedingly difficult. How can we have logical discourse if we cannot precisely define our terms?

AUTHOR: I will attempt to deal with your objection a bit later, Protagoras, but for the moment allow me to continue my diatribe against the literal. Let's say that you look at a man who is a bus driver. You say, "He is a bus driver." Can you actually say "He is a bus driver" without thinking of Ralph Kramden, without having him appear right there on the screen in your brain?

PROTAGORAS: What is a bus? Who or what is a Ralph Kramden? And when will you tell me why we do not have purely literal language?

AUTHOR: Bad choice of examples. Our life experiences have been a bit different and thus also our models.

PROTAGORAS: Please forget the models for a moment. I know that human language was once more metaphorical than it is now, but I must believe that the literal—the precise and logical—has come to predominate. When I made speeches I saw the effects of what I said—in the faces and gestures of my audience, and in their later actions—and what I saw was what I intended.

AUTHOR: I don't think so, Protagoras, and I intend to show that we humans are not precise and logical, even when the problems we face demand that we know what we are talking about, that we have conscious control of our models. Some will argue—have argued—that, yes, at one time language was less literal than it is now, that is, much more metaphorical, but that as the human race and its languages developed and increased in sophistication, the metaphorical gave way to the literal.[13] That is, the metaphorical sources of words and larger expressions were gradually forgotten, and the words and expressions, having disavowed their parents, are now taken to be self-sustaining, that is, *literal*. Indeed, we do forget our metaphorical sources, our models, archetypes, prototypes, or even figures, if you wish, and that is the core of the problem I am trying to address. But those sources are still there—buried in the unconscious—and forgetting them, that is, failing to consciously examine them from time to time, has led us into great error. Some scholars, in describing this process of forgetting, speak of *dead metaphors*. Now there is a metaphor worthy of some attention! Otto Jespersen, a famous linguist of another age and a man of considerable humor and wit, spoke of *dead metaphors* without saying that he was aware of the irony, and I think he would have said so if had been.[14] Take care that a dead metaphor does not rise up and get you.

PROTAGORAS: I do not fear the dead, but I do fear that you have wandered far from your argument. Did you not set out to show that your system of justice is hopelessly flawed, as you yourself so modestly put it? You have said even that weighing, as of evidence, is really just magic. Even in my present generous frame of mind—brought on no doubt by the pleasant company of these ducks—that proposition seems exceedingly strange.

CHORUS: You are surely one of us, Protagoras.

AUTHOR: Tell me, Protagoras, is metaphor rooted in logos, as Aristotle seems to imply, or in mythos?

PROTAGORAS: In both, perhaps. I know that I choose my metaphors —with the intention of causing some effect. It is rhetoric of which I speak. But you are surely going to say mythos.

AUTHOR: It is mythos of which I am thinking. What is it that happens to the psyche when man is startled into awareness of something he has not experienced before? A conception—the incipient myth—that will be the memory when the new experience is no longer seen or heard or tasted? Or words that will symbolically capture the experience and communicate it to others? Many scholars of my time have pondered these questions.[15]

PROTAGORAS: You are going to say both, of course.

AUTHOR: Yes, I am going to say both. Man experiences as man, that is, anthropomorphically. Remember that you yourself have said so. A great tree bends in the wind and makes a sound. The tree moans, a man moans. The tree moans as a man moans for his fallen comrade. Perhaps at this very moment a myth is born, a conception of the action of the indwelling spirit of the tree comes into being. Thus forever after when I say the wind moans in the trees, I am evoking a mythic conception. We hear again the indwelling spirit.

PROTAGORAS: You would claim, then, that when I use metaphor I invoke myth? Suppose I do not even know of the myth, cannot recall it or recite it?

AUTHOR: Not consciously, no. I am saying that somewhere in the roots of your metaphor myth may be found, just as somewhere in your brain the most primitive brain is still to found. The mythic origin of your metaphor is by now lost among a million other submerged memories, but we can deny that origin only at our peril. To deny it is to deny us any hope of ever knowing what we are talking about; it is to cut us off from what we were and thus from what we are. It is not just that a tree and a man can make a similar sound that is attested by this metaphorical use of the word *moan*; also attested is the conception that both man and trees moan, that the tree moans as man does because in the depths of its being it is moved to do so. Could we have poetry if this were not so?

PROTAGORAS: We do have poetry—and thus is your argument proved.

AUTHOR: I find often in metaphor the stuff of myth, just as I think I often see your hand in what now passes for the practice of law.

PROTAGORAS: Metonymy.

AUTHOR: What?

PROTAGORAS: Your metaphor was an example of metonymy. The part for the whole, the whole for the part. You said that you see my *hand* in the practice of law. You really mean that you see *me* in the modern practice of law, or my methods, rather. Do you know nothing of rhetoric?

AUTHOR: What do you know of the part for the whole or the whole for the part? Is this knowledge included in your rhetoric?

PROTAGORAS: Men speak thus and thus it is well to examine the way that men speak.

CHORUS: And whence the quack? Was this the sound that made the universe?

AUTHOR: Did you know that ancient men found all water in the smallest drop of it, and thereby proposed to make rain? That to have a lock of your hair gives one power over you, because all of you is in the lock? That in each grain of the harvest the daemon of the harvest resides and that some part of the harvest must therefore not be eaten so that the daemon may live? Thus, when I say that I see the hand of Protagoras in this business of the law, my tongue is controlled by the most ancient part of me. For that part of me, the hand of Protagoras *is* Protagoras, and I do not contrive a metaphor when I speak thus. An untidy notion, I admit, but so it is with all that is mythic, and I hardly need other justification for saying that we do not know what we are talking about. What we are talking about is hidden behind the myth. No, Protagoras, this metonymy of yours is not the invention of rhetoricians but a conception of early man.[16]

PROTAGORAS: As you wish; it is hardly worth arguing. But rhetoric does not claim metonymy as it own but only offers an explanation of it.

AUTHOR: But your explanation is too simple. It says little of what it is and even that as if it were a rational making of words.

We should be less the creatures of our words if we were at least to acknowledge their mythic roots. If you taught your students this article of rhetoric—this metonymy—did you also teach them that it was a principle by which their distant ancestors beheld the world? That what these distant ancestors were and did was in them and will be in all generations of man, so long as man shall be?

CHORUS: Where is the first quack that is the father of all the quacks you hear?

PROTAGORAS: Where is Author's argument? What does any of this have to do with the balance scales?

AUTHOR: Everything and nothing.

PROTAGORAS: Wonderful! He will take both sides again.

AUTHOR: When I say everything, I mean that I have led you to a way to comprehend what I have learned about the scales. When I say nothing, I mean that what I have learned about the scales is effective to my argument without any understanding of the mythic roots of metaphor.

PROTAGORAS: You intend to present evidence, then?

AUTHOR: Yes. And there is much evidence to support my view, Protagoras. With the help of my computer, I have been able to search quickly through the written records of human utterances —from the earliest times of writing to this very day—and I have found the language of law particularly revealing. It is apparent from the language of lawyers that they have lost sight of the source of their principal metaphor. There is much talk of *weighing* but almost nothing of what they weigh with. The balance scales are seen and heard much in popular images and language but only rarely in legal language. Having forgotten the instrument of their *deliberations*, lawyers clearly do not know what they are talking about!

PROTAGORAS: And, of course, only lawyers, your favorite goats, are at fault.

AUTHOR: When I said that lawyers do not know what they are talking about, I meant that they are unconsciously under the control of a magical model that seems to have appeared first in ancient Egypt.

PROTAGORAS: Then lawyers are not the only goats.

CHORUS: What are goats? Do they eat corn?

PROTAGORAS: They eat anything.

CHORUS: We feared as much.

AUTHOR: Of course, not. I have said that I want to limit myself to this one problem—of metaphorical weighing in legal matters—but I have found evidence of others. Tell me, Protagoras, how you understand the expression *strike a balance*.

PROTAGORAS: That of course refers to finding a compromise between opposing concerns.

AUTHOR: Yes, of course. But the expression is clearly a metaphorical use of the balance scales.

PROTAGORAS: So?

AUTHOR: How do you weigh opposing concerns? Do you know how to weigh something, Protagoras? You put something in each pan and then see if the balance beam is exactly level. I know how to do that with gold, for example: I put the gold in one pan and a standard weight in the other. How do I do this with your exceedingly vague *opposing concerns*?

PROTAGORAS: We are speaking metaphorically! You yourself have said that our models are always imperfect. What is your concern?

AUTHOR: My concern is that we do not know what we are talking about. We say that we have done something, but we cannot say what it is that we have done.

PROTAGORAS: Let me ask you this: Is it wrong to find a compromise between opposing concerns?

AUTHOR: I don't know. Since I do not know what has been done, how can I know whether the result is right or wrong?

PROTAGORAS: Nonsense! Your metaphor is dead and *strike a balance* literally means to find a compromise between opposing concerns.

AUTHOR: No, I say, dead metaphors are not dead but only unconscious, peacefully reposing in the collective psyche of our race, and thus in our individual brains, but always awaiting a call to further service. We need to call this one back to find if this really is what we want to do when concerns are opposed. Perhaps we can find a model that does not render us incapable of saying just what it is that we have done.

PROTAGORAS: Again I remind you that you yourself have said that our models are always imperfect.

AUTHOR: But some more imperfect than others. Since we have no choice but to use our pitifully limited set of models—no matter what we must do—perhaps it would be good for us to consciously examine them and consciously choose those that are most appropriate. We have so far allowed them to rise up and take control as they will.

PROTAGORAS: Perhaps you should continue with your argument, Author. I find your ideas uncomfortably strange, but I am condemned to listen. Make the most of the time you have left. When the sun sets I will be gone.

CHORUS: Take the goats with you when you go.

AUTHOR: These are not my ideas, Protagoras. I told you that I would tell you what I have read and heard, and you did agree to listen. Much of what I have said is the work of Carl Jung, a person I have already mentioned and one of the great intellects of my time. In your own time, he would have stood in the rank just behind Sophocles, Plato, and Aristotle. He would have understood exactly what I meant when I said that I do not know what I am talking about and that no one else does either.

PROTAGORAS: A great intellect, indeed. Demosthenes stood in that rank.

AUTHOR: And Protagoras?

PROTAGORAS: Perhaps. But enough of ranking; you were speaking of weighing.

AUTHOR: In a little while I will describe at some length another balance-scales metaphor that has apparently reposed in the collective unconscious for thousands of years and has exercised a control over human language and behavior that needs to be examined even if it is beyond remedy. I mean, of course, the one you just asked me about, the weighing of evidence and other such legal matters. I do not doubt that there are many such metaphors, but I want to restrict myself to this and just a few others of the same kind. At the moment, though I am loath to waste time, I would like to explore, with your help, another matter. Tell me, Protagoras, how you choose your metaphors?

PROTAGORAS: Very carefully.

CHORUS: This is the last straw! We shall endure no more!

PROTAGORAS: Silence! You are ducks, not camels. Better to say that you can eat it but cannot bear to hear it.

AUTHOR: Would you consider that—usually—you do not choose, carefully or otherwise? That a metaphor is out of your mouth before you have so much as tasted it? Witness these ducks, as fine a bunch of interlocutors as one could assemble. Out of their mouths came straw, without so much as a wheeze.

CHORUS: Bunch? Are we carrots? We are a flock.

AUTHOR: Who is your minister then?

CHORUS: You are on thin ice, Author! And the pond is deeper than you are!

AUTHOR: Do you mean deeper than I am deep or deeper than I am tall?

PROTAGORAS: You press your luck, Author! Nonsense! I was a teacher of rhetoric for many years and practiced the art very well. But if you mean that I can choose a metaphor deliberately but still not know what it truly means, or from where it came, then I agree.

AUTHOR: No, I mean that *sometimes* you can choose a metaphor deliberately but never always. Suppose I said that, on pain of death, when you speak you will use no metaphor at all.

PROTAGORAS: Then I would be speechless.[17]

AUTHOR: Ah. I have made my point, part of it, at least. If the literal that you have defended did exist then you should be able to say something.

PROTAGORAS: Of course. And I could should I give it thought enough. But I am no longer inclined to take such risks. Or do I mean that I no longer take my stand on slippery slopes? Or do I mean...

AUTHOR: Protagoras! Please! Come back to us. I have already said that not knowing what we are talking about is perilous, but I want to say it again—at the moment of your capitulation.

PROTAGORAS: I have hardly surrendered! Or were you referring to my list of alternative metaphors?

AUTHOR: When we do not know what we are talking about, we are in danger of being deceived. And if we are deceived, we do not know that we are or in what way. Our model becomes confused with the thing itself, and I believe you have agreed that our models are all imperfect, that is, not wholly capable of accounting for the thing itself. In your own day, Protagoras, you professed to understand the world of men and how to be successful in it. Do you still make that claim?

PROTAGORAS: If I say yes, I fall into your trap; if I say no, I defame myself.

CHORUS: Your choice, Protagoras. One horn or the other.

PROTAGORAS: How did this dilemma get horns?

CHORUS: Bulls have horns. When they catch you, you are sure to get one or the other.

PROTAGORAS: Very well, Author. I choose your trap.

AUTHOR: Could you consider, Protagoras, that what you understood so well was your *model* of the world of men and not that world itself?[18]

PROTAGORAS: I suppose. But I detect a problem here. If we cannot know the logos except by mythos, how can we ever know that the model—which is in the mythos—does not fit the thing itself, the logos, very well?

AUTHOR: We cannot. We can only consciously call up other models and compare them. Perhaps we can find one with a better fit to what we think our intentions are, perhaps not. Yes, man is the measure of all things, but we know too little of man to measure anything very well. I will tell you more of this later, for there is a way out of this quandary. We have not yet come to the real meat of the matter.

PROTAGORAS: I grow weary. And thank you for the perfect excuse. If I erred it was because my model was flawed, not for want of intellect.

AUTHOR: And so it is with judicial weighing.

3

Archetypes of the Collective Unconscious Become Prototypes of the Neural Networks

PROTAGORAS: You are discursive, Author.

AUTHOR: What? Rambling? I know very well where I am going!

PROTAGORAS: I mean only that you have passed from one topic to another.

AUTHOR: I am only following the steps of my argument, and it goes this way and that.

PROTAGORAS: Your argument went on before you then. Curious.

CHORUS: Where did it go? Will it come back? Must we wait for it?

AUTHOR: It has been my method, Protagoras, to attempt an understanding of my fellow humans by listening to what they say—and to some extent watching what they do—in order to discover what lies under the words— and under the actions. What I find in the words and in the actions is metaphor, and under metaphor archetype—or, perhaps, prototype. In a word, I am seeking models. These are the controllers of our words and deeds.

PROTAGORAS: Alas! We have lost our freedom!

AUTHOR: You have lost nothing. You never had any. But you might discover models less tyrannical than those that now enslave you.

PROTAGORAS: Please lead me to these lesser tyrants.

AUTHOR: Sarcasm cuts the tongue, Protagoras. May I proceed? Carl Jung's psychological concept of archetypes—inherited ideas distilled from the total of distant human experience—has been around now for several generations. Whether or not the concept has scientific validity—and some have argued most persuasively that it does[1]—it has certainly gotten itself well established in our culture. One finds the term, used more or less in the sense that Jung intended, everywhere in popular speech and literature. This idea does not seem likely to go away. It seems to me that interest in and acceptance of Jung's ideas may be waning but that general interest in the findings of neuroscience is growing. Is the archetype of Jung to be replaced by the prototype of the neural networks of our brains? As I have told you, Protagoras, I have no independent knowledge; I only watch, and listen, and read. Still, I can tell you that such a prospect thrills me, for I have a much better chance of understanding a computer in my head than the murky and mystical thing that Jung wrote about. But because ideas stemming from the discovery of the neural networks of our brains must certainly to some extent assimilate Jung's archetypes, and perhaps also the collective unconscious in which they exist, we need to begin with Jung. To say what I need to say I must employ metaphor, of course, knowing all the while that I will miss the mark, by much or little, but certainly miss. I suggest that we think of a vast computer that we are all plugged into as smart terminals. We can do a little on our own—a little independent processing, that is—but for all that we do we must depend on the primary programs that are stored on the great whirling hard disk of that vast computer. If we are to have any way of proceeding— any models to follow—we must first retrieve these programs.

PROTAGORAS: Stop! You have followed your argument and left me standing here. Vast computers? Great whirling hard disks? You not only don't know what you are talking about, you don't know who you are talking to.

AUTHOR: A moment, Protagoras, a moment. I love this metaphor. Let me follow it for a moment and then I will come back to get you. That vast computer is Jung's collective unconscious. It is always there in the background, but we are almost never aware of it. When we need to say something, or do something, and don't know how, we make a call to it for a program. That program is an archetype, or a prototype, and we put our own data into it to accomplish what we will. We thus never experience the archetype or prototype as it actually is, for when it is copied out to our terminal, and fleshed out with our data, it is changed. When that fleshed out copy becomes our personal tool, we can examine it closely and know it very well, but we still do not know that from which it came. Wonderful!

PROTAGORAS: Have you recovered from your seizure?

AUTHOR: Tell me, Protagoras, are you aware at this moment of everything you have ever done, every word you have spoken, every sight you have seen, every sound...

PROTAGORAS: Soon you will exhaust the universe! Of course I am not!

AUTHOR: Then all that is Protagoras, except for these momentary thoughts, is gone from your psyche—from your mind, roughly speaking.

CHORUS: Is he speaking roughly? We thought he was kind and gentle. He gave us corn and may yet give us more.

PROTAGORAS: Of course not. I can remember if I try hard enough.

AUTHOR: Yes. All that you are and have been that you are not thinking about at the moment is what Jung called the personal unconscious. Under the right conditions you can retrieve much of what is there. Now tell me this: What is woman?

PROTAGORAS: Great Zeus save me! Not in a million words could I tell you, nor in a million times a million!

AUTHOR: Then you do not know what woman is?

PROTAGORAS: Nonsense. I know that almost as well as I know myself, but words fail me simply because there are not enough of them. When you speak the word *woman* a sort of image rises in my mind, but it is far too complex for words. Nor do I need to put woman into words, for every man knows what I know and every woman knows herself as I know myself.

AUTHOR: You are speaking of an archetype of the collective unconscious that Jung called the anima. It is the universal, racial memory of all that man has had to do with woman since the beginning of humanity—and perhaps since before that.

CHORUS: Perhaps even since humans were ducks.

PROTAGORAS: And how do women know men?

AUTHOR: In the same way. Jung's name for that archetype is animus. It is all that woman has had to do with man since the beginning of time. And all that is the Protagoras that Protagoras knows he called ego, but that is not part of the collective unconscious. For all that you are, Protagoras, you are not universal.

PROTAGORAS: But perhaps some of my ideas are.

AUTHOR: Like saying whatever is necessary to achieve one's ends?

PROTAGORAS: Please! That is a terrible perversion!

AUTHOR: I withdraw the statement.

PROTAGORAS: Thank you.

CHORUS: How do we ask for corn and actually get it?

AUTHOR: Allow me to continue. Jung seems to me uncertain about where archetypes come from[2], and I am not at all comfortable with his speculations in this matter. He says that we of this age who talk about atoms, who have described them in great detail and even broken them into pieces...

PROTAGORAS: Wait! If you have broken them into pieces, they cannot be atoms. Do you know what the word means? It means *cannot be cut, indivisible.*

AUTHOR: I know that, but I am stuck; I have no other word. If I am to believe what I have read, we have found that which cannot be cut but have given it another name. That is one of the problems with these ancient archetypes; they are very persistent and the bond between word and archetype seems quite strong. Can I evoke the atom archetype with some other word? I think not. Now, as I was saying, Jung says that we who now talk about atoms, describe them in detail, and even break them into pieces are able to do so because our culture has brought to us the idea of the indivisible piece of matter, perhaps from the scientist Democritus of your age, Protagoras, perhaps from someone else. But, Jung asks, how did Democritus or that someone else get the idea? From archetypes unconnected with any real events, he says, risen without cause within that universal psyche, the collective unconscious.[3]

PROTAGORAS: Then these are the ideal forms of Plato.

AUTHOR: No. The ideal forms of Plato stamp themselves onto matter; these impress only the searching mind.

PROTAGORAS: But like the ideal forms of Plato they are simply there—as first causes.

AUTHOR: Or so Jung seems to have believed. I respectfully disagree.

PROTAGORAS: Then you must know something that Jung did not. Is that not quite arrogant if—as you say—Jung would have stood in the rank just behind Socrates and Plato and Aristotle?

AUTHOR: No. Not at all. One thing about these archetypes of ours, Protagoras, is that they guide us ever onward. Quite simply, I have knowledge that Jung did not have, and I tremble to think what he might have done had he possessed it. I mean what we now know of our brains—the knowledge that has come from the discovery and study of their neural networks. Isn't it ironic, Protagoras, that the ancient Egyptians dismissed as so much blubber the organ they would have most treasured had they known what we now know. It is the brain, not the heart, that is the seat of the soul.[4] I do not care to challenge their conception of the essence of a human being, but they gave the wrong organ the credit, and we shall perhaps never rid our thoughts and our language of that error. Hear how I clank, Protagoras, when I say that you know in your brain of brains that what I say is true.

CHORUS: We ducks have a word for all this.

PROTAGORAS: Which is?

CHORUS: Quack.

AUTHOR: Please! Let me continue. I have already said that the idealists, Plato and others, thought that ideal forms stamp out material realities.

CHORUS: We can think of some we would like to stamp out.

AUTHOR: I would like to turn that around and say, contrary to Jung's view, that material realities stamp archetypes into the collective unconscious. Now, Protagoras, I would like to carry forward my argument by telling a little tale, as you once liked to do.

CHORUS: You are going to lie?

AUTHOR: Come back with me now a million years or more, to the very beginning of the old stone age. Ducks are already ducks, resplendent in bright feathers, flying gracefully above a lake and swimming serenely on it. Nearby, on the shore, sits early man, without any tools or weapons that he himself has made, pondering how to catch and eat the ducks.

CHORUS: Quack! Quack! Quack!

PROTAGORAS: Please! You are spreading alarm, and we have been so civil till now!

AUTHOR: He holds in his hand a stone that he would throw at the ducks, but they are too far away and the stone is far too large. In anger he strikes the stone against another and it breaks in two. Puzzled, he picks up one of the pieces and strikes it again against the larger stone. Again it breaks in two. He strikes again and again and then—in a profound instant—he sees a small splinter of stone, long and thin, sharp at the end. Perhaps even more profoundly he sees it attached to the end of a stick and sees himself throwing it a great distance to strike a duck. The spear is born! An industry is born! And men go on breaking stones into smaller and smaller pieces to make all sorts of tools and weapons. Finally, after many, many years, he realizes that at some point he could not break them into smaller pieces. The atom archetype is born!

CHORUS: Quack!

PROTAGORAS: And you have complained of Jung's speculations.

AUTHOR: Then I shall say that a prototype has been written into the neural networks of their brains. Then forever after every human has this same prototype written into the neural networks of his brain because that prototype is in his culture and it therefore cannot be otherwise.

PROTAGORAS: That is no improvement at all. We can see neither.

AUTHOR: But we can *see*. We can now see in ways that you never dreamed of, Protagoras. And speaking of seeing—as well as of our other senses—what do you suppose that is except the gathering of data for our neural networks? Do you see?

PROTAGORAS: I see.

AUTHOR: Ultimately, all metaphors must be based on the tangible and visible things that provide the data. Thus images recorded in the mind are the substratum of linguistic metaphors.[5] The images—through the mediation of metaphor—become models for thinking about and acting on matters not related to that from which the model arose. And when these images are primordial, fundamental, they are what Jung called archetypes— and what we will surely come to call prototypes of the neural networks of our brains.

PROTAGORAS: I am puzzled by your assertion that the models may not be related to what we are thinking about and saying and doing.

AUTHOR: It is not my assertion, Protagoras. It is Jung's. Could you believe that a scientist solved a difficult problem by seeing snakes dancing in a fire? Jung offered this as support for his assertion.[6]

PROTAGORAS: Outlandish, I should say. But I recall now the strange conceptions of my own time.

CHORUS: Imagine what dancing ducks might accomplish!

AUTHOR: Of course, what we are talking about now—if I may presume that I have any idea what I am talking about—is analogy. Jung thought that the words *even as*—as we say in stating an analogy—were vastly important in the development of human thought.[7] Consider this: primitive man making fire by boring a stick into another piece of wood. Was coitus the archetype of fire making? Jung himself posed the question.

PROTAGORAS: I would like to hear the metaphor this primitive man made before he made the fire!

CHORUS: We are embarrassed. We have seen, on the banks of our pond, how you humans carry on.

AUTHOR: I think we should not suppose that in any particular instance language controls action or that action controls language but rather that an underlying archetype controls both. It seems unnecessary to suppose that there are archetypes that mediate language and only language. It seems much more likely that an archetype would serve whatever activity of the brain it is called on to serve. Language, after all, is only a species of brain activity, as no less an intellect than Noam Chomsky has said[8], although I am sure he would insist that this activity, the workings of the deep structures[9] of language—the primordial models, I would call them—belongs to language and language alone.

PROTAGORAS: In which rank do I put this Noam Chomsky?

AUTHOR: Possibly in the first, perhaps in none at all. Somewhere in that range.

PROTAGORAS: Very edifying. What is it that you lack in this instance, courage or judgment?

AUTHOR: Neither, but rather knowledge of the future.

PROTAGORAS: His work is still unfolding, then?

AUTHOR: No, but his deep structures now stand arrayed against the neural networks.[10] The outcome of this conflict will surely shake many a scientific edifice to the ground. Whole ranks of scholars will lie dead on the field. Their leaders will be as the battlefield trophies of old. Their shields and their...

PROTAGORAS: Enough! How far afield we have come! Were we not discussing weighing and archetypes, justice and the balance scales?

AUTHOR: Yes. And along this rutted road I see yet another digression.

CHORUS: A digression? Oh, surely not! This whole thing has been so coherent till now.

AUTHOR: I have said that this search should take me where it will, and it has brought me to this point of curious convergence. We have this word *yoke*, Protagoras. At the beginning of its long history, it was no more than a stick of wood. In another form, *zygon*, you know it well. In my language its immediate predecessors are Middle English *yok* and Old English *geoc*. Its ancestry includes Old High German *joh*—yoke—, Latin *jugum*—yoke—, Greek *zygon* —yoke—, Latin *jungere*—to bind or join—, and Sanskrit *yuga*—yoke. Scholars have theorized an Indo-

European root, *yeug-*, as the beginning of this line, and while it is known only by its descendants it is as real as you are, Protagoras. With it the beasts that do our pulling are bound together, and in earlier times it was laid upon the defeated, the perfect symbol of subjugation. But much more important to my argument, when it is borne across our shoulders it allows us to carry balanced loads. It is this use of the word yoke that I draw your attention to at the moment, but there are others I will mention. Then there is this English word *justice*. English got it from the Latin word *justitia*, which came from *jus*—meaning right, law, or justice—and perhaps from *jungere*—which, you will recall, is also a descendant of *yoke*.[11] Finally, a scholar of the balance scales, one Bruno Kisch, proposed that the invention of the kind of yoke that is put upon our human shoulders must have led to the invention of the balance scales.[12] Thus, even etymologically, it seems that justice and the law and the balance scales are connected.

PROTAGORAS: A tenuous proposition at best, but I will entertain it.

CHORUS: Why do you not entertain us with a little corn? Can you not see that you have worn us thin?

AUTHOR: Perhaps I could fatten it with this little tale.

CHORUS: Oh, help us! You humans fatten only to kill.

PROTAGORAS: Peace. I think we have merely come to another digression. Or perhaps I should say diversion.

CHORUS: But either way we turn aside and make our journey longer.

AUTHOR: Some early humans, looking at two oxen bound together by a wooden bar, a yoke, saw that with this device they had subjugated powerful beasts. These oxen were thus made to do the most arduous work of humans. But they also saw that together the oxen could do things that no single ox could do. Later, when they conquered their enemies, they held yokes—or arches of spears—above their heads and required them to thus acknowledge their subjugation. Even later, when they found that they had in some matters yielded to the welfare of the group and were thus subjugated by it, they said that this yielding was just.

Of course it was just for the just is the child of the yoke. When they forced all to yield to the welfare of the group, they said that was justice, the quality that is the yoke. It is all there in the history of the word. You may see for yourselves.

PROTAGORAS: Perhaps you make too much of history. Perhaps with more wit you would judge better.

AUTHOR: I see. You object to the way I fill in the blanks. Speculative, yes, but surely not without honored precedent. You know the word *fossil*, Protagoras. You yourself...

PROTAGORAS: Please!

AUTHOR: Of course. I go too far. In my age scientists dig them up in great numbers—I mean of course the rocks that are the graven images of something that once existed. From them, by filling in the blanks—many, many more blanks than rocks—they make wonderful histories. And we do not object, especially when they make histories of dinosaurs. How we love those great lizards!

PROTAGORAS: Zeus save us! You love lizards? The scaly monsters that we have so long feared?

AUTHOR: Yes. If they have been dead for seventy million years. But surely you can see that words are also fossils.

PROTAGORAS: In that they are made by things we do not know, yes, things that may no longer be, yes. But surely you do not mean that words are dead.

AUTHOR: Of course not. I meant only that they give some hints of what made them. You see how imperfect my metaphor was. It meant more than I wanted it to.

PROTAGORAS: Imperfect, indeed! I should not want to be more so! When my metaphors do not mean exactly what I want them to, I eschew them.

AUTHOR: You *shun* them?

PROTAGORAS: I meant I *avoid* them!

AUTHOR: Forgive me. For some reason I heard *shun* and shunning seemed to me severe, seeing as I did a useful servant driven from your rhetorical house, simply for having uses other than those you wanted.

PROTAGORAS: A master must be severe.

54

AUTHOR: You teach the metaphors and they do not teach you?

PROTAGORAS: Bah! Can we get on with this?

CHORUS: To that we add a very definite and unambiguous quack!

AUTHOR: Very well. Now where was I?

PROTAGORAS: You were speaking of metaphor and archetype but of which I am not sure. Of archetypes you have mentioned two. What others can you name?

AUTHOR: I have so far named four. Anima and animus, made of the endless contentions of man and woman, and also law and justice, both born of the yoke.

PROTAGORAS: Did you not also make the balance scales from the yoke?

AUTHOR: I would give the ancient Egyptians credit for that—and for much more that has to do with weighing. I will say more of that in a little while, but for now let me do as you have asked. This will be no easy task for I must proceed by indirection. As in looking at that which is very faint, I must look a little to the side or never see it.

PROTAGORAS: Or at that which is very bright, as the sun is, and will blind you if you dare to look directly.

AUTHOR: Name them I cannot, though I can name that which might have brought them into being, at least a few. Perfect union, as of man and woman; the mother; the father; the egg; the tale told by old men of the paradise that earth once was; chaos, as of war; water, of the sea and of the great river; explosion, as of a volcano perhaps; the quest, as for that which is won only by mighty effort; fall from grace, as from favor of the king; redemption, as given by the king; fire, as of the hearth and of destruction. You see how this is done, Protagoras. Now you can name a few.

PROTAGORAS: Yes. Gods, as of kings and heroes at a distance; heroes, as of adventurers and warriors at a distance; law, as of wishes of the king; blood, as of the slain; death and resurrection, as of Osiris born again at the flooding of the Nile.

AUTHOR: Very good but so cynical.

PROTAGORAS: My cynicism is hard-won, as of a quest.

CHORUS: We can name a few. May we speak up? Up, as of rising on our wings from this pond or of coming up from the bottom; down, as of going to the bottom or of coming back from the sky.[13]

AUTHOR: Very good but so down to earth.

PROTAGORAS: We can name no more?

AUTHOR: We could if we tried but we would come to end very soon. It seems possible to me, Protagoras, that all of our human ideas and understandings are derived ultimately from a very small set of basic and primitive experiences, the archetypes of Jung or—to be more modern— prototypes of our neural networks, written there by the fundamental content of our culture or perhaps even transmitted genetically. It would follow that extending this basic set—through space travel, for example—would change our ideas and understandings in very profound ways. Thus, though the set is small wholly new experiences are surely adding to it, and when we discover profound changes in our ideas and understandings we should search for new archetypes or prototypes.

PROTAGORAS: Space travel?

AUTHOR: I mean to journey away from this planet earth to other planets and some day to other stars. We do this now in ships you might have dreamed of. But you hear how words fail me! Journey indeed! Underlying this word is the sun's daily course across the sky, and it of course does not course the sky; the whole planet, as it spins, turns toward the sun and then away. You Greeks knew that, I think. I might say *travel* but would gain nothing; I would think then of the sweat of toil, and the sweating our space travelers do has nothing to do with toil.

PROTAGORAS: Very good. Let us find a metaphor in some worthy piece of writing and then find the archetype that made it, so that we may see how this making is done.

AUTHOR: Very good. There is in this land, once a colony of a great power, a very worthy piece of writing that marks its separation from that great power. It was written by one of our greatest solons, one even you would have placed very close to the front rank. To grasp the import, imagine that the colony of Thurii, for which you are said to have been law giver, had broken its bonds with the great Athens.

PROTAGORAS: I can well imagine but may find less import than you desire.

AUTHOR: We call this piece of writing The Declaration of Independence. Metaphorically, it is a judicial proceeding— perhaps a divorce proceeding— in a court in which God is judge and the world is jury. The bill of charges is presented for all the world to hear, and the bands are therefore declared dissolved. The appeal is to the higher law of God and nature, which the king of England has broken. The world remains hierarchical with God at the top and a place for kings, but America will henceforth be independent of the king of England and report only to God. Listen to the words: "When, in the course of human events, it becomes necessary for one people to dissolve the political bonds which have connected them..." And then, just before the bill of charges, this: "The history of the present King of Great Britain is a history of repeated injuries and usurpations, all having in direct object the establishment of an absolute tyranny over these states. To prove this, let facts be submitted to a candid world." In summation, there is this: "We, therefore, ...appealing to the Supreme Judge of the world for the rectitude of our intentions, do, in the name, and by the authority of the good people of these colonies, solemnly publish and declare, that these united colonies are, and of right ought to be free and independent states..." Can there be any doubt?

PROTAGORAS: Your great solon contrived this metaphor, was aware of exactly what he was doing?

AUTHOR: I do not know whether he was aware or not, but a better question is this: Is it an archetypal metaphor? Did an image that is in us all spring unbidden to consciousness and offer itself to our solon? I think so. He surely became aware of it once it came, and just as surely made the most of it, but I do not think that he in any way contrived it because he did not need to; it was there, at this crisis, waiting for a call. It is in us all; we cannot doubt that we are aware of it or of the archetypes that lie underneath.

PROTAGORAS: Some metaphors are archetypal, then, and others are not.

AUTHOR: You see, Protagoras, that I hesitate to respond. When we first met here by this lovely pond, you called me an aged sophomore.

PROTAGORAS: My apology if that still smarts. I usually choose my metaphors with more care.

AUTHOR: No. No. I did not take offense, but I do wonder if you chose at all. The metaphor you now regret perhaps rose up unbidden from the depths of your unconscious mind as you looked at me. Perhaps you saw a student of your own school, one who learned the lessons that you taught but not the virtues you intended. It must be a very ancient image, perhaps archetypal. What else could you have said if this is what you saw? At that moment you simply did not know what you were talking about. The archetype was in control.

PROTAGORAS: Thank you. I accept your reprieve, two-edged though it is.

AUTHOR: I surely did not mean to cut. You offered confirmation of my argument, and I wished to acknowledge that.

PROTAGORAS: Our friends the ducks spoke of up and down, but you seemed to dismiss them as frivolous.

CHORUS: Well said, Protagoras. Let no one forget that we have feathers and are thus of little weight!

AUTHOR: Indeed I did not. I merely noted their levity. But speaking of up and down, may I tell another tale?

PROTAGORAS: You certainly can tell a tale.

CHORUS: May we live till the end of it!

AUTHOR: One summer day as I sat outdoors, I saw a host of insects swarming inside the parasol under which I sat. In their efforts to escape, those insects crawled and flew toward the top, where there was no opening, but though they went in circles and

58

thus occasionally downward they did not venture near the bottom, which was completely open and therefore offered deliverance from doom. Flying up, I saw, would save them from the frog but not from the parasol. One by one they exhausted their tiny reserves of energy and fell through that broad opening at the bottom to lie dead on the table at which I sat. Perhaps, I thought, those insects could not escape because the insect *collective unconscious* does not include a *down* archetype or prototype that can be evoked in the context of escape. Given this example I could not but ponder the fate of man. Do we also lack some obvious model that would allow us to escape our doom? Until something external happens to add content to the unconscious we can only proceed with what is already there, but—clearly—what is already there may not be sufficient. Even as we speak, new disasters gather up their powers while we follow models validated by old disasters we have survived. We are under the parasol but cannot go down to find deliverance. Still, I do not mean to say that our old models avail us nothing. Albert Einstein, you may recall, employed a railroad train to discover relativity[14], and relativity still must be comprehended in terms of the archetypes of the collective unconscious that were there before Einstein bent the universe into a novel shape. In future times it may be understood in terms of archetypes yet to come, but if that is to be we must as a species survive, even though the history of life on this planet teaches us that extinction is the destiny of all species. No matter how many models we may have to guide us, some disaster will eventually overtake us and put us down.

CHORUS: Never shall we fly up again! This parasol we call the sky, under which we all must die, we cannot escape by flying high, and we shall seek deliverance in water.

AUTHOR: Horrors! The disaster that I feared! You shall have deliverance only if you drown.

PROTAGORAS: Albert Einstein? Railroad train? I should recall these?

AUTHOR: I am sorry, Protagoras. Once again I have imposed on your innocence of this modern world. Albert Einstein changed the shape of the universe; once we could comprehend the starry heavens and all that we see but now we cannot. He was truly of the first rank and you must place him there, with Aristotle, Plato, Socrates. A railroad train is...

PROTAGORAS: Please! I can endure no more! Albert Einstein has taken away your understanding and you praise him! Aristotle, Plato, and Socrates opened our eyes, and this man you place beside them has closed them! You are all about to perish, and you grow ecstatic as you say so! How am I to remain in this new world of yours, even until I hear you out?

AUTHOR: He has not closed our eyes; he has merely gone beyond our archetypes, beyond our metaphorical ability to grasp the universe as he has found it to be. We shall some day catch up—if we survive. And if I seem ecstatic it is because I see man shrinking in significance as the universe grows larger. When we are small enough we shall slip easily through the bars that now imprison us.

PROTAGORAS: I am listening to a madman! I shall take my leave!

AUTHOR: Forgive me. I did slip into a reverie. To see so much and understand so little is a bit maddening. I long for comprehension but simply have no model, no archetype. Give me just a moment and I shall again find comfort in the here and now.

PROTAGORAS: I shall find comfort in Hades as I never have before. In these past few hours you have slipped from logos to mythos, and I think you shall never come back again.

AUTHOR: Mythos was the beginning. Perhaps I am at a new beginning.

PROTAGORAS: To think that you can do nothing except by means of an archetype is an end, not a beginning.[15]

AUTHOR: Perhaps I did not mean what I said and perhaps what I said did not have meaning for you—or for me.

PROTAGORAS: Perhaps?

CHORUS: Perhaps? What did he say? Did he mention corn?

AUTHOR: I know I made the subjects agree with the verbs— although I do not know why I did so. Something in me simply compels me to do so. I know I had some sort of vision when I spoke as I just did and thus felt compelled to communicate, but at this moment I cannot recall that vision.

PROTAGORAS: Perhaps your Noam Chomsky can explain why you feel compelled to make subjects agree with verbs, but who can explain these strange fantasies of yours. But I forget myself! You have previously prepared your defense. You do not know what you are talking about.

AUTHOR: When I say that we do know what we are talking about, Protagoras, I am not implying culpability but rather inevitability. That which controls the content of our speech—as opposed to the structure of it—is for most of us most of the time unknown and thus beyond the fine control you think I should have. And if Chomsky is correct, we also have no direct knowledge of why we structure it as we do.

PROTAGORAS: Then your speech is merely the noise of an automaton— and I should ignore it, as I ignore the quacking of these ducks?

CHORUS: You listen to this madman and ignore our quacking? May Zeus cast you out of your precious Hades!

AUTHOR: Perhaps you now understand how I regard your judicial weighing.

PROTAGORAS: It is not my judicial weighing. It belongs to all mankind and you, I dare to say, have thus accused yourself. You cannot persuade me that you do not engage in this venerable practice.

AUTHOR: Venerable, indeed! Why did you not say sacred practice? I shall soon show that you might have said that with justification.

PROTAGORAS: Ah! At last a new topic.

AUTHOR: Yes, a new topic, but before we move on I would like to tidy up a bit.

CHORUS: Is he looking at us?

PROTAGORAS: I think he means that he is going to summarize.

AUTHOR: Yes, I will summarize. This is what I think I have successfully argued. Metaphor, far from being exclusively, or even mostly, the darling of you rhetoricians, is fundamental to all language, that of the greatest of poets and of the humblest bus driver. To be without metaphor is to be speechless, for without metaphor there is simply nothing to say. Under metaphor, providing both its power and its form, are those models deep within us that we now call archetypes and will surely come to call prototypes of our neural networks. Some metaphors may arise merely from images that we possess in common, but on this point I waffle and prefer to await the discoveries of neuroscience. But the essence of my argument remains the same: metaphors, instances of underlying models or prototypes, guide both our speech and our actions. We do not, as a rule, say one thing and do another. But these metaphors that control us are only more or less fitted to their tasks; they are most likely never perfectly so. Thus our speech and our actions are most likely never perfect responses to the problems that we must solve and are most likely often entirely inappropriate, even perilous. When our metaphors deceive us we err, and in erring we seem to be no more than the automatons of which you spoke, Protagoras. Judicial weighing is, I believe, an instance of a metaphor that has led us into great peril. There are others that I shall soon present for your consideration, but for the moment this is the hot center of my concern.

PROTAGORAS: And of course you are prepared to demonstrate that judicial weighing is a deceptive—and perilous—metaphor.

AUTHOR: Yes. I shall demonstrate.

4

Weighing Through the Ages

PROTAGORAS: Perhaps you could explain to us the meaning of your actions.

AUTHOR: You can see what I am doing.

PROTAGORAS: I know what I see but I do not know what you are doing.

CHORUS: We know what he is doing but we hardly believe what we see.

AUTHOR: Tell me what you see, Protagoras.

PROTAGORAS: Very well. I will play your little game of make a point. You went to the water's edge with these two buckets and there you filled them. You carried them up to these bushes and there you emptied them. Then you went back to the water and filled the buckets again. And again you carried them to these bushes and emptied them again. And again and again and again. What have I missed?

AUTHOR: The most important thing.

PROTAGORAS: About midway you began to use a stick.

AUTHOR: Yes, a stick. But let us call it a yoke.

PROTAGORAS: Very well. With ropes you tied the buckets to the ends of the yoke, at the pond you filled the buckets, you put the yoke across your shoulders, and then you continued to carry water. I almost forgot your lecture on etymology.

AUTHOR: And the carrying became much, much easier. My back is stronger than my hands.

CHORUS: Perhaps even stronger than your brain.

PROTAGORAS: Then you emptied one bucket by half and leaned to one side to show us that one bucket was heavier than the other. Marvelous! You have invented the balance scales again!

AUTHOR: Yes. And a wonderful model they are, too, these balance scales.

PROTAGORAS: But not for everything, I believe you are about to say.

AUTHOR: Yes, not for everything. Not for deciding such matters as criminal culpability, for example. Evidence is what we see; it has no weight.

PROTAGORAS: Is not evidence also what you hear?

AUTHOR: What I hear evokes images which I see, and what I see I should inspect, not weigh.

CHORUS: He sees with his ears! He must be a bat!

PROTAGORAS: Evidence, then, is soldiers arrayed in ranks and you inspect them. And if one of them has his helmet on crooked you dismiss him?

AUTHOR: Very well. I *examine* them.

PROTAGORAS: Ah, examen! You evoke the tongue of the balance. You have come back to weighing after all.

AUTHOR: No! I *contemplate* them and this I do as in the temple, as the augur directs.

PROTAGORAS: Do you really mean to say that we should *not* weigh evidence!

AUTHOR: Yes. I do mean to say that.

PROTAGORAS: Astounding!

AUTHOR: Not so astounding as your metaphorical *weighing*.

PROTAGORAS: It is not my weighing. It has always been done. Since the beginning of time. It is simply human judgment.

AUTHOR: Tell me about weighing. What is this human faculty and how do I know that I have it? What are the operations I perform?

PROTAGORAS: You judge. You get the facts and then you judge them. Great Zeus! Is this so difficult?

AUTHOR: Please do not tell me about judging. If I follow the etymology back to yoke—which in one form or another is the source of the balance scales—I get right back to weighing. Did you know that our English word *weigh* is a descendant of a very ancient root word that means *to transport in a vehicle*? A yoke, like this one across my shoulders, is of course a vehicle of sorts, and in it, as you have seen, I transport things. When in a blinding flash of invention this vehicle becomes the balance scales, how logical to call what it does *weighing*.[1] But back to matters present.

How do I weigh in my mind? If someone asks me to get the product of 4 times 23, I know just what to do. First, I multiply 4 by 20. This is easy; I have it memorized. It is 80. Then I multiply 4 by 3. Also easy, also memorized. It is 12. Then I add 80 and 12 and get 92. Very easy. But when you tell me to weigh the facts, I do not know what to do. What is the first step?

PROTAGORAS: Get the facts.

AUTHOR: And the second?

PROTAGORAS: How is it that all other humans have had no problem with this fundamental faculty?

AUTHOR: I know that better than you since I have examined their utterances about this matter since the time of the ancient Egyptians. I have examined more than a few of the utterances of your own countrymen. Your own countryman Epictetus said this: "When we intend to judge of weights, we do not judge by guess: where we intend to judge of straight and crooked, we do not judge by guess." Discourses. Chapter 28.

PROTAGORAS: Ah ha! You have facts! Let us have the facts.

CHORUS: First, let us have some corn.

PROTAGORAS: No. First, let us contemplate. Let him tell us how he contemplates the evidence.

AUTHOR: I see the facts—things that have been done—and I ask of them, What do you portend? Where do you point?

PROTAGORAS: These are not the facts I meant

AUTHOR: Very well. These are the facts I think you meant, but I found them in a place far away. Come with me now to a place you ancient Greeks knew very well. I mean ancient Egypt. Five thousand years ago, more or less, there were treasury buildings in that land where the Pharaoh's gold and silver were kept. Look, in this picture copied from the wall of a tomb we see some of the government offices of the nomarch Chnemhotep who served the pharaoh Amenemhet II. Here, on the left, we see balance scales in the treasury building.[2] The treasurer, an official of the highest rank,[3] sits here on his divan and watches the proceedings while this worker weighs the money and the scribe here on the right records the results. Since we are told that Amenemhet II began his reign in 1876 BC, we cannot consider this scene to be any older than that, but the treasuries of much earlier pharaohs have been described, though in lesser detail,[4] and it seems altogether reasonable to assume that those very early treasuries of perhaps 5,000 years ago did not differ greatly from what we see here. In this picture we see the weighing of treasure in more detail. Here in one pan of the balance we see ring-like ingots of gold while in the other pan are the known weights against which the ingots are to be weighed.[5]

PROTAGORAS: In this picture, in the pan you say holds the known weights, I see the heads of oxen. These are the known weights? How do you know?

AUTHOR: The heads of oxen I think are heads of bulls, and bulls were worshipped by the ancient Egyptians.[6] The pharaohs liked to think of themselves as mighty bulls. Perhaps these are in the shape of the heads of bulls because they were the property of a pharaoh, perhaps because the weights themselves were thought to be sacred. We know of at least one weight for weighing gold that is inscribed with the name of a pharaoh. In our museums there are many surviving examples of the weights the Egyptians used for weighing, and we know something of how they derived them, that is, their system of weights.[7]

PROTAGORAS: Then they knew how much these weights weighed?

AUTHOR: At least they thought they did, for much as we inscribe our known weights they inscribed some of theirs to show their weights. Regrettably, the actual weights of their units varied from time to time, and we apparently now have difficulty in saying just how much a weight recorded by the Egyptians actually weighed.[8]

PROTAGORAS: Is this technical matter actually germane to your argument? I thought you were concerned with magic.

CHORUS: We have begun to think of butcher shops and would much prefer to hear of magic.

AUTHOR: It is important only as a way of showing that accurate weighing was well known to the ancient Egyptians and that it was important to them. But it is quite important to my argument that we look closely at what is going on here. During the use of the scales the ancient Egyptians probably placed the known weights against which something was to weighed into the pan which rested on the floor or perhaps on a platform of some sort.[9] Then, when the thing to be weighed was placed in the other pan, the pan with the known weights would rise if the thing being weighed were heavy enough. The gold weighed in the treasury would presumably be in ingots of standard weights, and the purpose of the weighing was therefore to test the truth of the assertion that the weight of the ingot was indeed standard or that it weighed as much as the maker said it did. If the gold weighed at least as much as the maker of the ingot said it did, then the known weight in the other pan would rise and the truth of that assertion would thus be demonstrated. The known weights—the test—could, then, have been regarded as representing truth, and even now our idea of truth is tinged with magic. The truth shall make you free, we say.

PROTAGORAS: And thus a metaphor is born, I think you are going to say.

CHORUS: Yes! The truth is golden! And the truth is that we hunger for the golden corn.

AUTHOR: Yes, I think so, though I do not have all the evidence I could wish for. What I have seen is compelling, but what I need to clinch this part of my argument is some piece of writing in plain view—a few hieroglyphs— that has yet to be discovered for what it is.

PROTAGORAS: And what have you seen?

AUTHOR: You shall see it too. Here is a painting from what we now call the Egyptian Book of the Dead.[10] The Egyptians themselves seemed to have called it *Going Forth by Day* for it represented their hopes of returning to life from the underworld of death.[11] It was a scroll of papyrus that was placed in the coffins of those Egyptian dead wealthy enough to afford it and was intended to assist them through the terrible tribulations of the afterlife, especially the judgment. It contained illustrations such as this one and many incantations, prayers, instructions, and similar short pieces, what we now call spells. This painting is an illustration of the judgment of the dead. Here, on the left, is the dead man to be judged in the great Hall of the Two Truths, in this case a man named Ani, a scribe and without doubt one of considerable importance and wealth. Behind him is his wife, and we shall hope that she is not dead just because he is. In the center is the centerpiece, the balance scales on which his heart is being weighed. Anubis, the old jackal-headed god of the dead, manipulates the scales while on the right the ibis-headed Thoth, god of many things and inventor of the scales and of writing, records the result. In the pan on the left is the heart of Ani while in the pan on the right is an ostrich feather, the symbol of Maat, Goddess of Truth. On the far right here is Amemit, the monster with the head of a crocodile who devours the condemned.

PROTAGORAS: We have seen much of this before, but where is the treasurer, the lord of this scene.

AUTHOR: Here the lord is Osiris, sitting on his throne, here, far to the right, the new god of the dead as well as of vegetation and thus of rebirth. He is the central figure in a famous myth that gave much structure to ancient Egyptian religion.[12] He is a god of immensely greater stature than Anubis. He has been regarded as the sun-god Re in another guise.[13] He has even been called the King of Kings.[14]

PROTAGORAS: Then you would have us believe that we have come from the pharaoh's treasury to this Hall of the Two Truths only by casting new players in the principal roles.

AUTHOR: I think it was not that simple. You must recall that the treasury was an office of great importance, and ancient Egyptians must have been in awe of it, but still I am not altogether satisfied. Surely this august scene produced metaphors quite early in the life of ancient Egypt, but the earliest I know of appeared in hieroglyphic texts, on the inside of coffins, only about 4,000 years ago. In these texts we find such metaphors as *this balance of Re in which he weighs Truth*.[15] The weighing-of-the-heart metaphor in the Book of the Dead appears later, perhaps 3,300 years ago. If I could find something like *his heart is as precious as that which the lord of the treasury weighs* or like our modern expression *he has a heart of gold*, say, about the end of the Old Kingdom or early in the Middle Kingdom, at least early enough to make it an ancient notion by the time the weighing of the heart first appears[16], then I would have not only the source of the metaphorical scales of the mortuary rites but also an evolutionary link that would confirm my argument beyond reasonable doubt.

PROTAGORAS: Beyond reasonable doubt, indeed! Even what you wish to find would not yet persuade me. How does the practical business of weighing become the magic of the funeral rite? How could the quite substantial known weights of the treasury be replaced by a feather? A weight in the shape of a goddess, as in the shape of a sacred animal, I can accept, but not one in the form of a feather.

AUTHOR: You will recall, Protagoras, that in the treasury the desire was to see the known weights rise as the gold was placed in the other pan. In the weighing of the heart scene, the known weights of the treasury—the *truth* of the treasury—are replaced by another kind of truth, the moral *truth* of Maat, represented by Maat herself or by her feather. And in the context of the weighing of the heart, as in the context of the weighing of gold in the treasury, the desired result was to see the *truth* rise. Thus the feather, when it substitutes for Maat, should not be thought of as suitable in this context by virtue of *lightness*—although such a connection is altogether reasonable— but rather by virtue of its association with flight or rising. This idea of truth rising I think may be found in judicial thinking even now.[17]

PROTAGORAS: And this judgment after death is the source of judicial weighing? I cannot yet accept that.

AUTHOR: A noted scholar of ancient Egypt, one whose work I have already referred to, translated an ancient Egyptian tale which he called *The Eloquent Peasant*.[18] In this tale, a peasant had gotten himself into deep trouble because his donkey had eaten corn that belonged to another.

CHORUS: We have eaten corn that belongs to another! Fly! Fly!

AUTHOR: Come down to earth. I gave you the corn and thus it was your own. In the tale of which I speak the corn was not given, but neither would the donkey have eaten of that corn if it had not been forced from the path on which it traveled by an unconscionable act of the owner of the corn. Nevertheless, the owner of the corn, for compensation, seized all that the peasant had. If you think this was a great injustice, be assured that the peasant thought likewise and straightway appealed his case to a high official. Though he seemingly was not answered, he would not give up, and nine times he petitioned, many times metaphorically calling forth the balance scales to show justice rightly done. "Is it not wrong, a balance which tilts, a plummet which deflects," the peasant asks. "Does the balance deflect? Does the stand-balance incline to one side?" he goes on. "Speak not falsehood," he says to the official, "thou art the balance."[19]

PROTAGORAS: Then this is the first metaphorical use of the balance scales in the halls of justice?

AUTHOR: Our scholar did not think so. He recalled an even earlier metaphor which I have already mentioned, the "balance of Re." This he thought was the first appearance of that metaphor.[20]

PROTAGORAS: And do you agree?

AUTHOR: Yes and no. I agree that the first appearance was likely earlier than the time of the tale of *The Eloquent Peasant*— perhaps no more than 3,900 years ago[21]— but, no, I do not agree that the metaphor he cited was necessarily that first appearance.

PROTAGORAS: Ah! You have found another.

AUTHOR: Yes, I think so. At least one that seems to me to be much more in accord with the drama of judgment.

PROTAGORAS: Drama? Now judgment is drama? But again I do not pay attention enough to etymology. Yes, drama. Actions on a stage, and surely the hall of justice is a stage. What is this dramatic metaphor, then?

AUTHOR: "Who is this god whose eyebrows are the arms of the balance?"[22]

PROTAGORAS: Eyebrows! Eyebrows are the arms of the balance?

AUTHOR: Watch my face, Protagoras. Watch my eyebrows *mirror* the arms of the balance, one rising as the other falls, just as the arms of the balance do. I cannot do this as well as a god might, but imagine Thoth, who is this god whose eyebrows are the arms of the balance, standing there by the scales of judgment waiting to record the judgment. I cannot say which eyebrow held the feather of Maat and which the heart of the dead, but the expression on the face of that god—a cold sneer or a benign smile beneath the eyebrows—left no doubt as to the outcome of the judgment. Now that is a fit beginning for the balance of justice![23]

PROTAGORAS: And a fit ending for this exposition. The sun is sinking and you have far to go. But tell me, why do you make so much of *rising* truth?

AUTHOR: Because it establishes a link with the ancient treasury from which I think this judgment scene came. The known weights—the truth of the treasury—rise to affirm the assertion of a certain amount of gold; the truth of judgment—the feather of Maat—rises to affirm the assertion of righteousness. The two scenes are consistent as regards the behavior of the scales.

PROTAGORAS: Interesting but hardly persuasive.

AUTHOR: But you will admit it is the sort of thing a lawyer would make much of.

PROTAGORAS: Bah! You are too eager to connect justice with commerce.

AUTHOR: I will not make the connection; the connection has been there for thousands of years, as I intend to show. And you should say that the connection is between the *administration* of justice and commerce; justice is sacred but the administration of justice is suspect.

PROTAGORAS: May we move on? By your own reckoning we have 5,000 years of history to traverse, and we have not made progress since the sun began to sink.

CHORUS: Put down a trail of corn and we shall make great progress!

AUTHOR: We shall soon go to your native Greece, Protagoras, but before we do I want to jump ahead several thousand years to medieval Europe. There is not a more striking example of the transfer of this judgment scene to other cultures than the sculpture to be found on the cathedral of Saint Lazarus at Autun in France. Here is a picture of a small part of the tympanum of the west doorway.[24] Here we see the scales of judgment, quite recognizable. The ancient Egyptians represented the dead in this scene with the emblem of the heart, but this reticence seems to have disappeared by the time the weighing-of-the-heart notion got to medieval Europe. Here the horror of the judgment is quite explicit, and—absent Egyptian certitude—the soul at this last judgment is shown, in clearly human form, sitting in a scale pan. The figure in the other pan is a gruesome devil. The Archangel Michael, on the left, is doing the weighing while this devil, on the right, attempts to rig the outcome by putting his hand on the beam of the scales. Here you see that some of these souls ascend into heaven while others—depending on the outcome of the judgment—are doomed to hell. Oh, forgive me, Protagoras! I spoke without thinking!

PROTAGORAS: Yes. Of course. And your excuse is that you do not know what you are talking about.

AUTHOR: Or to whom. Perhaps I can make amends by taking you now to ancient Greece. Look now, Protagoras, across this wine-dark sea to the battlements of Troy. There is the plain where the Achaean armor flashed, where Achilles defiled the poor, dead Hector, where great Zeus, sleeping, failed his sacred duty.

CHORUS: Wine-dark sea? It's a duck pond.

AUTHOR: I was trying to be poetic.

PROTAGORAS: I am not familiar with your meter.

AUTHOR: You know this passage well, Protagoras. The *Iliad*, Book 7. Apollo speaks to Minerva, daughter of Jove, saying, "Have you no pity upon the Trojans, and would you incline the scales of victory in favour of the Danaans?"[25] Are these not the metaphorical scales of the ancient Egyptians, now in all Homeric splendor? Can you imagine that the translator did not find the metaphorical scales in this passage? That he did such violence to the great Homer?

PROTAGORAS: Have you read the original Greek, and do you know that Homer himself used this metaphor? Perhaps your translator supplied it, daring to put words into the mouth of the great Homer.

AUTHOR: You are right, Protagoras. Our translator did put these words into the mouth of the great Homer. In this passage, in the original Greek of the immortal Homer, the word for the balance scales is not to be found. In the English of another translator, perhaps more precise, the passage is: "Is it that thou mayest give to the Danaans victory to turn the tide of battle, seeing thou hast no pity for the Trojans, that perish?"[26]

CHORUS: Pluck his feathers and roast him!

PROTAGORAS: May Zeus cut off his tongue!

AUTHOR: Yes, I have read the original Greek, and I have read another passage of the Iliad in which the metaphorical scales unambiguously appear, as I shall soon show you.[27] But for the balance scales in these lines we must look elsewhere. I plead for our translator, a respected man of letters, that there is no culpability here. As he pored over the words of Homer, the image of the balance was somehow evoked, and he could not but translate as he did. Perhaps it was the word *niken*, sometimes used in the context of law and justice.[28]

PROTAGORAS: Perhaps, but a question remains. Even if Homer himself did use this metaphor, how do you know that it is Egyptian and not Greek?

AUTHOR: We of this age, Protagoras, universally acknowledge our debt to ancient Greece—indeed, some find it fashionable to say that we *are* Greeks—and I think you Greeks should acknowledge your debt to Egypt. You are as much Egyptian as we are Greek.

PROTAGORAS: Then you yourself are also Egyptian.

AUTHOR: Yes. And my heart swells with pride, to think that I have in me such conceptions as can raise those vast monuments—out of flesh and stone and little else. Were not the pyramids an omen, Protagoras? After Khufu there could be no turning back. Magnificence of scale was chiseled into our

73

brains—or should I say our hearts—and we should henceforth be driven by it.

PROTAGORAS: You are poetizing again, and you have evaded my question. How do you know that the balance scales metaphor is Egyptian and not Greek?

AUTHOR: I cannot be sure, of course, but the historical evidence certainly suggests that the Egyptians had this notion while you Greeks were still in your cultural infancy. We first find the metaphorical scales in Egyptian literature and painting—to say nothing of the actual scales of the treasury— more than a thousand years before we first find them in Homer, if indeed they are there.

PROTAGORAS: Perhaps we got the scales and the metaphor from the Sumerians, also a very ancient people.

AUTHOR: Perhaps. We have good evidence that scales of some sort existed more than 5,000 years ago among the Babylonians and Assyrians.[29]

PROTAGORAS: Then why are you of the opinion that the Greeks got the scales from the Egyptians?

CHORUS: Do Greeks have scales? Are they fish?

AUTHOR: Another picture, Protagoras. Here is a scene on a Greek cup of the sixth century BC, shortly before your civilization reached its zenith. Here are the balance scales, here the workers doing the weighing, here on the left a high official of some sort.[30] Do you see his scepter here? Where have you seen all this before?

PROTAGORAS: Yes, of course, in the Egyptian Book of the Dead, but must you be so patronizing? I am quite capable of weighing evidence on my own.

CHORUS: Scold him, Author! He is weighing evidence again!

AUTHOR: Yes, in the Book of the Dead and elsewhere in Egypt.[31]

PROTAGORAS: Where else in Greece?

AUTHOR: The *Iliad* again. Your Homer said, in the English of our errant translator, "...the sire of all balanced his golden scales, and put two fates of death within them, one for the Trojans and

74

the other for the Achaeans. He took the balance by the middle, and when he lifted it up the day of the Achaeans sank; the death-fraught scale of the Achaeans settled down upon the ground, while that of the Trojans rose heavenwards."[32] On the other hand, our perhaps more precise translator rendered it thus: "...the Father lifted on high his golden scales, and set therein two fates of grievous death, one for the horse-taming Trojans, and one for the brazen-coated Achaeans; then he grasped the balance by the midst and raised it, and down sank the day of doom of the Achaeans."[33] This time there is essential agreement, for the word is there: *talanton*, the balance. How can you now doubt, Protagoras, that the Egyptian scales are there in Greece?

PROTAGORAS: You press me too hard, Author. You cannot make your argument by force. In this court you must present evidence. Even if they are there, how can you be so strongly of the opinion that they came from Egypt? If the Greeks had the actual scales, as they certainly did, could they not have conceived the metaphor on their own? It seems almost inevitable to me.

AUTHOR: Such a conception is of course possible once the scales are known, but I do not think that it is inevitable. Let me explain my opinion.

CHORUS: Let you? Do you mean in the same way we *let* you give us corn?

AUTHOR: The metaphorical—ritualistic, magical—use of the scales might have arisen from the observation that he who had and understood the scales—priest, officer of the king, or even the king himself—had the power to confidently resolve disputes involving the quantity of something precious, and those granted such an observation could well have attempted to apply the power of the scales to other matters of judgment. But while this scene seems likely to have occurred in some form and at some time everywhere the scales existed, we do not always find the metaphorical scales in such places. In some of the writings of the ancient middle east—Assyria, Babylon, Sumer—I have found much use of the scales but none metaphorical.[34] This suggests to me that the appearance of such a conception as the metaphorical scales is not inevitable but only likely, especially when a culture without the metaphor closely associates with one that does. You have seen that the earliest evidence we have of this conception is Egyptian, that the Greeks knew the Egyptians well and traded with them. Certainly it was in trade that the actual scales were most important. How can we then imagine that the Greeks could have known the Egyptians and their scales so well and not have known of their magical conceptions?

PROTAGORAS: Perhaps you could tell me of other examples of this magical conception that you have with certainty found in the Greek writing of my time. Perhaps you could stop castigating Greeks and give me examples of the metaphorical balance in other cultures.

AUTHOR: Yes, I will. But first one example from the *Iliad*.

PROTAGORAS: I grow weary and the sun is far advanced.

CHORUS: We have advanced to starvation.

AUTHOR: The sun does not advance, Protagoras. It is the earth that...

PROTAGORAS: ...advances. Now I am exhausted!

CHORUS: Only exhausted? See us perish?

AUTHOR: It is an important matter or I would not impose on you.

PROTAGORAS: Impose then and be done with it!

CHORUS: Impose some corn on us. Be really severe.

AUTHOR: From our more precise translator, this: "...the Father lifted on high his scales, and set therein two fates of grievous death, one for Achilles, and one for the horse-taming Hector; then he grasped the balance by the midst and raised it; and down sank the day of doom of Hector..."[35]

CHORUS: You forget your lines. You recited this only moments ago.

PROTAGORAS: No. Our epic bards spoke thus. Once they found a way to say something, they used it again and again. This is another passage in a familiar pattern. It is of no great significance.

AUTHOR: It has significance for me. It suggests to me the ritual incantations of the Egyptians. Homer and the other bards had the

76

image of the magical balance in their unconscious minds, and every occasion that evoked it brought forth a metaphor with certain blanks to be filled in.

PROTAGORAS: You make too much of trifles.

CHORUS: We make short work of trifles.

AUTHOR: Very well. I will leave it where it is. Aeschylus comes now from Marathon to speak his words upon this tragic stage.

CHORUS: Tragic stage? It's a muddy shore.

PROTAGORAS: Ah! Now to my own time. Now we shall be done with trifles!

AUTHOR: Agamemnon is the play. "Justice inclines her scales so that wisdom comes at the price of suffering."[36]

PROTAGORAS: Yes, I know it well. You will not find *talanton* here, but the image of the balance is in *epirrepei*.

AUTHOR: Now Demosthenes. A little after your time but one whom you admire, I believe.

PROTAGORAS: Yes. Perhaps the greatest orator of all time—and Greek. But before you leave the great Aeschylus, I must ask you why you have not mentioned his play entitled *Psychostasia*.[37] In it we have...

AUTHOR: *Psychostasia?* I have never heard of such a play! How wonderful! I must read it, but where will I find it?

PROTAGORAS: Where you found the others—unless, like so many others, it has been mislaid somewhere. There is a wonderful scene with Zeus himself and the weighing of souls. But, please, you were speaking of Demosthenes.

AUTHOR: Yes, I was! I am nearly breathless! From his second Olynthiac: "...fortune is indeed a great weight in the scales..."[38]

PROTAGORAS: Yes, I know the speech well. The scales are there, but this is fate, not justice.

AUTHOR: Then once more for justice. Aeschylus, your contemporary, in the most telling of the balance metaphors I have found, has this in *The Libation Bearers*: "...the balance of Justice keeps watch..."[39] That phrase is there, unambiguously, in the Greek words of Aeschylus.

PROTAGORAS: It is there, but it is art, not magic, as you would have us believe. And it is surely Greek, not Egyptian.

77

AUTHOR: Yes, just as surely as I am modern and not Greek.

PROTAGORAS: We should get to the end of your argument before the end of the world if we do not argue this point.

CHORUS: The end of the world! Do we have time for corn?

AUTHOR: Very well. In deference to the world I abandon that particular point, but I cannot yet abandon Greece. Do you remember that I said Plato called you a skillful weigher? Well, I took too much liberty. What Plato actually said to you, in his dialog, in the English translation that I have, was: "Like a practised weigher, put pleasant things and painful in the scales..."[40] This was admonition, not accusation, and I must therefore believe that Plato was also given to metaphorical weighing.

CHORUS: Give him a cup of hemlock!

AUTHOR: In this passage I find the Greek *histanai*, among the uses of which is *to place in the balance*, *weigh*, but more exciting for me is the word *zugon*. Here is the yoke of the oxen, the beam of the balance, the whole balance.[41] Here in this passage is the whole history of the balance scales!

PROTAGORAS: Again you exaggerate. And again your excitement adds unjust weight to your discourse.

CHORUS: Let him be stoned!

AUTHOR: I said that I found no metaphorical scales in certain writings of the ancient middle east, but there is a notable exception in this part of the world. I mean the Hebrew texts that in my age have become what we call the Old Testament. In these the balance is to be found in abundance, in both actual and metaphorical uses. Let me give you some examples. Genesis 23:16. "And Abraham hearkened unto Ephron; and Abraham weighed to Ephron the silver, which he had named in the audience of the sons of Heth, four hundred shekels of silver, current money with the merchant." Genesis 19:36. "Just balances, just weights, a just ephah, and a just hin, shall ye have: I am the Lord your God, which brought you out of the land of Egypt."[42] Ezra 8:29. "Watch ye, and keep them, until ye weigh them before the chief of the priests and the Levites, and chief of the fathers of

Israel, at Jerusalem, in the chambers of the house of the Lord." Surely these passages establish that the balance was well known and widely used among the Israelites.

PROTAGORAS: That I grant but I have not yet heard a metaphor.

CHORUS: Did they weigh corn?

AUTHOR: Then this: Second Samuel 2:3. "Talk no more so exceeding proudly; let not arrogancy come out of your mouth: for the Lord is a God of knowledge, and by him actions are weighed." Job 6:2. "Oh that my grief were thoroughly weighed, and my calamity laid in the balances together!" Job 31:6. "Let me be weighed in an even balance that God may know mine integrity." Can there be any doubt?

PROTAGORAS: How is it that the Israelites had this conception and others in their part of the world did not?

AUTHOR: Because they came out of Egypt.

PROTAGORAS: And with them brought Egyptian scales.

AUTHOR: And the imagery of judgment! Hear this: Proverbs 16:2. "All the ways of a man are clean in his own eyes; but the Lord weigheth the spirits." Can this be else than the weighing of the heart?

PROTAGORAS: You seem certain of this connection. From this came the judgment carved in stone on the temple of Lazarus at Autun?

AUTHOR: As certain as I can be without reading the Hebrew, and of course I cannot. By many twists and turns the sculpture of the cathedral of Saint Lazarus might have come from these words, but there are many other routes: those plowed by Greek ships of commerce, those made by Alexander and Caesar. Whatever the route of passage, I cannot doubt that the judgment of Saint Lazarus is the weighing of the heart in Egypt, that the weighing of the heart is the weighing of the gold in the treasury of the pharaoh.

PROTAGORAS: Let us press on, then, by whatever route you choose. And let it take us near Hades, for there I end this journey.

CHORUS: Where is Hades? Is it far from here?

AUTHOR: It is just beneath your feet.

CHORUS: Fly! Fly!

PROTAGORAS: Come back! Come back! Your jest is no better than Author's and I have no time for either. Better to eat corn than to be it!

AUTHOR: You grow querulous, Protagoras. Should I take this to mean you cannot refute my argument?

PROTAGORAS: Now you speak Latin. May I suggest we go to Rome?

AUTHOR: Very well! Here is Rome.

CHORUS: A field of grass? We had better visions of it.

PROTAGORAS: I think he means you must imagine. Just as I must imagine that I am a sane man listening to rational discourse. What is it in this citadel of Caesars that you think worthy of my attention?

AUTHOR: A little of Egypt. Much of Greece. The law of my world. And the progress of the balance scales. There is also a lady, much courted and little honored.

PROTAGORAS: Yes. I think I know who you mean; I know her well. Here and there, in stone or bronze, on a pedestal. In this city she is called Astraea, I believe, but sometimes Themis, her name in my native Greece. She holds the scales and in later times often also a sword. Whether she is an immigrant here or a fugitive I cannot say, but the lady is much traveled˙ She is the law and order that you in your time lament. Without her the Greece that you know could not have been.[43]

AUTHOR: But she was not the only one to hold the scales. Here, Protagoras. I show you these coins.

PROTAGORAS: Ah, you practice for the law. Very well. I have examined them. I see figures of women holding scales. Themis? Astraea? Whose coins are they?

AUTHOR: No, not Themis but perhaps Dike, daughter of Themis by Zeus and thus a goddess of justice, or Tyche, Greek goddess of fortune. This one was struck by Antoninus Pius of Alexandria and is of course Roman. This one appears to be Greek.[44]

PROTAGORAS: What little of Egypt have you found here?

AUTHOR: The metaphorical balance, of course.

PROTAGORAS: And, of course, whatever metaphorical balances you have found you consider to be Egyptian.

AUTHOR: Yes. Because we have good evidence that the balance scales were invented by the Egyptians and because we know that they used them metaphorically. And certainly you cannot deny that there was much contact between Greece and Egypt, between Rome and Greece, and between Rome and Egypt. It seems to me that we should have a puzzle only if we did not find metaphorical balances here in Rome.

PROTAGORAS: May I hear them?

AUTHOR: Plutarch, writing of your Pericles: "...taking them apart by themselves and uniting them in one body, by their combined weight he was able, as it were upon the balance, to make a counterpoise to the other party."[45] I have not seen the original Latin, but the translation was done by a famous Englishman, a literary person of great stature. I think he would not have mistreated the Latin of Plutarch. Tacitus, *Histories*, Book 1: "...a body of troops which, to whatever side they might incline, would, whether as allies or enemies, throw a vast weight into the scale."[46] Epictetus, *The Discourses*, Book 1, Chapter 11: "What is the matter presented to us about which we are inquiring? Pleasure. Subject it to the rule, throw it into the balance."[47] Book 2, Chapter 26. "For Socrates knew by what the rational soul is moved, just like a pair of scales, and that it must incline, whether it chooses or not."[48] Shall I go on?

CHORUS: Tell him to stop, Protagoras! We are becoming unbalanced!

PROTAGORAS: No. Unless you mean to move on to wherever you are taking us. I do not doubt that the metaphorical scales are here. I wonder, though, that you have not yet found them in law. That is your concern.

AUTHOR: But I have. I have wondered when this marvelous invention first got into English law and thus into the law of my own land. I do not know with any certainty, but I think I have found a clue. There is a treatise on English law called Glanvill, written in Latin more than 800 years ago.[49] In it I found this: "Ac per hoc et laboribus hominum parcitur et sumptibus pauperum. Preterea, quanto magis ponderat in iudiciis plurium idoneorum testium fides quam unius tantum..."[50] The clue I referred to is *ponderat*, it weighs. If one weighs, the scales are present; it cannot be otherwise.

PROTAGORAS: Strange Latin, but allow me to translate, haltingly, I fear. "And through this also sparing hardship of mankind and expense of the poor. Besides, as the testimony of many fit witnesses weighs more in trials than that of one..."

AUTHOR: Excellent!

CHORUS: Excellent? We heard a grievous error!

PROTAGORAS: What else shall I translate for you?

AUTHOR: That is all.

PROTAGORAS: What? You have only this in an entire treatise, and you want to draw a conclusion?

AUTHOR: Why should I not draw a conclusion? Is *ponderat* there or is it not? If it is there, then metaphorical weighing—metaphorical use of the balance scales—had gotten into English law at this point. Testimony can be weighed only on metaphorical balance scales. Where would you put it on the butcher's scales? How would you get it into the pan? And even if you could get it into the pan, against what would you weigh it? A cylinder of brass? No, Protagoras, this single word betrays that ancient book. The scales were there in the mind of whoever it was who wrote this treatise, and surely he was a lawyer. That he was learned in Roman law there can be no doubt,[51] and there as we have seen he surely would have found weighing—*ponderare*— though possibly nothing of what the weighing is done with—*bilancia*— the balance scales.

PROTAGORAS: A single word in a whole treatise leads you to conviction?

CHORUS: We would certainly convict him.

AUTHOR: If that single word can be explained in some other way, I will recant. Otherwise, I must be convinced. The metaphorical balance scales got into English law at least 800 years ago, and perhaps sooner.

PROTAGORAS: What other metaphorical balance scales of this time?

AUTHOR: Just a little later, but first this, because our medieval English lawyer might have read this. Epictetus again, *The Discourses*, Book Three, Chapter 22. Cynicism: "It is necessary also for such a man to have a certain habit of body: for if he appears to be consumptive, thin and pale, his testimony has not then the same weight."[52] I cannot vouch for the translation, but we again seem to be weighing testimony.

CHORUS: Where is justice?

PROTAGORAS: Where is justice, indeed! I cannot get this sophomore to advance a year!

AUTHOR: I shall advance one hundred and fifty years! Giovanni Boccaccio, *The Decameron*, The Eighth Day: "I must borrow the selfe-same courtesie of you, which in equity you cannot deny mee, weighing the wrong you have sustained by my wife."[53]

PROTAGORAS: And was this weighing done by Giovanni Boccaccio or by his English translator?

AUTHOR: I cannot say.

PROTAGORAS: Then your testimony has little weight!

CHORUS: Where are the stones?

AUTHOR: Let them weigh what they will! All together weigh enough; I cannot be wrong in every instance.

PROTAGORAS: Perhaps if you gave me examples from your own language your illiteracy would be less apparent. Do you not have a dramatist who would stand not far behind the Greeks?

AUTHOR: Shakespeare! And he would stand beside, not behind! "Why, man, he doth bestride the narrow world Like a Colossus, and we petty men Walk under his huge legs and peep about To find ourselves dishonourable graves." The play is *Julius Caesar*. Cassius speaks to Brutus—about Caesar, not Shakespeare, but I am sure you get my drift.

PROTAGORAS: Do you mean that you have once again drifted from your subject? What has this to do with weighing?

AUTHOR: Nothing! Now hear this: *All's Well That Ends Well.*

The King says, "My honour's at the stake; which to defeat, I must produce my power. Here, take her hand, Proud scornful boy, unworthy this good gift; That dost in vile misprision shackle up My love and her desert; that canst not dream, We, poising us in her defective scale, Shall weigh thee to the beam..."

PROTAGORAS: I do not know the play. Perhaps you could translate.

AUTHOR: Forget the play. Consider only the passage. What could be more simple? Oh, very well. A pretty woman has cured the King of an illness. To reward her the King gives her in marriage to a count that she has always loved. But the count refuses her and the King is quite upset. We, the King says—the royal *we*—if the two of us are weighed in her defective scale—defective because she is blinded by love and thinks he is heavy when clearly he is not—then I shall cause you to rise up so fast that you shall strike the beam of the balance, or perhaps cause you to rise up to the beam—of the house—where you shall hang. You see? Even though the scale is defective, the King would still be so much heavier than the count that the count would still rise up quickly, perhaps up to the beam to be hanged. Is this not judgment most excellent? A little later on the King says...

PROTAGORAS: Please! A little later on I should hang myself! Perhaps another example from your great playwright would be better.

CHORUS: Perhaps a hanging would be better.

AUTHOR: Very well. Then this: *Richard II*. The gardener says to the Queen, "Pardon me, madam: little joy have I To breathe this news; yet what I say is true. King Richard, he is in the mighty hold Of Bolingbroke: their fortunes both are weigh'd: In your lord's scale is nothing but himself, And some few vanities that make him light; But in the balance of great Bolingbroke, Besides himself, are all the English peers, And with that odds he weighs King Richard down."[54] Is that not monstrous judgment? And do you see how dreadful to be light in the balance, as the Egyptians knew?

PROTAGORAS: It is certainly a better example. Please do not translate. Perhaps now we could move on a few years.

AUTHOR: Very well. Another fifty years. John Milton. *Paradise Lost*. Allow me to recite:[55]

...Of Heaven perhaps, or all the elements
At least had gone to wrack, disturbed and torn
With violence of this conflict, had not soon
The Eternal, to prevent such horrid fray,
Hung forth in Heaven his golden scales, yet seen
Betwixt Astraea and the Scorpion sign,
Wherein all things created first he weighed,
The pendulous round earth with balanced air
In counterpoise, now ponders all events,
Battles and realms: In these he put two weights,
The sequel each of parting and of fight:
The latter quick up flew, and kicked the beam,
Which Gabriel spying, thus bespake the Fiend.

PROTAGORAS: Golden scales? "In these he put two weights..."? This we have heard before. Homer. Your Milton pays tribute to a Greek.

AUTHOR: Your Homer owed tribute to the Egyptians.

PROTAGORAS: Move on, Author. Move on.

AUTHOR: In Shakespeare's *Measure for Measure* there is this curious line: "Go to, sir; you weigh equally; a feather will turn the scale."[56] Could this be the feather of Maat? Does Shakespeare pay tribute to Egypt?

PROTAGORAS: Move on, Author. Move on.

AUTHOR: To another time or to another language?

PROTAGORAS: As you wish, but remember that in another language you know even less of what you are talking about than you do in your own.

AUTHOR: French. Voltaire. *Candide*. "I know not," said Martin, "in what balance your Pangloss could have weighed the misfortunes of mankind, and have set a just estimation on their sufferings..." Rousseau. *Confessions*. "...I weigh in the scale of reason every action of my life." German. Nietzsche. *Thus Spake Zarathustra*. "In my dream, in my last morning-dream, I stood today on a promontory—beyond the world; I held a pair of scales, and weighed the world."[57]

PROTAGORAS: I weigh all this against my time and see it tossed into the sky!

AUTHOR: Your time is tossed?

PROTAGORAS: The scales are tossed!

CHORUS: Could you weigh out a pound or two of corn?

AUTHOR: We are weighing evidence, Protagoras. Am I not, like you lawyers, to wear you out with tedium?

PROTAGORAS: You have certainly lessened me. Pray that enough remains to fill my place in Hades!

AUTHOR: American. Ralph Waldo Emerson. *Essays.* "The world is full of judgment-days, and into every assembly that a man enters, in every action he attempts, he is gauged and stamped. In every troop of boys that whoop and run in each yard and square, a new-comer is as well and accurately weighed in the course of a few days, and stamped with his right number, as if he had undergone a formal trial of his strength, speed, and temper. Nathaniel Hawthorne. *The House of the Seven Gables.* "What is there so ponderous in evil, that a thumb's bigness of it should outweigh the mass of things not evil which were heaped into the other scale!"[58] Herman Melville. *Moby Dick.* "What of it, if some old hunks of a sea-captain orders me to get a broom and sweep down the decks? What does that indignity amount to, weighed, I mean, in the scales of the New Testament?"[59]

PROTAGORAS: Indignity, indeed! I should rather scrub a deck!

AUTHOR: What do you conclude, Protagoras?

PROTAGORAS: What should I conclude? Simply tell me and I will concede. Name your price for mercy and I will agree!

AUTHOR: That we have followed this trail of scales from ancient Egypt.

PROTAGORAS: Yes!

AUTHOR: That these metaphorical scales are in us all and are evoked when we think of judgment.

PROTAGORAS: Yes!

AUTHOR: That the further along in time we go the less we hear of what this metaphorical weighing is done with. We surely go on with our weighing, but we forget what we do it with.

PROTAGORAS: No.

AUTHOR: No?

PROTAGORAS: No! I recant and concede no more. You push me too hard; I must have more evidence of this last point.

AUTHOR: And you shall. The language of the lawyers of my time is the evidence that you want, and you shall surely have it. We have come all this way to prepare for that.

PROTAGORAS: Yes, we have come far but have not yet gotten to judicial weighing. That, I believe, is the point of all of this. Do you have examples?

AUTHOR: Yes, many, but before we come to them there are other matters we must consider. Otherwise, I fear, my argument will become unreasonably disconnected.

PROTAGORAS: Then at the moment it is only reasonably disconnected.

5

The Marketing of Crime

CHORUS: Quack! Quack! Quack! Quack!

PROTAGORAS: What are you doing to that duck?

CHORUS: Quack! Quack! Quack!

AUTHOR: I am wringing its neck.

PROTAGORAS: In the name of Zeus, why?

CHORUS: Quack! Quack!

AUTHOR: To make a point.

CHORUS: Quack!

PROTAGORAS: This is an outrage! A crime! Surely you can make your point without such violence!

AUTHOR: If it is a crime I shall pay for it.

CHORUS: You surely shall! Our friend here is nearly dead—of mortification—and ruffled feathers.

AUTHOR: Tell me, Protagoras, what a duck is worth.

PROTAGORAS: I cannot. I never bought a duck.

AUTHOR: I can tell you. In my currency, no more than ten dollars, I assure you. Thus, I can pay no more than ten dollars for this crime—if the duck dies—and except for a feather or two he looks fine to me.

PROTAGORAS: You speak nonsense. You do not pay for a crime with money. At least not in this way. You simply do not commit a crime and then offer payment for it. You are thinking of fines, of civil penalties, altogether different from paying for a crime.

AUTHOR: I think otherwise, and of course I shall offer evidence. Do you see this stick, Protagoras? If I should become angry with you and thus strike you with it and injure you severely, what must I pay?

PROTAGORAS: Not less than your life, barbarian! You are dealing with a Greek, not a duck!

AUTHOR: Not so! I must only swear that I did not mean to hurt you and then pay the physician who treats you. It is the law. And if you should then die, I must pay about one hundred and sixty dollars, that is, one half a mina.[1]

PROTAGORAS: What law is this? What law makes of Protagoras a lump of silver?

AUTHOR: This is the venerable law of Hammurabi, king of Babylon, but I assure you that Protagoras is no more than silver under any law, that even if I am put to death for killing you I pay no more, as I shall prove, than half a mina.

PROTAGORAS: You make your plea under laws now thousands of years without a court to enforce them. Your jest does not amuse me, but I hold my breath as I await the point you will now make.

AUTHOR: To be sure, Protagoras, 3,800 years have passed since this law of Hammurabi was written, and that king is dead, but there is little else to make my plea invalid. The price of crime is still reckoned on the balance scales—in silver, or in liberty to be taken away, or in life to be given up—and paying for it, as for bread or meat in the marketplace, is still the established principle. And the logic of this seems to me inexorable. If I kill you but swear I did not intend to do so and thus only pay in money half a mina, what then is the value of Protagoras on these scales? Half a mina. What else can it be? But if I kill you and am convicted of murder, I must pay with my life. That is, I pay a life, my life. How much then do I pay in money? Half a mina, for that is the value of my life. How so? It has already been determined that your life is worth half a mina, and if my life for yours satisfies the scales, then the value of my life must also be half a mina, and that is what I pay if I pay my life. And how does my life for yours balance the scales? Suppose that you kill me and plead that you did not intend to do so and thus pay half a mina for my life. My life on these scales is worth, as your is, half a mina. You know, Protagoras, logician that you are, that things equal to the same thing are equal to each other. The scales attest our equality.

PROTAGORAS: Logic was not made for such arguments as this.

AUTHOR: Nor were the scales made for judgment, for weighing the value of human life. To weigh a loaf of bread is to make equity in the marketplace, but to weigh a life is to make meat of what we value most.

PROTAGORAS: I do not weigh life but evidence; it is only evidence I weigh.

CHORUS: He weighs evidence again! Put him on the scales! Weigh him! Weigh him!

AUTHOR: Not so. If the evidence is in one scale of the balance and my life—or my freedom—is in the other, then you weigh life. If this were not so, then I would fly away, these ducks would swim again, and you would go to Hades.

PROTAGORAS: We argue scales again, but you were speaking of how we pay for crime.

AUTHOR: I meant to say that where we find the metaphorical scales we may also find this metaphorical paying, as in paying for a crime.

PROTAGORAS: If one follows from the other, then why not always? Why do you say we *may* find metaphorical paying?

AUTHOR: The scales are everywhere but of metaphorical paying I am not quite certain. In the Egyptian tale *The Eloquent Peasant*, which I have already mentioned, there is this, as translated by a distinguished scholar of the Egyptian language: "Deal punishment upon him who should be punished..."[2] Another scholar every bit as distinguished has: "Deal punishment to him who ought to be punished."[3] The word *deal* is their rendering of an Egyptian word that means *count, reckon up, assess, pay, allot*, and other similar counting words.[4] Still another distinguished scholar has said that *deal* can be rendered *pay* in this passage, though not literally. That is, the Egyptian word can be rendered *pay* in the metaphorical sense.[5] Thus, we could have, "*Pay* punishment to him who deserves it..." This is not exactly paying for a crime, of course, but it does tend to establish metaphorical paying in the context of wrongdoing.

PROTAGORAS: A useful but not persuasive example. If the scales were carried far from Egypt, why not also this metaphorical paying, as in paying for a crime? Surely your metaphorical paying for crime is also to be found in Egypt, though you have not yet found it. Why one and not the other?

AUTHOR: I have not, as I have said and you have heard, found such paying in Egypt, but I have found the balance scales there and also among the Israelites, who came out of Egypt. If I were to find metaphorical paying also among the Israelites, might I infer that this notion also was brought from Egypt?

PROTAGORAS: You might but such evidence would have little weight. You have already said that if you find the scales you do not necessarily find paying.

CHORUS: Again he weighs! Make him pay, Author!

AUTHOR: I pay no attention to your criticism.

PROTAGORAS: You might have said that in Greek but for your illiteracy. We also had that expression, and it sounds much better in Greek.

CHORUS: Could you say corn in Greek? We are certain it would be tastier.

AUTHOR: Here. The Old Testament again. The Book of Exodus. "And if men strive together, and one smite another with a stone, or with his fist, and he die not, but keepeth his bed: If he rise again, and walk abroad upon his staff, then shall he that smote him be quit: only he shall pay for the loss of his time, and shall cause him to be thoroughly healed." Does this not sound familiar?

PROTAGORAS: It does. It is much like a law of Hammurabi, but what is the point?

AUTHOR: The point is that this is not metaphorical paying but actual paying. Here is the metaphorical. Again the Book of Exodus, Chapter 21, Verses 18 and 19: "If men strive, and hurt a woman with child, so that her fruit depart from her, and yet no mischief follow: he shall be surely punished, according as the woman's husband will lay upon him; and he shall pay as the judges determine. And if any mischief follow, then thou shalt give life for life, Eye for eye, tooth for tooth, hand for hand, foot for foot, Burning for burning, wound for wound, stripe for stripe."

PROTAGORAS: You know Hebrew, then. How could you know that you have found metaphorical paying in this Hebrew writing unless you know Hebrew. Your linguistic accomplishments are indeed impressive.

AUTHOR: No, I do not know Hebrew, but I have asked certain scholars of Hebrew about this matter. They have told me that the

Hebrew word for *give* in "give life for life" is *natan* and that in this passage it may be read as *pay*.[6]

PROTAGORAS: Well! You might have said so before you recited! This bit of information was certainly worthy of my attention.

AUTHOR: This from the first Book of Kings is also worthy of your attention: "And as the king passed by, he cried unto the king: and he said, Thy servant went out into the midst of the battle; and, behold, a man turned aside, and brought a man unto me, and said, Keep this man: if by any means he be missing, then shall thy life be for his life, or else thou shalt pay a talent of silver."[7] Here we have a much higher price placed on a life, a talent of silver, about $20,000 by my reckoning.[8]

PROTAGORAS: It is not altogether clear to me that metaphorical paying is here, or by inference in ancient Egypt, but it certainly is to be found in Greece.

AUTHOR: Yes, I know. Aeschylus. *Agamemnon.* "The spoiler is despoiled, the slayer pays penalty."[9] Could you give me the Greek word?

PROTAGORAS: I think you mean *ektinei.*[10]

AUTHOR: And this: Euripides. *Andromache.* The Chorus speaks. "Perished is Atreus' son by the hand of his wife, and she in her turn received death, in exchange for his murder, at the hands of her children."[11] *In exchange* is of course *in payment.* Could you give me the Greek for *exchange* ?

CHORUS: Oh, that a Chorus could speak of such things!

PROTAGORAS: It is *enallaxasa*, but to make *to pay for murder by death* you also need the word *thanaton.*[12] But enough of this. The metaphorical paying for crime that you seek is there in Greece.

AUTHOR: Please! Reward me for my diligence in searching by listening to one more. Aeschylus. *Eumenides.* "I will wither you alive and drag you down, so that you pay atonement for your murdered mother's agony."[13] Would you once again give me the Greek?

PROTAGORAS: I think it would be *apaxomai*, which can mean *pay*.[14]

AUTHOR: Good! From Egypt have we come, through Israel and thence to Greece, finding uses of the language of the marketplace in matters clearly judicial. Now let us wend our way, example by example, to the very modern times of these gracious ducks.

CHORUS: That is not the corn we want!

PROTAGORAS: And it seems to me that we begin our wending on perilously infirm ground. You leap like a gazelle in reaching your conclusions, and I would like to tidy matters up a bit before we go further.

AUTHOR: And you leap like a kangaroo from metaphor to metaphor!

CHORUS: Kangaroo?

PROTAGORAS: Kangaroo, indeed! Not even these pious ducks know what a kangaroo is, and you dare to chide my metaphors!

CHORUS: Pious?

AUTHOR: Forgive me. Once again I have forgotten to whom I speak. I have wandered too much in time and hardly know where or when I am.

PROTAGORAS: You are forgiven but not excused from answering my concerns. How do you think we came to pay for things that are not goods in the marketplace? If this came to be by error, as you seem to think, then in your wanderings through time you must have seen or heard something that would explain that error.

AUTHOR: Yes. I think so. What do you think of this? We were already in the marketplace where the balance scales are used. We were there when first we used the scales for judgment of moral matters. Having done that, it was no more than an inevitable next step to *pay* for what the scales had charged us with. If it seems to you, as it does to me, that early laws, such as those of Hammurabi, were largely civil and thus mostly matters of money, or at least of wealth or property, then the use of the metaphorical scales in judgment seems natural enough, and the paying in money for what is charged must surely follow. What is the paying of a fine other than the paying of the debt the scales have charged in the moral realm? Do you know the etymology of *fine*,

Protagoras? You pay the money and that is an end to it; it is *final*. If you struck a free-born woman in the time of Hammurabi and thus caused her to lose her unborn child, you paid ten shekels and were home free.[15]

PROTAGORAS: Home free? You paid ten shekels and also lost your home?

AUTHOR: No. Another modern expression, I fear. I meant that ten shekels settled the account entirely.

PROTAGORAS: And therefore, you will say, in the time of Hammurabi the price of an unborn child was ten shekels.

AUTHOR: What would you say, Protagoras?

PROTAGORAS: I would say that it was not Hammurabi's intention to set such a price, or any price at all.

AUTHOR: What was the effect of that law, Protagoras?

PROTAGORAS: Very well! Perhaps we should know more of this law. We Greeks made our laws through careful deliberations.

AUTHOR: That is to say through weighing. And I dare to say you made the same grievous errors as you did so. Well, I can tell you what I have read, Protagoras. I can tell you that even in its own time this law of Hammurabi was old law, not new. It assimilated much older law and custom, even tribal custom. We thus expect to find the law of retaliation and we do. An eye for an eye. A life for a life. I can tell you that the death penalty was common, imposed in ways we might think unreasonable, although I cannot tell you whether the Babylonians considered death a penalty or simply a way to prevent crime. If a man built a house for you and it then fell on you, he could be put to death. If you made love with a tabu woman—mother, daughter-in-law, or even any other woman if the affair was adulterous—you could expect to pay with your life. Burglary or receiving stolen goods likewise could terminate forever your criminal and other undertakings. A woman who proved to be a bad wife could also be terminated. Though you must have concluded by now that these Babylonians practiced draconian control of the size of their population, I can tell you that the most frequent penalty was the fine. It was money or its immediate surrogate that most often satisfied the scales of justice.[16] And, I believe, this was so because ancient law first concerned itself with property; it was in the marketplace that property was exchanged, and it was in exchange that the balance scales certainly found their first use.[17] If I must pay you money, or exchange something whose value we agree on, for something of value I receive from you—bread or beer or a hat—does it not seem almost inevitable that you would demand like compensation for a wrong I did you? Should I take your dignity from you, and you certainly value your dignity, would it not occur to you to charge me according to its weight, rather than to take my life? Would it not be better for you to take my money rather than my life? If you take my life, the king, having forbidden killing on such grounds, may very well take yours, and you will have gotten a very bad bargain indeed.

PROTAGORAS: Now I hear you justifying the very thing to which you say you are opposed: the use of marketplace metaphors in matters of justice. Do you take both sides again?

AUTHOR: I meant to explain, not justify, and I have not yet said that I am opposed to the use of marketplace metaphors in matters of justice. I have said that I fear that the use of such metaphors is in error. It is error because we have come to think that what we do in judicial matters—these practices that have come from the marketplace—best serves the order in human affairs that we all long for, what we have long called justice. To this end—of order in human affairs—I must believe that the language and the practices and the images of the marketplace simply will not work. Would I willingly exchange my eye for your eye? Your eye would be of no use to me, and I would rather keep my own. And I would find no justice in being forced—by you and by the magistrate who hears your plea—to make such a trade.

PROTAGORAS: What then? How do you propose that I be punished, that I pay for my crime?

AUTHOR: If you take my eye through no fault or intention of your own, then nothing. To live at all is to live in hazard, and no law or magistrate or king can change that. But if you would take it because you are simply so disposed, because taking it would serve some end of yours, because you are a barbarian who values nothing not his own, then I would kill you if I could before you were able to take it. Killing a dog for killing a sheep is the same sort of precaution.

CHORUS: We trust that this is mere digression, to make a point.

AUTHOR: I do not digress. I anticipate.

PROTAGORAS: I think that you regress. You have gone back not to the law of retaliation but to something worse, and I do not know what to call it.

AUTHOR: I must remind you, Protagoras, that the law of retaliation—the *lex talionis*—is a law of weighing. My eye is put in one scale and yours in the other, or my life in one scale and yours in the other. And if I have indeed gone back to something worse that has no name, then I think you have no model to evoke. It is as though I had burned the marketplace before you got there and thus forced you to look elsewhere to find some way to bring order to the world.

PROTAGORAS: You said you would present evidence but you only harangue. You are surely a lawyer.

AUTHOR: I throw myself on your mercy! And again I will present evidence.

PROTAGORAS: And what do you intend to prove?

AUTHOR: Let us allow the evidence to speak for itself.

CHORUS: This evidence does not speak but must be spoken.

AUTHOR: Then I shall speak the evidence itself. William Langland. *Vision of Piers Plowman*. "So with wikked wil and wrathe my werkmen I paye!" William Shakespeare. *The Tempest*. "He that dies pays all debts." John Milton. *Paradise Lost*. "...He, with his whole posterity, must die, Die he or justice must; unless for him Some other able, and as willing, pay The rigid satisfaction, death for death." Daniel Defoe. *The Fortunes & Misfortunes of the Famous Moll Flanders*. "...that he should ever acknowledge his happiness owing to me; that he would be debtor to me as long as he lived, and would be paying that debt as long as he had breath." Edmund Burke. *Reflections on the Revolution in France*. "No theatric audience in Athens would bear what has been borne in the midst of the real tragedy of this triumphal day: a principal actor weighing, as it were, in scales hung in a shop of horrors, so much actual crime against so much contingent advantage; and after putting in and out weights, declaring that the balance was on the side of the advantages. They would not bear to see the crimes of new democracy posted as in a ledger against the crimes of old despotism, and the book-keepers of politics finding democracy still in debt, but by no means unable or unwilling to pay the balance." Alexander Hamilton. *The Federalist Papers*, Number 5. "The history of Great Britain is the one with which we are in general the best acquainted, and it gives us many useful lessons. We may profit by their experience without paying the price which it cost them." Nathaniel Hawthorne. *The Scarlet Letter*. "All that dark treasure to be lavished on the very man, to whom nothing else could so adequately pay the debt of vengeance!" Herman Melville. *Billy Budd*. "The criminal paid the penalty of his crime. The promptitude of the punishment has proved salutary. Nothing amiss is now apprehended aboard H.M.S. Indomitable."

PROTAGORAS: What is this babble?

AUTHOR: Please do not interrupt! It is evidence. Henry David Thoreau. *Walden*. "My excuse for not lecturing against the use of tobacco is, that I never chewed it, that is a penalty which reformed tobacco-chewers have to pay..." Charles Dickens. *A Tale of Two Cities*. "My faith!" returned madame, coolly and lightly, "if people use knives for such purposes, they have to pay for it. He knew beforehand what the price of his luxury was; he has paid the price." Samuel Butler. *The Way of All Flesh*. "That vice pays homage to virtue is notorious; we call this hypocrisy; there should be a word found for the homage which virtue not unfrequently pays, or at any rate would be wise in paying, to vice." Oscar Wilde. *The Picture of Dorian Gray*. "Each man lived his own life and paid his own price for living it. The only pity was one had to pay so often for a single fault. One had to pay over and over again, indeed. In her dealings with man, destiny never closed her accounts." Joseph Conrad. *Heart of Darkness*. "It was an affirmation, a moral victory paid for by innumerable defeats, by abominable terrors, by abominable satisfactions." Arthur Conan Doyle. *The Valley of Fear.* "We pay the price, Watson, for being too up-to-date!" he cried. "We are before our time, and suffer the usual penalties." Henry James. *The Ambassadors.* "Her affairs would go to smash, but hadn't one a right to one's snatch of scandal when one was prepared to pay?" W. Somerset Maugham. *Of Human Bondage.* "She never ceased reminding him that he was under a debt of gratitude to her which he could never repay." E. M. Forster. *A Room with a View.* "Under the rug, Lucy felt the kindly pressure of her cousin's hand. At times our need for a sympathetic gesture is so great that we care not what exactly it signifies or how much we may have to pay for it afterwards."

PROTAGORAS: In the name of Zeus, evidence of what?

AUTHOR: How peppered my language is with this metaphorical paying.

PROTAGORAS: Peppered? Is this a fit metaphor?

AUTHOR: Pepper is seasoning for food, and in eating food one should not notice the seasoning.

PROTAGORAS: He is mad! He has left us to wander in the mountains with the Dionysians!

CHORUS: We are so embarrassed!

AUTHOR: It is everywhere and everywhere unconscious. We simply do not notice it, unless of course it is called to our attention.

PROTAGORAS: And how does all this serve your argument?

AUTHOR: You may not know, Protagoras, but all these writers of my language, whose words I have just spoken, were scribes of great stature in the temple of their culture. They were the linguistic mirrors of their times. Of this you may be certain. They wrote the language of the people, fine words, yes, but words that all who heard and read them would recognize as their own. The groundlings of Shakespeare's audience heard in the verse of their great bard the very words that daily buzzed in the streets of London, better turned without doubt but common words and teasing images they all knew well.

PROTAGORAS: Not all of what you recited had to do with paying for crime.

AUTHOR: True. But it all had to do with the metaphorical paying of metaphorical prices and debts. And, of course, crime has a *price* and thus incurs a *debt*. In all of what I recited the clearest example was, "The criminal paid the penalty of his crime." Herman Melville in *Billy Budd*. But this is only another instance of metaphorical paying, and as you have demonstrated, it attracts no more attention than any other. And even when one's attention is drawn to it, it requires some effort to see that it is metaphorical. It seems so natural to say this—because it has been said and heard so often and because the image that is evoked does not quite rise to full consciousness. I see a hand extended with the payment and another hand extended to receive the payment, but only with conscious effort do I see what the payment is.

PROTAGORAS: You make too much of this one word *pay*. There are other ways to say that the criminal is punished for his crime.

AUTHOR: The particular word that evokes the image does not matter; it is the image that you must consider. Is it appropriate or is it not? To be punished is to pay a penalty; it is this for that, and I see no way to avoid the weighing, the handing over of something of value, something of value taken in exchange. Say payment or expiation or atonement or punishment. Say it as you will, you will find it to be a transaction in the marketplace.

PROTAGORAS: Atonement? Is this also to be a transaction in the marketplace? Is not the temple the place for this?

AUTHOR: Temples have always been places of commerce. You Greeks paid the gods for their favors.

PROTAGORAS: Do you know what a price I paid for such blasphemy?

AUTHOR: I know. I know too that such words as *atone* and *expiate* are not much used in my language and would hardly do for common discourse. Once again, etymology may suggest a reason. Our word *pay* came from the Latin *pax*—peace—and thus we *pay* to *pacify* a creditor. But we English made *atone* from *at one*, by which we meant *to reconcile*, not much different from *pacify*, though it has a distinctly religious flavor. Likewise *expiate*, which we got from Latin *expiare—to appease*, as by sacrifice to the gods—and which also seems more religious than judicial—or commercial.[18] Why do you frown, Protagoras?

PROTAGORAS: Indigestion. A surfeit of etymology. It will pass.

AUTHOR: Let us hope. Etymology is history and what is my argument without history?

CHORUS: We have served your argument well, for we will soon be history!

PROTAGORAS: I am history but will not serve this argument! A slave of madness I am not, nor will I be any man's menial!

AUTHOR: You have forgotten, Protagoras, what I have asked you to do. I want you to refute this argument, not to serve it. It is I who am slave to it, and I wish to be free.

PROTAGORAS: You should better wish to be free of madness! You have spurned the Olympian gods and joined the mad women of Dionysius! You revel in the hysterical music of the Bacchantes, and you shall surely find your doom!

AUTHOR: Such strange images! Such wild metaphors! Do you see, Protagoras, how these can take control? But I think this outburst of yours may well serve my argument. Perhaps now you may find some plausibility in what I next present.

PROTAGORAS: I shall find plausibility in what you say when my reason applauds yours.

AUTHOR: Good! I accept your terms. You will recall, Protagoras, that we found in ancient Egypt the image of judgment by a god by means of balance scales. We heard also in Egypt a high official exhorted to "pay" punishment to those who to deserve it. We found in ancient laws that the guilty paid for their misdeeds with their money, their property, and often with their lives. We found that these beginnings found expression in the images of later times, as in the sculpture on the cathedral of Saint Lazarus at Autun. It should not shock us, then, to discover that these also found expression in customs quite as bizarre as your most recent evocation of ancient Greek images.

PROTAGORAS: I can no longer be shocked by anything.

CHORUS: We are nearly dead of starvation and quite beyond sensations of any kind.

AUTHOR: Can you imagine a price list of crimes?

PROTAGORAS: You mean so much for this crime, so much for that. Have we not found that already in the Code of Hammurabi[19]?

AUTHOR: No. I do not mean the law itself but rather a separate document that gives the prevailing prices of the various crimes, a document the criminal might consult as a sort of shopping guide.

PROTAGORAS: You jest, of course. You are going to make some point or other.

AUTHOR: No, I do not jest. I am talking about an invention of my own time, what we call sentencing guidelines. Such a document can be found in the library of the local jail, only a few miles from this pond. It is there for the convenience of the prisoners. They can consult it to determine whether they were charged too much or how much they are likely to be charged for their next crimes—if they should happen to be caught. Rather than *consult* I should say *study* for these documents are extremely sophisticated and detailed. Nothing seems to be left to chance. And while the names of these documents suggest that they are not strictly followed, the judge who does not follow them had better have his ducks in a row.[20]

CHORUS: What! Ducks in a row? The judge will shoot us? We have done nothing! We are innocent!

AUTHOR: You have not been paying attention. It is just an expression, a metaphor. It means nothing. Just an exercise in wit.

PROTAGORAS: Yours is surely an age of brilliance. That you could do this on your own, without guidance from my age, astounds me. But you are aware, of course, that Plato himself wished punishment to be appropriate. I recite. *Laws*, Book IX: "No criminal shall go unpunished, not even for a single offense, nor if he have fled the country; but let the penalty be according to his deserts—death, or bonds, or blows, or degrading places of sitting or standing, or removal to some temple on the borders of the land..."[21]

AUTHOR: Hades has, then, a library?

PROTAGORAS: Yes. The other place does not need one.

AUTHOR: Well, if you insist on making so much of origination, I must admit that the barbarians of medieval Europe had similar documents. These were their law codes, simply long lists of crimes and their prices—almost always cash fines.[22] They were certainly influential in the making of our own sentencing guidelines but far too simple to account for the sophistication of our own.

PROTAGORAS: Sophistication? Do you admire this trait? I have been under the impression that you hold sophistry in contempt.

AUTHOR: I do. I do. I did not mean sophistication in the sense of sophistry but in the sense of subtlety, intellectual appeal.

PROTAGORAS: I see. I see. And, of course, we sophists utterly lacked subtlety and intellectual appeal.

CHORUS: We also see and we are ashamed!

AUTHOR: Why would you say that? I was only using the word in its modern sense. I did not mean to offend.

PROTAGORAS: If your modern sophistication is anything like your sentencing guidelines, I am offended. But, tell me, have the prices of crimes gone up or down since the time of the barbarians?

AUTHOR: In recent times, at least, down, down, down.[23] What happens, Protagoras, when there is a surplus of any commodity?

PROTAGORAS: The price goes down, of course, but surely you do not mean to say that crime is a commodity.

AUTHOR: Why should I not say so? A commodity is an economic good, and is not crime an economic good for lawyers? For policemen? For prison keepers? And, as the prices go down and down, crime goes up and up, the number of criminals to be serviced goes up and up, the numbers of gainfully employed lawyers and policemen and prison keepers go up and up, and only victims and taxpayers are unhappy.

PROTAGORAS: I cannot endure such cynicism! Please. Tell me more about the laws of the barbarians.

AUTHOR: I will, Protagoras, but first let me tell you more about our crime price lists. Suppose I intend to commit a crime for which I will be tried in a federal court—should I be caught. In that case I would consult a table of prices. I would find that there are forty-three levels ranging from the very high to the very low. For each level I would find that there are six categories of prices reflecting the points awarded for previous crimes. For example, if I intend to commit a crime that would have a price at Level 15 and I have been awarded enough points for previous crimes to be in the third category, then I would expect a price of twenty-four to thirty months in prison.[24] Let's say that I intend to murder someone I do not care for. Well now, I consult the table or the guidelines and find that the price for that is at Level 43, life imprisonment, very stiff indeed—should I be caught—but I do not have to be concerned with any murders I may have committed before because I am already at the top level. Very well, I will sell illegal drugs, say about four kilograms of cocaine—at one time, that is. Here the price is at Level 32, a bit high but tolerable. Or I could sell only about 150 grams at a time and pay only the price at Level 20. Since I have no prior convictions, I would be in the first category and thus charged the lowest price. I would have to do much more selling, of course, but not a bad deal at all.[25]

PROTAGORAS: I detect a flaw in this wonderful scheme. If the price of a duck in your currency is ten dollars and you buy six of them, then the price of all six is sixty dollars, or your shopping guide is of no use. What merchant would sell you six ducks for the price of one?

CHORUS: An outrage, that ducks should be sold at all! Additively so, if they should be so discounted!

AUTHOR: Yes, you are right. I remember now. One must be careful with these shopping guides and price lists. One must always read the fine print. The merchants want you to come and buy. Fungible items.

CHORUS: Fungible items?

PROTAGORAS: Fungible items? Fungible items? Oh, yes. Countable things, weighable, measurable. Lawyers have not changed, I see. They still prefer the word that obscures rather than the one that illuminates.

AUTHOR: Yes. Fungible items must be added, and one must consult the price lists or tables additively. They definitely say that fungible items must be added and that the guides apply to the total amount. But if my memory serves I would certainly get a discount.[26]

CHORUS: One does not discount ducks!

PROTAGORAS: Nor does one fool the goddess Justice!

AUTHOR: But one does take full advantage of whatever the merchant offers! If I sold 150 grams of cocaine twenty-six times to make a total of almost four kilograms, I would not then be charged twenty-six times the price of one sale. The price would then be at Level 520 and there is no Level 520. No, no! I would surely get a steep discount, surely less than the price for four kilograms sold only once.[27]

PROTAGORAS: It is of course unthinkable to murder twelve at once, but if you were to do so I suppose the price would be somewhat less than twelve times the price of one. And if the price of one is death, as I suppose it sometimes must be, then the discounted price of twelve would be less than death.

AUTHOR: In my time that is not at all unthinkable. Quite often one can buy many lives for the price of one. Truly a bargain-hunter's paradise!

PROTAGORAS: Atrocious metaphor! And is the price the same no matter who you murder?

CHORUS: And name the price for murdering a duck! Could it be as high as the number of drops of rain that fall from this sky?

AUTHOR: No. Not so. If you murder a government official, the price goes up three levels.[28] It is clearly cheaper to murder a common person.

PROTAGORAS: Again I see that there has been no change. The ruling class provides for its own.

AUTHOR: There has not been a change since the time of the barbarians whose law you want to know more about. In those times the price for the murder of an ordinary freeman was 150 gold *solidi*, not much when you consider that the price for stealing a bull was 45 *solidi*. But the price for killing one of the upper class was twice that for killing an ordinary freeman, and for killing a freeman who worked for the king the price was three times as high, an enormous 450 gold *solidi*. It is enough to give one pause. You see, in this time every man who was not a slave had a sort of official price, the *wergeld*. One would do well to know a man's rank before murdering him.[29]

PROTAGORAS: I doubt that your own price lists are as appreciative of rank.

AUTHOR: To be sure, they are not. Democratic sentiment would not allow such discrimination, and persons of rank must be satisfied with the little that our modern price lists give them.

PROTAGORAS: A pity! And all of this is the work of those abominable balance scales.

AUTHOR: Yes. I fear so.

PROTAGORAS: Has anything else so simple done such mischief?

6

The Tools of Life

AUTHOR: I too have wondered.

PROTAGORAS: The balance is but one of many ancient tools. If it has done the mischief that you claim, then surely others likewise have. Other tools must have led to other metaphors and models that have also been misapplied.

AUTHOR: I too have thought so.

PROTAGORAS: Then we must examine them. I demand rigorous scrutiny.

CHORUS: Fetch a black hood! Protagoras has become the inquisitor!

AUTHOR: I too have done so.

PROTAGORAS: We must examine them as in a court of law. If they have done foul deeds, then they shall surely pay.

AUTHOR: Let us so examine tools and other useful devices found in the caves and camps of our stone-age ancestors, for these are truly primitive and thus much older than the scales.

PROTAGORAS: You mean from the time before there were Greeks. I shudder a bit, but please continue.

AUTHOR: Thank you. Let these tools also be represented by Egyptian hieroglyphic signs, for those so represented are companions of the balance scales.

PROTAGORAS: And certainly in league with them.

AUTHOR: Let us therefore bring before the court the ax, the bow and arrow, the knife, the adz, the drill, and the sickle. And though they are not what we would call tools, perhaps also the cooking pot and the door. If there is another such as the balance scales, perhaps we will find it here.

PROTAGORAS: Why must these be represented by Egyptian hieroglyphic signs? Why do you attach significance to such representation?

AUTHOR: The images of these must have been important to the early Egyptians, just as the image of the balance scale was. They must also have been important in our common proto-culture; for most of these there are words in our common proto-language, Indo-European.[1] We may therefore with confidence believe that the names of these tools have been spoken by many every day for thousands of years and that this speaking was often metaphorical. If any of these became what the balance scales are, we should find some hint in the language we will examine. In short I say the image of these tools has been in the minds of our species for thousands of years.

PROTAGORAS: And if there is an image we may expect a metaphor?

AUTHOR: Yes. I think so.

PROTAGORAS: And if there is a metaphor, there is a model to be misapplied?

AUTHOR: If it please the court, that is what we are to determine. I intend to show that these tools, truly the tools of life, not only extended the hands of man but also his mind and tongue as well. That they have not done the mischief that the scales have done. That there is no edifice built on them except the life of man.

PROTAGORAS: Very well. Bring the first.

AUTHOR: Here is the ax, an ancient one indeed. It first appeared during the late paleolithic period, so says at least one scholar of such matters.[2] That is to say perhaps thirty thousand years ago.

PROTAGORAS: Which ax? The woodsman's ax, the battle-ax, the executioner's ax?

AUTHOR: Just the ax. Before there was the woodsman's ax, the battle-ax, or the executioner's ax, there was just the ax. We often say just ax to refer to any of the special uses.

PROTAGORAS: What are the metaphors? What are the models?

AUTHOR: How about this one: "Give him the ax."

PROTAGORAS: Do you mean let him have it?

AUTHOR: Precisely!

CHORUS: Ohhhhhhhh!

PROTAGORAS: Is that a metaphor?

AUTHOR: Of course. It means removal from employment, and for some people removal from employment is almost as bad as removal of the head. It is a sort of execution.

CHORUS: Ooooooooh!

PROTAGORAS: Thus the model to be followed is the swinging ax. Anything or anyone we find objectionable is destroyed with terrible violence. Executed as with the headsman's ax. Foul, indeed!

CHORUS: Eeeeeeeeh!

AUTHOR: Well, yes. But there is a tinge of humor. You see, we no longer use the ax for executions; we use more civilized methods.

PROTAGORAS: I fear to ask what these may be.

AUTHOR: Electrocution, lethal injection, and sometimes hanging.

PROTAGORAS: I know what hanging is. Please tell me how the other two, more civilized, accomplish their ends.

AUTHOR: Well, ah, I suppose I would have to say that electrocution, in a sense, fries the executionee's body.

CHORUS: Uuuuugggh!

PROTAGORAS: Fries the executionee's body! Well, the invention of cooking was progress. Certainly we could not have had civilization without it.

AUTHOR: Lethal injection is the squirting of poison into the body, with a large hollow needle.

CHORUS: Butter, yes. But poison! Uuuuugggh!

PROTAGORAS: Socrates drank his poison, holding the cup in his own hand! We should have only half a martyr had he been treated so civilly! Better the headsman's ax than to live in such a time!

AUTHOR: In my time few axes are to be found and no Socrates at all.

PROTAGORAS: Would you say, then, that the ax, withdrawn from many of its former employments, has begun to lose its power and may someday disappear altogether?

AUTHOR: I think that it might have begun to lose its power in your own time, Protagoras. Your great Homer made some sparing use of the ax as simile, but the great dramatists of your time—Aeschylus, Sophocles, Euripides, Aristophanes—made no metaphors on the ax that I have found.[3] But, no, unless we stop saying chop, cut down, and split, the ax will be with us always. These words often evoke the image of the ax, and though the ax is no longer a tool of life in our hands, in our brains it will continue to do its work. One of the greatest writers of my time—a bit before my time—could write that "...mourners split and moved to each side of the hole..."[4] and, though he was working on the very precipice of language, he could not be misunderstood. He could also say, "A split is gone for the flatties..."[5] and only be misunderstood by most. I can say that *I split*, and none who know the English language of my time could fail to understand that I had left a gathering of some sort, had thus been cut off from it. I cannot say that such expressions inevitably evoke the image of the ax, but I think that deliberately becoming conscious of them does. And deliberately evoking the image of the ax will, I think, always have a telling effect. Consider this: A famous writer of my own land, speaking of politicians who had recently won office, wrote that "...when they strike, the ax may be sharp indeed, but its edge is seldom poisoned with ill-will; nor is it their custom ignominiously to kick the head which they have just struck off."[6]

PROTAGORAS: Enough! What edifice has been built upon the ax? What dangers does it hold for us? How does it mislead? Please summarize. Briefly.

AUTHOR: None. None. It does not. If there is evidence to the contrary, I have missed it. The ax is an honest tool, needing only the touch of stone to keep its edge, but the scales—and the buying and selling that they oversee—are full of conceit. That the balance scales, and the marketplace in which they were supreme, have rolled more heads than any headsman's ax we cannot doubt. The woodsman's ax has not felled more trees nor the battle-ax more soldiers.

PROTAGORAS: We shall reserve judgment. Call the next of these to be examined, the bow and arrow, I believe.

AUTHOR: Yes, the bow and arrow. Not so ancient as the ax but ancient still. It first appeared, we are told, during the mesolithic period and no doubt greatly extended the hand of man.[7]

PROTAGORAS: And his brain as well, if I am to follow this argument. He now comprehends the swift and true.

AUTHOR: Yes. And the darting and the far reaching as well. This can only be good.

CHORUS: No! The arrow could only be bad...for ducks.

AUTHOR: Your lament has missed the mark by far. Many more men than ducks have fallen to the arrow. If you have shot your bolt, we shall go on with this.

CHORUS: Your words pierce us to the heart!

PROTAGORAS: Hark! Echoes of my own time! Aeschylus wrote such words and so did Euripides.[8] These are the metaphors, harmless enough they seem. What need have men—or ducks—to fear a model arrow?

CHORUS: Yes, the metaphors only sting but the arrows kill. Your point is barbed. Have you forgotten Cock Robin?

AUTHOR: Your tongues would have no twang without the arrow. Why do you disparage it? And Cock Robin was not a duck!

CHORUS: We know Cock Robin was not a duck! We are not dull! And we do not disparage; we merely wish to be blunt.

PROTAGORAS: No. You wish the arrow to be blunt. But why do we speak only of arrows? Do we not examine bow *and* arrow?

AUTHOR: Truly, for the bow without an arrow but with a few more strings is a lyre, and an arrow without a bow is a dart. But the bow as it shoots is one model, and the arrow as it flies is another.

PROTAGORAS: I see. If I pluck my bow I make music, but if I draw it I make war.

CHORUS: You two do not know pizzicato from pizzle. Pluck the strings or draw the bow over them and you make music.

AUTHOR: Yes. And it is war you make if you shoot an arrow but play if you throw it—at least in my own time.

PROTAGORAS: In my time the dart was a spear, and I should not take pleasure in such play. It was said that in the hands of Abaris

110

it was a thing of magic; he flew through the air upon it, as you do, Author. The dart of Abaris it was called, a gift of Apollo. Nonsense, of course, but I take note of how it presaged your age. Look there in the sky, Author. The dart of Abaris still flies!

AUTHOR: In my time even the arrow has become a toy. Could such a thing be sinister?

CHORUS: Only in the wrong hand. One holds the bow in the left hand and draws back the string and the arrow with the right.

PROTAGORAS: Clearly the bow and arrow—these tools of life— are fraught with mischief, but they have done nothing truly foul. Let us have the next of these we are to examine.

CHORUS: Ugh! Protagoras has become your student, Author, and a very bad one, indeed!

AUTHOR: Perhaps we could examine some metaphors. You know that the flight of the arrow by day is deadly; by night it is far deadlier because we do not see it coming. Sir Francis Bacon wrote that "...base and crafty cowards, are like the arrow that flieth in the dark."[9] Similarly, a biblical proverb evokes the arrow: "A man that beareth false witness against his neighbour is a maul, and a sword, and a sharp arrow."[10] You know also that when we feel pain in the heart we think often of the arrow. Lord George Byron wrote: "The devil hath not in all his quiver's choice An arrow for the heart like a sweet voice."[11] And surely you know that our eyes, trained by long experience, must follow the flight of the arrow. Benjamin Franklin—philosopher, scientist, statesman, founder of a nation—in a treatise on water spouts invited us to "...look...in the Direction of the Arrows..." that he had drawn in a figure in the margin of the paper.[12] Look across the street, Protagoras, at that black and yellow device. It is what we call a traffic sign. Do you see the arrow curving? It tells us truly to turn to the right, to follow the flight of the arrow.

PROTAGORAS: I will concede whatever point you are trying to make.

CHORUS: And by point you mean of course the point of the arrow that Author makes with his finger as he punctures the air.

AUTHOR: Perhaps he means the point of this knife!

CHORUS: Help us, Protagoras! Author threatens us with one of his points!

PROTAGORAS: Perhaps we could examine this knife—without violence.

AUTHOR: Very well. The knife. It also first appeared during the late paleolithic period.[13] It was first made of stone, of course, and was used, for example, for cutting up food, cutting ducks into bite-sized pieces.

CHORUS: Horrors!

PROTAGORAS: What are the metaphors? What are the models?

AUTHOR: If you offend me with your words, I might say, "You have cut me to the quick."

PROTAGORAS: Surely you can do better than that!

AUTHOR: I mean your words but in my imagination I see your knife slashing at me. I might also cut you off! Or cut you down to size!

PROTAGORAS: These are allusions to the knife?

AUTHOR: I no longer know what they are allusions to, nor does anyone else. They are too deeply submerged in the unconscious—or lost in the neural networks. This is why I say we do not know what we are talking about. Any of us might say that something is *cut and dried* without any vision at all of wood being cut with the ax and then stacked and dried so that it is ready for whatever use it is to be put to.[14] And who knows now that to *cut and run* is to escape by cutting with a knife the mooring or anchor rope of one's ship so that it may run with the wind?[15] Dead metaphors the scholars call these, but I wonder. Perhaps these words now evoke another image, a mugger cutting his victim with a razor and then running away. We cut with many tools—knives, axes, razors, scythes, scissors—and their images are surely evoked as we speak of cutting. Surely your great Homer had in his mind a vision of the knife—or something very much like it—when Patroclus *cut off* the front phalanxes of the Trojans[16], or as Zeus, in guarding Hector, *cut* the string of Teucer's bow.[17]

PROTAGORAS: You say Patroclus *cut off* the Trojans with a knife? Remarkable! You would think he would have used a sword, nay, a thousand swords.

AUTHOR: No, no, Protagoras. Homer was writing metaphorically, though he very likely did not know he was. You see, we think of soldiers in battle as a body—a unit—and when a line of soldiers sticks out from the main body, like an appendage of your own body, that part may be *cut off*, as with a knife. All this is unconscious, even for Homer.

CHORUS: Could we cut this short? We see no end.

PROTAGORAS: Please! Give me something else from literature that I may judge the true weight of this blade.

AUTHOR: I cannot think of any.

PROTAGORAS: There are too few?

AUTHOR: Too many. This knife, I have told you, is a tool of life; it is everywhere, part of the eternal background; we simply are not consciously aware of it. I might more easily recall the images to be found in wallpaper.

PROTAGORAS: Wallpaper?

AUTHOR: I should have said wall paintings.

PROTAGORAS: I recall certain goddesses.

CHORUS: Cut! Whatever the tool, we shall have an end to this!

AUTHOR: Surely you can agree that this tool has not done what the scales have done.

PROTAGORAS: I agree. Bring the next. The adz, I think.

AUTHOR: Yes, the adz, an ax with the blade turned to right angles with its handle. It is used for the rough shaping of wood. Many a log house of my ancestors came from its work. I can see them yet, standing on a log, slowly, rhythmically swinging...

PROTAGORAS: You are out of order as no doubt your ancestors were! You continue to chip away at my patience! Get on with the examination.

AUTHOR: Late paleolithic but if there is an Indo-European word I do not know it.[18] Ancient Egyptians used them and represented them with signs that look like adzes.[19] Homer knew them. Metaphorical use, I must conclude, however, is uncommon.

PROTAGORAS: Is that all?

AUTHOR: A rough-cut piece of work, I agree, but I can think of no more.

PROTAGORAS: So much for the adz. It is guilty only of obscurity. Call the drill.

AUTHOR: The drill. Paleolithic.[20] A tool for boring holes by a spinning motion. A cord is wrapped around a shaft with a cutting point and drawn back and forth to make the shaft spin. The cord might be the string of a bow, though Homer described a different arrangement. Or the shaft might simply be spun between the hands.

PROTAGORAS: Homer still! I do not need to be drilled in matters of my own culture.

AUTHOR: Drilling always makes heat, and many cultures used an adaptation of the drill to make fire. We call these fire drills.

CHORUS: Where is the exit? Ducks first! Be orderly!

PROTAGORAS: Be calm! What was the different arrangement Homer described?

AUTHOR: In that wonderful passage in which Odysseus and his men destroyed the single eye of Polyphemus the Cyclops, Homer tells us that Odysseus plunged a burning stake of olive wood into the eye and with his weight upon it twisted it around. This he did, Homer tells us, the way a man drills a hole in a ship's timber, that is, by putting his weight on the top of the drill while others wrap a cord around the shaft, grasp the cord at both ends, and pull it back and forth.[21]

PROTAGORAS: Ghastly! I remember! The eye hissed as does a hot adz plunged into water! The high rocks rang in chorus to the terrible screams of Polyphemus!

CHORUS: Protagoras blanches. Does he attest the power of Homer or his own weakness? We ducks could tell you of being plunged into boiling water to remove our feathers, of being...

AUTHOR: Cease! He knows well this drill. He was the greatest of orators.

PROTAGORAS: It was not oratory. I revealed this weakness long ago even though my teachers drilled into me that to pity

Polyphemus was to despise Odysseus, unthinkable for a Greek. Enough! Bring the next.

AUTHOR: The sickle. A blade for reaping grain. Neolithic.[22] It is now curved, like an arm reaching out to pull in stalks of grain, but in neolithic times it was surely made of stone and thus more like the corn hook we sometimes see in museums. One reaches out with the sickle to grasp the grain and then smartly pulls it back. The scythe, of course, is only a larger form of the sickle, held with two hands instead of one.

PROTAGORAS: I think I know what a sickle is and how it is to be used.

AUTHOR: Your disposition sours, Protagoras.

CHORUS: We never thought his disposition was anything like sweet corn.

PROTAGORAS: Cease! Or I will mow you down like so many blades of grass!

AUTHOR: With a sickle or a scythe? The image you have evoked in me is of Death, personified in the form of a human skeleton bare of all flesh and armed with a scythe. Ghastly!

PROTAGORAS: Then with a scythe!

CHORUS: Get on with this, Author, before he finds a scythe—or a machine-gun. The sun is sinking in the west and there we see the sickle moon.

AUTHOR: Let us examine the cooking pot.

CHORUS: We agree only if it is empty. Protagoras has a big pot and he looks hungry.

PROTAGORAS: I am lean and not hungry! I wish only to be gone to Hades.

AUTHOR: This discussion has gone to pot, and I want no more of it.

PROTAGORAS: Very well. It would seem that none of these have done wrong. But what of those we have not examined? Surely there are others as miscreant as the balance scales, others that have built monstrous edifices.

AUTHOR: Surely.

PROTAGORAS: Well? Name one.

AUTHOR: I cannot name one as old these we have examined, but I am sure there are more modern tools with the power of the balance scales. Because their work is unconscious, it is very difficult to recognize them. I fear that if we were to attempt to discover them the sun should have set many times before this argument would end.

PROTAGORAS: Before the sun sets once I shall be gone to the refuge of Hades.

CHORUS: And we shall be simply gone. No longer in this world. Faded like the light that shines for yet a while from the ripples of this our pond. Purged forever from the rolls of...

AUTHOR: Enough! Or I shall cut you...

CHORUS: Help! Help! He is going to kill us!

AUTHOR: I intended to say off.

PROTAGORAS: I think that is what they feared.

AUTHOR: For the purpose of a quick conclusion to this argument, let us conclude that among the contemporaries of the balance scales there is no other that has done great mischief.

PROTAGORAS: Then we shall close an argument to close an argument. Wonderful.

AUTHOR: Then what is it that you wish to argue?

PROTAGORAS: I am not content. Why is it that the balance scales have done what you contend? Why not the ax, or the bow and arrow, or the knife, or even the cooking pot or the door?

AUTHOR: The sun still sinks, but if it might ease your discontent we could play this game: we could chose one of these other tools that we have examined and build upon it an edifice much like that built upon the balance scales. An edifice dedicated to the regulation of human behavior. We shall solve in another way the problem of evil!

PROTAGORAS: Excellent!

CHORUS: Wonderful! We shall in ten thousand years make Protagoras content!

AUTHOR: No! No! We shall only make a brief outline. We shall not actually build. We shall not recruit legions of functionaries. We shall not...

PROTAGORAS: Please! The sun! The sun! Get to the shall!

AUTHOR: Choose one you have named, Protagoras, and we shall.

PROTAGORAS: Very well. I choose the...door.

AUTHOR: The door?

PROTAGORAS: Yes, the door. The door is everywhere in all times. The humblest hut has one as does the grandest temple. Why not the door?

AUTHOR: Very well. The door. Where shall we begin?

PROTAGORAS: We shall ask this question: What is a door?

AUTHOR: It is that which keeps things out. The cold and the wind and the wolf.

CHORUS: And the thief!

PROTAGORAS: It is that which keeps things in. The children and the chickens and the warmth of the fire.

CHORUS: And the thief!

AUTHOR: If it is in a wall it is called a gate.

CHORUS: If it is in a fence it is called a gate.

PROTAGORAS: If there is man, there is a city; if there is a city, there are many doors.

AUTHOR: It is seen by all. All speak of it. Open the door. Close the door. Lock the door before you go to bed. Unlock the door for friends are coming. All treasure it. It is the protector of our secrets. It is the guardian of our sanctuaries.

PROTAGORAS: I sit by my door in the evening.

AUTHOR: I stand by my door to watch the sun rise.

CHORUS: We stand by your door...to ask for corn.

PROTAGORAS: Go! And do not darken my door again!

AUTHOR: Offend me and I shall show you the door!

CHORUS: Feed us and we shall leave your door.

PROTAGORAS: We stand now in the marketplace. We behold an evil man. We watch the merchant as he weighs his goods. We watch as he closes his shop and locks the door. What shall we do with the evil man?

AUTHOR: We shall shut him out as if he were the wolf.

PROTAGORAS: Shut him out of the shop? He will break in.

AUTHOR: Shut him out of the city.

PROTAGORAS: The gate is but a door. He will break in.

AUTHOR: Shut him out of the land.

PROTAGORAS: The land is bordered by a fence of soldiers, and in the fence is a gate of clerks. He will bribe them.

AUTHOR: Shut him out of the earth.

PROTAGORAS: And how would we do that?

AUTHOR: Cancel him! Cross him out! He shall not be and he shall commit no crimes tomorrow!

PROTAGORAS: There is but one way to do that. How shall we sanction this cancellation?

AUTHOR: We are in the marketplace at high noon. The people are all gathered to attend to business. Listen to me. This man is evil. Today I saw him steal the merchant's goods. Yesterday this good woman saw him kill a pilgrim on the highway. Tomorrow he will steal again or kill again for he has no other way to live, nor does he wish to live in any other way. What shall we do with him? Shall he be in or out?

CHORUS: Put him out and close the door. The ax that made the door shall keep the door.

AUTHOR: Why do you say so?

CHORUS: Behind the door is our sanctuary and he shall have no part of it. Neither wolf nor thief nor murderer shall share our sanctuary.

PROTAGORAS: I so order it. He shall be put out and the door shall be closed to him forever. The scribe shall write down what we have done this day.

AUTHOR: And when another evil man is discovered?

PROTAGORAS: He shall be seized and brought to this marketplace. The scribe shall read what we did this day, and we shall leave him in or put him out as the people shall decide.

AUTHOR: And how shall they decide? How shall they know with certainty that this man is evil?

PROTAGORAS: How do we know with certainty that the wolf is deadly?

CHORUS: We shall ask what this man has done in his life. What did he do today that caused him to be seized and brought before the people here assembled. What did he do yesterday? What did he do the day before yesterday?

AUTHOR: And the day before that?

PROTAGORAS: Suppose I tell you that this man did no evil thing yesterday or the day before that? That no one knows of any evil thing he did before this day?

CHORUS: We are not vengeful. Let him stay in. But we shall be wary and patience is not our greatest virtue.

AUTHOR: But let him bring recompense to the door of him he wronged.

PROTAGORAS: Suppose it was the city he wronged?

AUTHOR: Then let him bring recompense to the gate of the city.

PROTAGORAS: This too shall the scribe record, and if this man be brought again to marketplace the scribe shall read what he did this day.

CHORUS: Again we shall decide. Leave him in or put him out.

AUTHOR: In or out. We do not quibble. There is this side of the door and the other. There is no in-between.

PROTAGORAS: Enough! I am content. Long ago the scales became our guide in this business, but some other tool might have done as well. We shall never know.

AUTHOR: Or better. In my time the scales are obsession more than guide; they are balanced far too finely.

PROTAGORAS: A thoughtless moment marked forever all ages ever after? But what does it matter? Would the door have been a better guide? It so happened that early humans were taught—or learned—the virtues of the scales. If they had learned the virtues of the door instead, all would be as it is now. The difference between the two as guides for the problem of wickedness is unknowable, and surely it is best that we should keep the guide that we have learned.

AUTHOR: On that moment long ago our destiny is hinged. Should we do nothing if we find out in ten thousand years that we erred?

PROTAGORAS: We could not know for ten thousand years. Tell me, Author, had that moment long ago resulted in the door becoming our guide for the regulation of human behavior, would we just now have explored the scales as an alternative guide? What grievous wrongs would you have found in the edifice of the door?

AUTHOR: Then we do nothing?

PROTAGORAS: Nothing! Why should judging by the door be more virtuous than judging by the scales? I have stood here by this tranquil pond the better part of a day and have not yet been accosted by a robber or attacked by a barbarian. I must therefore conclude that, generally, the scales have accorded the miscreants their due. Our laws are generally just, and to abandon them or remake them because of imperfections that you alone seem to perceive is madness. Surely you will not argue that we have made no progress in the ten thousand years that aggrieve you so. Ten thousand years ago we were savages and would not have ventured abroad without a burden of weapons for our defense, yet here we stand—unarmed—in perfect tranquillity. Perhaps we could come back to this another time. It is surely time for something else.

AUTHOR: Then tell me no more of truth and virtue! You have told me that they are not worth pursuing. And as for judging, that is the business of the scales. The door does not make us judge but only keep in or out, accept or reject. It is perhaps too simple for your fine mind. You seem to say that once the metal has hardened and the mold has been broken it is better to see the flaws as inevitable than to throw the metal into the fire again and make the mold anew!

PROTAGORAS: I shall tell you no more! My words would pass through you as my hand passes through this air. And why do those soldiers approach us?

AUTHOR: They are not soldiers. They are police officers, the keepers of order in this land.

7

A Day in Court

AUTHOR: This is most distracting.

PROTAGORAS: This is most distressing! When I was sent here I was not told that I would be dragged into one of your courts on a charge of...

AUTHOR: Littering.

PROTAGORAS: Yes, littering. Is it akin to murder? It was for this that I was dragged here against my will? Humiliated? Have I committed sacrilege?

AUTHOR: No. It means carelessly tossing things about.

PROTAGORAS: Tossing things about! You were tossing corn about! I did nothing! I am innocent!

CHORUS: Tossing corn cannot be other than virtue. You must be the miscreant, Protagoras.

AUTHOR: Did you drop a page or two of philosophy, Protagoras? A scrap of virtue?

PROTAGORAS: I did nothing, I tell you! In these stately robes, I stood there by that pond and...

AUTHOR: Pontificated.

PROTAGORAS: Made a bridge? Made a bridge? I made nothing! You are the miscreant!

CHORUS: Hold! Let us make peace among ourselves, for we are all about to be processed by that device that you, Author, abhor and you, Protagoras, adore.

PROTAGORAS: Processed? I wonder if they know they cannot put me to death?

AUTHOR: They mean that the machinery of the scales will clank, will take us in, will spew us out. But they would not consider execution; that would cost far too much.[1]

PROTAGORAS: Spew us out! Outrage! I am a Greek!

AUTHOR: May I suggest that you not speak so loudly? Our case will soon be heard and I think we should not irritate the judge. For whatever reason, the lawyers call this one The Prince of Darkness, and I fear your orphic voice may not suffice to get us free.

CHORUS: Let us not hear any quacks at all, enchanting or otherwise.

PROTAGORAS: The Prince of Darkness does not carry a balance. But tell me, Author, what is that curious document hanging on the wall behind you?

AUTHOR: I do not know but the script is ancient. Let me see. Upon my word! It is a page or two from Jonathan Swift's *Gulliver's Travels*. I shall read a bit of it. "Upon what I said in relation to our Courts of Justice, his Majesty desired to be satisfied in several points: and this I was the better able to do, having been formerly almost ruined by a long suit in chancery, which was decreed for me with costs. He asked, what time was usually spent in determining between right and wrong, and what degree of expense. Whether advocates and orators had liberty to plead in causes manifestly known to be unjust, vexatious, or oppressive. Whether party in religion or politics were observed to be of any weight in the scale of justice. Whether those pleading orators were persons educated in the general knowledge of equity, or only in provincial, national, and other local customs. Whether they or their judges had any part in penning those laws which they assumed the liberty of interpreting and glossing upon at their pleasure. Whether they had ever at different times pleaded for and against the same cause, and cited precedents to prove contrary opinions."[2]

PROTAGORAS: Remarkable! Is this a jest?

AUTHOR: I think not. It is in such a prominent place. Perhaps no official of the court has ever read it.

PROTAGORAS: How ancient is it?

AUTHOR: Nearly three centuries. Half a century older than that document over there, the one that established this republic.

PROTAGORAS: I should hang another, truly ancient, document here. Again I recite. "Among our citizens there may be those who cannot be subdued by all the strength of the laws; and for their sake, though an ungracious task, I will proclaim my first law about the robbing of temples, in case any one should dare to commit such a crime. I do not expect or imagine that any well-brought-up citizen will ever take the infection, but their servants, and strangers, and strangers' servants may be guilty of many impieties. And with a view to them especially, and yet not without a provident eye to the weakness of human nature generally, I will proclaim the law about robbers of temples and similar incurable, or almost incurable, criminals. Having already agreed that such enactments ought always to have a short prelude, we may speak to the criminal, whom some tormenting desire by night and by day tempts to go and rob a temple, the fewest possible words of admonition and exhortation: O sir, we will say to him, the impulse which moves you to rob temples is not an ordinary human malady, nor yet a visitation of heaven, but a madness which is begotten in a man from ancient and unexpiated crimes of his race, an ever-recurring curse; against this you must guard with all your might, and how you are to guard we will explain to you. When any such thought comes into your mind, go and perform expiations, go as a suppliant to the temples of the Gods who avert evils, go to the society of those who are called good men among you; hear them tell and yourself try to repeat after them, that every man should honour the noble and the just. Fly from the company of the wicked—fly and turn not back; and if your disorder is lightened by these remedies, well and good, but if not, then acknowledge death to be nobler than life, and depart hence."[3]

AUTHOR: Plato again? I wonder what you would do without Plato.

PROTAGORAS: Yes, Plato again. I wonder what Plato would have done without me.

AUTHOR: Has this philosopher now become your teacher? I seem to recall that Plato was not one with you in scorning the gods.

PROTAGORAS: Pure posturing! Is there anything in that document there that might explain why we were put in a cage before we were brought here? Was it because we were in the company of these ducks? Because I, as does that judge up there, wear robes instead of those rags you wear?

CHORUS: Because the judge had gone to dinner and wanted to be sure you would still be here when he got back. He quite possibly knew that you are a fugitive. And you have not yet posted bail.

PROTAGORAS: Did you notice that a barbarian touched my robes? Outrage! And no one has asked me to post bail!

AUTHOR: Speak softly, Protagoras, or you shall find even greater outrage. You have not yet had a bail hearing.

PROTAGORAS: I shall find my refuge in Hades! I shall simply disappear in a puff of smoke!

AUTHOR: Before you have refuted my argument? And what would Zeus have to say about that?

PROTAGORAS: I shall stay only as long as this amuses me.

CHORUS: We hope they fry him. Better him than us.

AUTHOR: Please! I beg you! We must not annoy The Prince of Darkness. He has looked this way twice and we shall surely be thrown into the fire.

PROTAGORAS: I, for one, will conclude that he is no more to be feared than any other judge in this doomed temple. You should recall, Author, what we saw in the first room to which we were taken by mistake. Four young men stood before that judge and confessed that they had attacked another young man from behind and beaten him nearly to death. Another said that the victim, clearly a person of considerable virtue, still struggles with disabilities he cannot overcome. The record showed that all four of the accused had committed such crimes before. It was said that they had boasted of such crimes. Yet that judge released them, sent them away with nothing more than admonishment.[4] This is not the weighing that you fear but rather lack of it.

AUTHOR: Again you err, Protagoras! In this house of scales a human life has been discounted to virtual worthlessness, and virtually nothing is what they paid.

PROTAGORAS: Perhaps you need to repair the scales. In the second room to which we were taken by mistake, we saw one

124

person sentenced to eight years for stealing money—an amount far less than you have said a human life is worth—and another to almost nothing for taking a human life, for homicide by vehicle while intoxicated.[5] Forgive me, but I must recite Plato again. "Having an eye to all these things, the law, like a good archer, should aim at the right measure of punishment, and in all cases at the deserved punishment. In the attainment of this the judge shall be a fellow-worker with the legislator, whenever the law leaves to him to determine what the offender shall suffer or pay; and the legislator, like a painter, shall give a rough sketch of the cases in which the law is to be applied."[6]

CHORUS: And what sentence, your honor, would you have given?

PROTAGORAS: This woman did not seem to me a great threat to society, but the winebibber—who surely drank from his own cup and by his own leave—certainly did. Great Zeus! Must I recite again? "...let those who have been made what they are only from want of understanding, and not from malice or an evil nature, be placed by the judge in the House of Reformation, and ordered to suffer imprisonment during a period of not less than five years. And in the meantime let them have no intercourse with the other citizens, except with members of the nocturnal council, and with them let them converse with a view to the improvement of their soul's health. And when the time of their imprisonment has expired, if any of them be of sound mind let him be restored to sane company, but if not, and if he be condemned a second time, let him be punished with death. As to that class of monstrous natures who not only believe that there are no Gods, or that they are negligent, or to be propitiated, but in contempt of mankind conjure the souls of the living and say that they can conjure the dead and promise to charm the Gods with sacrifices and prayers, and will utterly overthrow individuals and whole houses and states for the sake of money — let him who is guilty of any of these things be condemned by the court to be bound according to law in the prison which is in the centre of the land, and let no freeman ever approach him, but let him receive the rations of food appointed by the guardians of the law from the hands of the public slaves; and when he is dead let him be cast beyond the borders unburied, and if any freeman assist in burying him, let him pay the penalty of impiety to any one who is willing to bring a suit against him."[7]

AUTHOR: Harsh, indeed! If this woman should steal again she shall be put to death, and the winebibber cast into prison until he dies and then his body cast beyond the borders of this land to be eaten by vultures.

PROTAGORAS: Plato himself has said so.

AUTHOR: Perhaps we should not leave the sentencing to these judges. Do you remember the sentencing guidelines I mentioned some time ago?

PROTAGORAS: Can you accomplish nothing without a Greek to guide you? Again I recite! "But when a state has good courts, and the judges are well trained and scrupulously tested, the determination of the penalties or punishments which shall be inflicted on the guilty may fairly and with advantage be left to them."[8]

AUTHOR: And if these qualifications—well trained and scrupulously tested—are not met?

PROTAGORAS: Then punishments cannot be left to them.

AUTHOR: Thus the guidelines we both seem to deplore. What other leash do we have on the conduct of judges?

PROTAGORAS: Again I recite. Plato. *Laws*. Book VI. "Every judge and magistrate shall be liable to give an account of his conduct in office, except those who, like kings, have the final decision."

AUTHOR: And if they give an account and be found wanting—as they surely will—then what?

PROTAGORAS: Book VIII. "But if any of the magistrates appear to adjudge the penalties which he imposes in an unjust spirit, let him be liable to pay double to the injured party. Any one may bring the offences of magistrates, in any particular case, before the public courts."

AUTHOR: And what would you do about juries?

PROTAGORAS: Do you refer to what we saw in the third room to which we were taken by mistake, the selection of twelve citizens to watch the trial?

AUTHOR: No, not to watch but to decide guilt.

PROTAGORAS: Wonderful! What then does the judge do?

AUTHOR: He decides matters of law—and punishment.

PROTAGORAS: Thus this jury of yours has usurped the powers of the judge! Little wonder this institution is unable to bring order to your land. And you would place the blame for this upon the scales!

AUTHOR: Perhaps your library in Hades has no volumes on this matter. Perhaps I should explain how this came about. You see, during medieval times—my medieval times, not yours—the accused were often tried by ordeal or by combat. The accused would be immersed in water or perhaps stretched on the rack, and if he could survive this torture he was of course innocent, for God had protected him. He might also be required to fight someone's champion, usually a highly skilled soldier or knight. If he won he was innocent; if he lost he was guilty—and of course dead. You have to admire the efficiency of this arrangement, but the folk of this time began to feel uneasy about certain more or less obvious flaws in the logic of it. It was in this setting, we think—no one knows for certain, that the idea of the jury arose. Those originally selected to serve on this jury were citizens of the neighborhood who knew a great deal about the crime in question. Twelve were selected, and I suppose they voted to condemn or not.[9]

PROTAGORAS: Ingenious, indeed. And I suppose these too, as Plato would have it, are well trained and scrupulously tested.

AUTHOR: Scrupulously tested without a doubt; well trained is another matter. The judge tells them what to do.

PROTAGORAS: May I ask you what are you reading?

AUTHOR: The Manual of Model Civil Jury Instructions. I found it here on this table.

PROTAGORAS: I hope you do not intend to add theft to your other crimes.

AUTHOR: Of course not! I will put it back when I have finished with it. It must have been put here for the elucidation of the public.

PROTAGORAS: Or by mistake.

AUTHOR: Mistakes are not made here.

PROTAGORAS: You grow more cynical by the moment.

CHORUS: Is he improving then? He says he is a cynic.

AUTHOR: Listen to this. Following the instructions for the judge found in this manual, the judge speaks to the jury. Ladies and gentlemen, he says, I will tell you what your duties are and give you your instructions. Before you retire to the jury room to deliberate, he goes on, I will give you more instructions that will control your deliberations. You alone will decide from the evidence what the facts of this case are, but I will tell you what the law is. You must, he says gravely, follow the law whether you like it or not. You must reach a verdict in accordance with the evidence. The evidence is the testimony you will hear, documents and exhibits that you will see, and any facts I tell you to accept. On the other hand, he continues, this is what the evidence is not. It is not anything the lawyers say. It is not anything that I tell you to disregard. It is not anything you hear or see when you are not in this courtroom. Furthermore, you should not pay any attention to anything I say or do that may suggest to you what I think of the evidence or what I think the verdict should be.

PROTAGORAS: Masterful! I have not heard what I know I have heard; I have not seen what I know I have seen! This is a monument to discipline even a Spartan would hold in awe.

AUTHOR: Listen! This judge is not yet finished. Nothing, he asserts, is evidence unless the rules permit it to be evidence. If a lawyer objects to evidence presented by the other side and I sustain the objection, then what was presented is not evidence. If I overrule the objection, then it is evidence. If I declare that anything you see or hear in this courtroom is not evidence, then you must strike it from your minds. You must not consider it when you decide this case.[10]

PROTAGORAS: The monument grows larger! Oh, shame, you Spartans!

AUTHOR: It is not yet large enough. Listen again! He is not yet finished! His voice rises. A finger—the barrel of the pistol of his mind—points menacingly at the jury. I will now, he intones sternly, tell you how you must behave. You shall not talk to each other about this case until you go to the jury room to deliberate. You shall not talk to anyone else about this case until I have discharged you from your duties as jurors. You shall not allow anyone to talk to you about this case. You shall not read or watch or listen to any news reports about this case. You shall not look into any book or paper that may explain to you the meaning of anything that transpires in this courtroom. You shall not decide this case until you go to the jury room to deliberate.[11]

CHORUS: What is it that these twelve could not do should they but set their minds to it?

PROTAGORAS: I scoff! As we watched in the fourth room to which we were taken by mistake, I saw jurors violate the first of these commandments. They passed notes to each other and the judge saw them do so. He called all the lawyers to his bench to tell them what he saw, but he did not punish the offending jurors. So much for instructions!

CHORUS: Let us speak. We know why the offending jurors were not punished. One of our number approached the bench with the lawyers, and no one thought that there was anything amiss. He heard the whole discussion. The offending jurors were not punished because they were not writing notes to each other but only playing tic-tac-toe. None thought that this was a great offense.

PROTAGORAS: Tic-tac-toe?

AUTHOR: A game played on paper. It is an antidote for tedium.

PROTAGORAS: If it is efficacious there should be no paper left in all the world. What would the judge have done if they had slept or come to court with their bellies full of wine?

AUTHOR: He would have dismissed them.

PROTAGORAS: Curious.

CHORUS: May we speak again? The judge said the jurors are allowed to take notes, but he could not decide where taking notes ends and tic-tac-toe begins. He said that he had carefully weighed the matter but could not decide. The jurors may not let each other see their notes, the judge explained, but clearly—this judge saw—tic-tac-toe marks are not notes. In brief, the judge could not tease the scales to answer.

AUTHOR: No notes at all but noting all should be required.

PROTAGORAS: Why should the jurors do their own recording of the proceedings. I watched as a scribe wrote all. Let the scribe tell all. I for one cannot both write and listen. Subjects and verbs demand my attention; gender and case and mood as well. I should not let even my eyes see my words were the rhetoric not good.

AUTHOR: This is the answer. It is in the book. You may write notes, but if you do you must not let the other jurors see them until you go to the jury room to decide your verdict. You may write notes, but you must miss nothing as you do. And whether you take notes or not, you must remember all.

PROTAGORAS: These twelve with perfect memory shall decide as perfect memory guides them. Could not the scribe read to them what he has written? Could they themselves not read the record?

AUTHOR: They may not read the record, and to have the scribe read to them is much too difficult and time consuming.[12] These twelve whose empty minds are poised shall decide as memory guides.

PROTAGORAS: This becomes more wonderful by the moment! Why twelve? What is it that they are expected to know by reason of being alive when the wrong was done?

AUTHOR: In medieval times everything; in my time nothing.

PROTAGORAS: Surely you jest. A jury that knows nothing! Not even Spartans had such self control. Where do you find such persons?

AUTHOR: Well, actually, you do not; you have to settle for as little as possible and that is not so difficult.

PROTAGORAS: You do make sport, and I thought the majesty of this place had made you serious!

AUTHOR: I am serious! You asked me why there are twelve. I cannot say and I think no one else can either. Perhaps because there are twelve lunar months in each year.

CHORUS: We know! The twelve days of Christmas.

PROTAGORAS: Perhaps because of the Twelve Tables of Roman Law. Perhaps because of all the twelves to be found in Plato.

AUTHOR: Perhaps because of the twelve arrows that English archers carried. But it really is not quite that simple, for grand juries may be twice that number and juries hearing minor cases half. Thus, the number can be six, twelve, or twenty-four, depending.

PROTAGORAS: I dare not ask what a grand jury is.

AUTHOR: And I choose not to say.

PROTAGORAS: You did say that they are scrupulously tested. How is that done?

AUTHOR: You watched that being done, Protagoras.

PROTAGORAS: I watched them being questioned about their knowledge of the crime in question, and—curiously—the less they knew the more highly they were regarded.

AUTHOR: Precisely. Their skulls are to be empty of all except what the witnesses are to put into them.

PROTAGORAS: And in this way you choose an impartial jury?

AUTHOR: Well, not quite. The judge wants an impartial jury but the lawyers do not. You of all people should know that, Protagoras. The lawyers do all they can to select jurors who will favor their side. In short, they do their best to get a biased jury, as you would no doubt have done. Did you not do anything to win?

PROTAGORAS: Nonsense! Vigor in arguing both sides was all I wished for. Rhetoric was my burden, not justice.

AUTHOR: I will agree that you were not much burdened by justice.

PROTAGORAS: You seem to know much about my crimes. Am I thus assured that you would not sit on the jury of my trial?

CHORUS: He is fully qualified to sit on your jury: he has only second-hand knowledge of your crimes—what your enemies have said—and, besides, he obviously does not like you. The lawyers for the prosecution will surely choose Author. But be grateful, Protagoras, that he cannot be judge; he sees no virtue in the scales and does not weigh. He himself is the measurer of all things.

AUTHOR: And the lawyers for the defense will reject me. I will not serve.

PROTAGORAS: Is this truly so? The lawyers may thus pick and choose?

AUTHOR: It is truly so, another refinement of my time. The balance scales have been at work here; the lawyers of both sides, like Anubis of ancient Egypt, stroke and tease the scales to get the outcome they desire. Surely you see that this weighing is a scrupulous business, that you do not simply pick a pebble from the beach and toss it into the pan. No, you must use a weight duly stamped by authority.

PROTAGORAS: Thus when you see a jury acquit a person everyone believes is guilty, as we did in the fourth room to which we were taken by mistake, you are neither surprised nor dismayed. It is what you expect.

AUTHOR: I was surprised and dismayed, but once you refute my argument I will learn to endure. I will climb a high hill to survey the ruins of this my land and perhaps to find solace in the certain knowledge that ruin is the destiny of all.

CHORUS: Thank great Zeus! We were afraid he would become maudlin.

PROTAGORAS: It was what I expected, but he might do well to be his own lawyer.

AUTHOR: I might not be able to do otherwise than be my own lawyer; I have no money.

PROTAGORAS: Another indigent philosopher! I have known many and all have hated me because I turned my knowledge into riches! This one too will soon have his hand in my purse.

AUTHOR: You may not pay for your crime here, but you will surely pay your lawyer.

CHORUS: Can you get us a discount? The regular customers seem to get discounts.

PROTAGORAS: Surely we are not to be regarded as regular customers. Are you, Author, one of those we have seen here who knows every door?

AUTHOR: I have not been here before.

PROTAGORAS: Never?

AUTHOR: Never! Why do you doubt me?

PROTAGORAS: You seem to have a professional familiarity with this place, yet you are neither lawyer nor judge.

AUTHOR: I have told you that I have watched and read. In this land I do not need to go anywhere to watch; a magic window shows me all. As for reading, well, a magic box fetches books for me. No, I have never stood in this place before but I have seen it still. All of us in this land are privy to almost everything. That is why this edifice cannot stand.

PROTAGORAS: This is truly a wondrous land! Sophomores are magicians and judges get their wisdom from a book of instructions!

AUTHOR: There is good reason for such timidity.

PROTAGORAS: Yes. Your judges are timorous and unencumbered by reason.

AUTHOR: The judge must instruct the jury before it deliberates at the end of the trial; he is required to do so. The jury pays no attention, of course, and does exactly as it wishes. But if the judge commits an error of some sort as he instructs, even a very trivial error, a higher court may nullify the outcome of the trial.[13] All judges hate to be overturned on appeal; it is simply a matter of pride. Now let us compose ourselves. The last case before ours has been heard.

PROTAGORAS: That defendant was sentenced to eighteen months for killing two persons with a vehicle, nine months for each.[14] How much is that in your money, Author? Has the price of a human life gone up or down?

AUTHOR: In this case the maximum is one year for each life. The discount was only twenty-five percent; it could have been worse. But did you hear? The judge said that he could "feel the weight of sadness in this room."[15] The scales are ever behind his words!

PROTAGORAS: A discount for one side and sympathy for the other. Would you say that he is seeking to balance the scales? A bit of mercy in this pan for the unfortunate offender, a slice of

133

kindness for the suffering victims in the other. Plato himself would have smiled on such judicial behavior. Does this not buoy your spirits?

AUTHOR: I sink further into despair. You find comfort in reciting Plato, but all I see in such wisdom of the ages is accumulated error. At some point the human race must reinvent itself or perish. Scientific discovery constantly results in the trashing of earlier notions of the physical universe, but no such refurbishing of some areas of human knowledge and practice ever occurs. The law, this law, thousands of years after its formal beginnings, is essentially what it was at the beginning, and it is now no more than what one would expect from unrelieved accretion. The frightening madness that issues from our courts does not inspire us to invention but rather only to hopeless tinkering. We who send our mechanical arms to the edge of our solar system cannot dream of daring to find new ways to regulate human behavior. I want to cry out to my compatriots that they cannot fix this thing that causes them so much grief; they must trash it and begin anew.

CHORUS: This is not a lawyer that we hear but a great tragedian! Sophocles despair!

PROTAGORAS: There is no despair for Sophocles for Author has it all. Surely he is a new Prometheus, whose much too bitter liver the vultures refuse to eat. Is he bound alone to this rock? What do others of this land say?

8

What the People Say

AUTHOR: Now that we are here again by this lovely pond, I shall tell you what the people say. With my notebook and my scissors, I have made a small collection.

PROTAGORAS: That sheaf of tiny papers? He holds them so loosely. Soon they shall be blown with the wind, and we shall be in court again.

CHORUS: The next time we shall be on the wind and you two will be on your own.

AUTHOR: Tell me, Protagoras, are we as one in understanding what we have just seen and heard?

PROTAGORAS: That can never be—unless you mean that we have but one pair of eyes between us, and one pair of ears.

AUTHOR: Very well! We did not see or hear exactly the same things, but surely in general we saw an institution run amuck.

PROTAGORAS: There is no *in general* when we see and hear. What we perceive...

CHORUS: ...is madness all about!

AUTHOR: We have no general impression then? Would you, Protagoras, be alarmed if this were your civilization?

PROTAGORAS: And as for running a muck, unless a muck is a race I have no idea what you are talking about. Yes. I would be alarmed but not enough, as you are, to sound alarm.

AUTHOR: I should have said that we saw a failed institution—although I have already said that I do not know what I am talking about.

PROTAGORAS: I should have said that we saw a failing institution—and I do know what I am talking about because in my mind I see a great building in need of much repair. That, I say explicitly, is my model and thus I do know what I am talking about. Men have built this edifice and they can restore it.

135

AUTHOR: Restore it? To what? To what it was in your time when Athens was bright and new and the barbarians had not yet come? To what it was in this land when there was little crime and one could walk about without fear of being robbed or murdered? And if we did that would it not fail again because it is built on fundamental error? But I digress. Let me tell you what people have said. You did ask me what others of this land say of this institution—failed or failing—that we both have witnessed.

PROTAGORAS: I wished to know if consensus could be found in this land. I should have asked a different question.

AUTHOR: A different question would not have gotten you a different answer. As for consensus, as much as can be found by this little pond.

CHORUS: Which is none at all. You two agree on nothing!

AUTHOR: Not so! We agree on almost everything but because we are contentious make much of our few differences. We are but a microcosm of the people of this land, the most contentious on this earth. We the people complain much and often, demanding that the people, in the persons of the ladies and gentlemen of the jury, hear the pleas of the people, in the persons of the complainants and the accused. Thus it is that nearly all trials by jury are here in this very land.[1] Thus it is that lawyers rule this land, that they have overwhelmed it by shear force of numbers, that nothing may progress without their ministrations. What shall save us from this ravenous horde?

PROTAGORAS: A few good lawyers.

CHORUS: Could we all agree to get on with the reading? And perhaps we will all agree that the people did not know what they were talking about.

AUTHOR: They did not know what they were talking about, but that we shall discover. That shall be our game—discover the model.

PROTAGORAS: That sheaf of papers you have in your hand. Do you have among them what lawyers have said? They too do not know what they are talking about, of course, and we shall have to tell them.

AUTHOR: I can tell you, Protagoras, without looking at one of my clippings, about the model that controls much of what lawyers say. It is to be found in the name that lawyers have given this institution. It is a system, a machine that does work. After notorious trials, lawyers almost always come from the courthouse to stand before the camera and say, "This proves that the system really does work." One could wonder why the lawyers find it necessary to say so. Has evidence to the contrary been introduced? But one need look no further than the nature of lawyers: they know very well that the system does *not* work—except for them. That is, they know that the machine—which is their model—cranks out not justice but money. The lawyer who speaks has earned his handsome fee, and for him the system truly does work.

PROTAGORAS: Perhaps, as is often the case, he has earned no fee, or but a small one.

AUTHOR: Then he has earned fame, which for him is money. The television camera looks upon him and thus so must we all.

PROTAGORAS: And if there is no fame?

AUTHOR: There is always some. At the troubling conclusion of a famous trial of my time, many lawyers were asked about the outcome, and many tripped over their defenses. Here among my clippings is an example. The lawyer in my city who is responsible for prosecutions and thus for public safety said in the same breath that the system had worked and that the accused had gotten away with double murder.[2] He certainly knew that the defense lawyers in this trial had made a grand fortune and much fame as well, that the system that gives him his place and his fee is the same that resulted in this travesty, and that the system is trembling under its burden of failure. So tell me, Protagoras, what I am to conclude.

PROTAGORAS: That you make too much of failure.

CHORUS: We conclude otherwise. The system is held to work because it gets the lawyers their fees. Justice is certainly not at issue, or we should have corn.

AUTHOR: Listen to this, Protagoras. The author of this one was once the local sheriff. The system "is severely flawed," he says.

What are flaws, Protagoras? Faulty parts? Gaps? Cracks? Because of these defects, he goes on, the system "is in need of refinement."[3] He saw a creaking old system that needs new parts. But if it is severely flawed how would refinement fix it? Would he, as if he were refining steel, burn out the impurities? Since he was once a part of the system, perhaps he felt a need to defend it. But he seems to me like a used-car salesman who admits obvious flaws but insists on general worthiness.

PROTAGORAS: A used-car salesman?

AUTHOR: I meant a horse trader.

PROTAGORAS: I see. The system is a lame horse then, one that shall never do its work.

CHORUS: No. That would be a lame duck.

AUTHOR: I withdraw the remark. Here is another clipping you might find worthy of your attention. A letter to the editor from an angry citizen. We let criminals "run rampant on the streets," he says. Perhaps he saw wild horses rearing in the street or war horses with barbarians mounted upon them. He also said "that the victims are between the law and criminals."[4] Perhaps he also saw the people, the law, and the criminals arrayed as on a field of battle with the people standing helplessly between the incompetent law, the supposed protectors, and the criminals, who commit atrocities in their war against society.

PROTAGORAS: Tell me what the judges of this land say about this institution over which they preside. Surely we may hope that they are lovers of truth and justice.

CHORUS: Not unless they are all ducks!

AUTHOR: Judges? Let me see here. Yes. Yes. Here is one. A man came home to find his wife in bed with another man.

CHORUS: Please, Author! This is a public place! No indecent jokes!

AUTHOR: No. No. This is truth. It actually happened.

CHORUS: And for that reason it is neither indecent nor a joke?

AUTHOR: Please! After several hours of argument and drinking, which one can imagine was conducted in the manner of a trial, he executed her with a hunting rifle. The judge in the case wondered how many men, in the same situation, could do otherwise than impose "some corporal punishment." He then sentenced the man to eighteen months in prison but only because, as he said, he felt compelled to in order "to make the system honest." It is interesting to note that this man left the prison every day to go to work and was thus not further punished by the loss of his job.[5]

PROTAGORAS: This was certainly not considered proper!

AUTHOR: In fact, this judge was accused of improper conduct and was judged by his peers. I do not recall the outcome, but many defended his actions.

PROTAGORAS: If he was judged by his peers in this land, I will guess the outcome. But perhaps you could balance this example with the view of a more distinguished judge.

AUTHOR: More distinguished? Let me see. Yes. Would you consider the highest judge in the land to be more distinguished?

PROTAGORAS: Let us hope he would be.

CHORUS: We will not so hope. We know very well what often distinguishes the highest duck!

AUTHOR: There is in this land, Protagoras, a court superior to all others. We call it the Supreme Court. At the head of that court of nine judges is one who is the highest in the land. We call him the Chief Justice.

PROTAGORAS: August indeed.

AUTHOR: Yes. Especially this one. He attended carefully to his augustness. But before I tell you what he said, I must tell you about a curious feature of my civilization. I believe I have already mentioned television and perhaps even have tried to explain it. The television camera is a great eye that looks on everything, and when it looks we all must look. It is as though we all have eyes everywhere. There was nothing in the myth or imagination of your time—no god, no monster—that ever came close in omnipotence to this thing. It is at once wonderful and abominable, at once both antidote and bane. Its great success is that it is no longer possible in this time to be wholly ignorant; its great failure is that it was no sooner invented than it was seized by those who built the Roman amphitheater and made to entertain the bored masses with bloody spectacle.

PROTAGORAS: And now this great eye has come to court. What has your great judge said about this intrusion?

AUTHOR: He said it was very "destructive," that it would "distort," not clarify, the proceedings of this institution that we are pleased to call a system of justice. Note that he said this when television had only recently come to court, very tentatively, one might say. The gist of what he said was that we must not combine court with Coliseum.[6]

PROTAGORAS: He was a prophet then?

AUTHOR: Some have thought so. A famous trial of recent time certainly became a very great spectacle—and the cause of much dissension. All across this land, as the sword was poised above the accused, many thumbs were up and many more were down. When the sword did not fall, the outcry was thunderous.

PROTAGORAS: As it was in Rome. Judgment by the mob. And the accused of course raised his sword in gratitude to his saviors.

AUTHOR: No. He did not acknowledge the cheers. It is said that he has been severely criticized for not doing so. It was said that he would be the greatest "ingrate" in the land if he did not do so.[7]

PROTAGORAS: Surely the people of this land did not say that this was justice!

AUTHOR: Those whose thumbs were up certainly thought it was and said so; those whose thumbs were down thought otherwise and said so with louder voice. I have told you about television, Protagoras. Now I must tell you of another such miracle. Imagine that you are standing in the agora and that you shout your displeasure about some such matter as this. How many would hear you?

PROTAGORAS: I would not shout, but if I did few would hear me. That was not the way to be heard in my land.

AUTHOR: Then imagine shouting so and being heard throughout the land, even in all the world. Not even the gods of your time had such voices.

PROTAGORAS: He raves! The great eye and now the great voice!

CHORUS: You do not know the worst. His great voice is in the tips of his fingers.

AUTHOR: No. No. My great voice comes *through* the tips of my fingers —and thence to all the world.

PROTAGORAS: I must leave this land! All here are oracles and monsters! Again the Minotaur roars for human flesh! Great Zeus give me the sanctuary of Hades!

AUTHOR: You have nothing to fear, Protagoras. It is as though a great spider had spun a web of glass and copper over all the earth.

CHORUS: Yes. And you know, Protagoras, how a spider's web works. When the prey falls into the web, the spider, sitting at the center, feels the shaking, at once knows whence the shaking comes, and pounces on its meal.

PROTAGORAS: Odysseus himself in the land of the Cyclops knew no such horror! Shall my sails find Hades ever again?

AUTHOR: No! No! That is not the image I intended! Listeners sit at every intersection, and every listener has also a voice.

PROTAGORAS: Praises to the gods! Happily between Scylla and Charybdis shall I sail!

AUTHOR: Listen, Protagoras! From this web I have taken these. This is what the people have said about the famous trial of which we just spoke. "I am physically sick," one said. Another said that money bought acquittal. A poisoned jury, another claimed. Still another said that infamous murderers of the past would have escaped justice had they possessed the wealth of this accused person. This one said the system needs an overhaul, like an automobile, I suppose. Acquittal from crime is a commodity that can be bought this one also said, happy that a more notorious murderer of our time did not have the great wealth needed to buy it. The trial was "the joke of the century" for this one. "We love you," said this one to the accused. "Moral decay" is the problem, said this one. This one was appalled. This one said the accused was guilty but the verdict was "fair," apparently because "reasonable doubt" is a moveable standard over which the prosecutors failed to leap. "No! No! No!" this person exclaimed.

For this one the jury thwarted "the injustice of bigots, racists, liars..." This one, of another land, is "very sorry" for us here. This one says our legal system is "a farce and a lie" and that trials by jury may need to be ended. The jury system suffers from "terminal cancer," said this former trial judge.[8]

CHORUS: Are you aware, Author, that you have been tossing those scraps of paper to the wind?

AUTHOR: I have no more use for them. None of these persons knew what they were talking about. Perhaps they can be playthings for the wind.

PROTAGORAS: I thought he was demonstrating something. Perhaps his contempt for judges.

CHORUS: Be warned, Author! We shall fly away and thus deprive this farce of yours of all moral probity!

AUTHOR: Forgive me. Notice how carefully I place this scrap back into the stack. I shall keep it forever though it is wholly illiterate!

CHORUS: Thank you.

PROTAGORAS: You threw these remarks away because the persons who made them did not know what they were talking about? I thought this was the purpose of your argument, to show that none of us do. You proposed just now to discover the models of which these speakers were ignorant.

AUTHOR: So I did. It slipped my mind.

CHORUS: Just as those scraps of paper slipped from your fingers.

AUTHOR: If I could see them again, perhaps I could discover the models. How many were there?

CHORUS: They are on the wind. Sixteen of them by our count. We shall have a fair sentence if we go to court again!

PROTAGORAS: Then we shall discover no models.

CHORUS: We shall bring them back. Any duck is swifter than this wind.

AUTHOR: How swift is the flight of the righteous!

CHORUS: Here is the first—and the most distant. And here is the second. You may expound while we put the others back into your hands.

PROTAGORAS: By my count sixteen that came from the tips of the fingers. Sixteen that you carefully selected to support your opinion.

AUTHOR: Yes. Yes. I now have sixteen again. No. No. I took them as they came to me. Let me see if I can get these into some kind of order.

PROTAGORAS: May you remember that these are all about a single trial.

AUTHOR: Yes. We may order these by primary concern. Of these sixteen, thirteen are primarily concerned with the failure of the criminal justice system. Of the other three, one treats the accused as a hero—above the law, I suppose—one finds a loophole in the reasonable doubt standard, and one holds that the jury thwarted racial injustice.

PROTAGORAS: These are models?

AUTHOR: No. Merely kinds of responses. A sort of straw vote. If we were to look further, I am sure we would find many more of each kind, perhaps in the same proportions. The models are another matter. They are images that we may infer were in the minds of these persons as they commented.

PROTAGORAS: Of course. Images of which they were not conscious. Thus they did not know what they were talking about. Are you now prepared to describe those images?

AUTHOR: You could do the same, Protagoras. You will recall that one of these persons mentioned a poisoned jury. What image do you suppose lurked beneath those words.

PROTAGORAS: A lawyer placing succulent but poisoned fruit before a hungry jury.

AUTHOR: Very good! The fruit is words and the poison is hatred and distrust.

PROTAGORAS: Very good, indeed! What fault do you find in this image?

AUTHOR: Suppose this person had said that the lawyers for the defense had *misdirected* the jury. What image—or model—might you find beneath such an expression?

PROTAGORAS: Very well. I will play your little game. I see an evil old man sitting by a fork in the road. The road to the left leads

143

to Hades, the one to the right to the temple of Apollo. A weary pilgrim approaches the fork and asks the old man the way to the temple of Apollo. The evil old man points to the left.

AUTHOR: Excellent! You have made my point! Perhaps overly elaborate, but excellent nevertheless. Now I shall try one. This one said that he was "physically sick" because of the verdict. He also wished that "horrible" things would happen to the accused. What image is hidden here? It must have been hideous indeed to make him physically ill. Perhaps, unconsciously, he saw the scales unbalanced and the very foundation of the universe trembling. That the Furies will pursue and punish him is his hope.

PROTAGORAS: Wonderful! Euripides himself could not have done better! And, of course, your image is not overly elaborate. I shall try another. Please give me one.

AUTHOR: Try the one that claims that acquittal can be bought.

PROTAGORAS: Very well. This person saw a marketplace. There was a great bench at which sat evil men dressed in black robes. On the bench were bags on which was written "Acquittal." The accused, bearing a loathsome burden on which was written "Guilt," approached the bench. He offered a great bag of gold.

AUTHOR: Wonderful! The high drama of the unconscious is once again revealed!

PROTAGORAS: Overly elaborate?

AUTHOR: Who knows what images lurk in the minds of men? Another of these speakers was standing in the same market when another murderer approached the same bench. That murderer also bore a loathsome burden on which was written "Guilt," but it was much larger than that of your murderer. This murderer opened a small bag and poured its contents onto the great bench. The evil men in black robes looked at those contents—a paltry amount of gold—and somberly shook their heads. No acquittal would be bought here! The speaker looked skyward and uttered a prayer of thanks.

CHORUS: This is not high drama. It is low comedy. And because of it your argument suffers, Author. We see it standing before the great bench searching through its tattered clothes for a few coins with which to pay for a sharp ax rather than a dull one.

PROTAGORAS: A dull ax would do quite well.

AUTHOR: Another said the system needs an overhaul, like an automobile. He saw it in a shop where such things are repaired. The mechanic lifted up its hood and looked inside. Sagely he shook his head from side to side. "Um, um, um," he said.

CHORUS: Another saw the trial as a joke. He laughed until he thought his sides would split. The judge thought he was on a roll. "A priest and a rabbi were walking down the street," he said.

PROTAGORAS: Please! Please! We have exceeded the bounds of decency! We are examining the very entrails of civilization!

AUTHOR: The guts, you say? Yes. And this is where the rot is that another saw.

PROTAGORAS: We were examining the balance scales. Did any of these speakers so much as mention the scales?

AUTHOR: Two of them, in speaking of the jury, used the word *deliberate*, which means, of course, *to weigh the evidence*. If they saw the jury *weighing* the evidence, then somewhere in their minds the instrument of weighing was to be found. All through this trial nearly every televised report of the proceedings began with the scales shown in the background, almost unconsciously. All who watched surely had this image in their minds.

PROTAGORAS: But none spoke of the scales.

AUTHOR: I have concluded that few speak of the scales, that some speak of weighing, which is done with the scales, and that many speak of justice, which is thought to be accomplished by weighing. Do you remember the etymology, Protagoras? Latin *jugum*—yoke—, Greek *zygon*—yoke— Sanskrit *yuga*—yoke. The stick that borne across our shoulders allows us to carry balanced loads. The stick that became the balance scales. All these words from the Indo-European root, *yeug-*, to join. The English word *justice* from the Latin word *justitia*, which came from *jus*—meaning right, law, or justice—and is perhaps related to *jungere*—to join. When we talk of justice all this is lurking in the unconscious, or perhaps now I should say it was captured in our neural networks thousands of years ago. When we speak of justice, all this is what we do not know. We do not know that we are talking about what we did with one of our earliest tools.

PROTAGORAS: None spoke of the scales.

AUTHOR: One did. He said he once thought of justice as a "blindfolded lady holding scales." But the lady has lost her virtue, and for him she is now "a greedy whore grabbing for money."[9]

PROTAGORAS: Who is this lady?

AUTHOR: You know very well, Protagoras. She is Astraea, or Justitia, or Carmenta, or Themis, or Dike. And who knows what other names she may go by? She is an image, nearly universal in our common culture. Her sculptured image with scales and sword is to be found on and in courthouses across this land, imitations no doubt of sculptures you knew well. Her kingdom is the collective unconscious. Her place in our neural networks is original and permanent.

PROTAGORAS: One woman, many names. She was born Themis in Greece.[10]

AUTHOR: No. She was born Maat in ancient Egypt.[11]

CHORUS: No. She was originally a duck born of pure water.

PROTAGORAS: Whoever she is or was or may be, she is not served in this land!

AUTHOR: Not so! In this land people often say, "Justice has been served," or "Justice has not been served," or something of the sort. Here. A newspaper clipping. This person wants to replace the jury with several judges who, he says, "would serve justice more efficiently, more honestly and more expeditiously."[12] Did you hear that, Protagoras? He said "serve justice." And not just serve, but serve efficiently, serve honestly, serve expeditiously. Surely in the mind of this person the goddess still reigns.

PROTAGORAS: In the mind of this person, perhaps, but I was not sensible of her presence in the courthouse we left within the hour.

AUTHOR: Here. Another clipping. An article about another judge who is called The Prince of Darkness. "Most defendants are in fact guilty...," he has said.[13] If a defendant refuses to testify, he has asserted, we may assume that he is guilty. Ah, this is efficiency! How can you suggest, Protagoras, that the goddess is not served in this land?

146

CHORUS: We are suspicious of your use of the word *served*.

AUTHOR: Do you know how to serve a duck?

CHORUS: Outrage! Just as we suspected! You have perverted this word, just as you have the others that you speak.

PROTAGORAS: Outrage indeed! But it is not words that are turned on their heads but rather ducks.

CHORUS: Horrors!

PROTAGORAS: Forgive me. So far has this discourse fallen from grace that I could not resist a jest. Perhaps you would seek redemption, Author, by telling me what your rulers say of justice.

AUTHOR: In this land we have no rulers—at least it is the fashion to say we have none—but we do have politicians. They always speak on occasions such as the acquittal of the famous defendant of whom we have spoken. One of them, the President of this land, whose rank and power is much like that of Pericles, the ruler of your Greece, said this of the jury's verdict: "...justice requires respect for their decision."[14]

PROTAGORAS: And the model is?

AUTHOR: An ancient one, I believe. Ruler and subject. Rulers can rule only obedient subjects. Thus rulers require obedience; they cannot rule without obedience. Thus this ruler *requires* us to accept a decision we believe to be unjust, a verdict in conflict with natural law.[15]

PROTAGORAS: I thought he meant that the rule of law *requires* you to accept the verdict.

AUTHOR: Perhaps he thought he meant that, but he did not know what he was talking about. He betrayed himself when he said *requires*. He was a ruler speaking to his subjects.

PROTAGORAS: You betray yourself! You argue for anarchy, not for justice!

AUTHOR: Another politician, one who only aspired to the office of President, said only that the verdict "must be trusted."[14]

PROTAGORAS: Not only do you not know what you are talking about, you also do not know what you hear.

CHORUS: Now hear us! Natural law is the law of ducks. And, verily, no duck has ever broken it.

AUTHOR: Perhaps I should tell you what our British cousins have said in commenting on this trial. It was "a three-ring circus," one said; "a Farce." Another said "...the justice system over there stinks." Still another said the trial was "a big film really, made for" television.[16] Can you describe the models, Protagoras?

PROTAGORAS: Do not offend me further!

AUTHOR: You asked me a little while ago, Protagoras, what lawyers have said of our system of justice, and I told you little. You may recall that we discussed sentencing guidelines some time ago.

PROTAGORAS: It was another day, nay, another age!

AUTHOR: New sentencing guidelines—the price lists of crime—have been proposed for my state, my province, that is. The new guidelines, it seems, reduce the prices even further. One person said that the "flimsy, weak sentencing" of judges made it difficult for her to understand why the new guidelines would reduce sentences. A judge—and thus a lawyer—who was chief of the creators of the new guidelines said that they "...are only supposed to describe what the judges have been doing." One could suppose that this judge simply wanted to post an honest list of prices. But prosecutors are unhappy with the price cuts; the new guidelines "...are terrible, just absolutely terrible...," one said, adding that he would ignore them. Another said feelings about them went from "...outraged to skeptical to disgust."[17] Even lawyers object to the cheapening of crime.

PROTAGORAS: Have you altogether forgotten the models? You would say that none of these people know what they are talking about. What is it that they did not know?

AUTHOR: The scales. One writer, apparently not a lawyer, said that what the lawyers who are responsible for the new guidelines had done was to examine the sentences judges had been giving for the past several years, "...compute them, and then refigure what a reasonable sentence under the guidelines should be."[18] This is pure commerce. It is done with the balance scales. These lawyers are putting crimes and prices in the scales, and they are unhappy with the proposed prices, for a lesser price marks a

148

lesser crime. They certainly do not seem to see that, as in the case of murder, a human life is further cheapened when it is balanced against even fewer months or years of a murderer's life.

PROTAGORAS: Enough! I am weary unto death of this new world.

CHORUS: We were going to mention how pale you look.

AUTHOR: Yes. I can see through you.

PROTAGORAS: Have you offended me again?

AUTHOR: No. No. I meant only that you seem transparent.

PROTAGORAS: I am too weary even to take offense.

AUTHOR: Have I answered you fairly, Protagoras? Are you satisfied that I have told you what the people of this land say?

PROTAGORAS: Yes. These people, as did the Romans before them, will have their vulgar diversions, circuses and games.

AUTHOR: Perhaps it would cheer you to see our circus.

PROTAGORAS: I have already seen what you call a circus. Show me rather Hades! But tell me, why did you go to the circus—the hippodrome—to get your imagery rather than to the Coliseum?

9

The Trial As Circus

AUTHOR: Why did we go to the circus? Because we of this time love our circuses, though I must admit that *circus* is a term of contempt when it is applied to anything else.

PROTAGORAS: The Romans also loved their circuses, but what do chariot races have to do with these trials of yours? Do you see the lawyers as charioteers racing madly around the course in search of glory?

AUTHOR: Ah! You speak of circus as in Circus Maximus of ancient Rome! Truly we do not know what we are talking about, for your circus is our racetrack and our circus is your Roman Coliseum—without the blood!

PROTAGORAS: Thus when in derision you call a trial a circus you do not mean that you see a chariot race?

AUTHOR: No. Rather something very different. There are animals, of course, as there were in the Roman Coliseum, and rings in which they perform. Perhaps it is the rings—the circles—that account for this misunderstanding. What we deride is certainly not the charioteers but rather farce or worse. When you pay to see the clowns, only clowns will do, but when it is justice that you want, you do not want to pay the clowns.

PROTAGORAS: Then I know what your circus is as well as I do know the public taste for conflict and commotion. Better pay to see the clowns than what we have seen this day. But if you think your circus is a bloodless Coliseum, I think you are confused. Perhaps you could refer again to that sheaf of papers in your hand. Confirm for us that the circus that you see in these trials of yours is not the Circus Maximus but rather a Coliseum that never was.

CHORUS: We are thankful he holds those papers still, for we are too weakened by hunger to bring them back again.

AUTHOR: Yes. Yes. Let me see. Let me see. My word! This person said that the famous trial of which we have been speaking was the Circus Maximus, strange entertainment for the masses!

CHORUS: Pay no attention to him, Author. He clearly did not know what he was talking about.

PROTAGORAS: Your argument is proved. I regret that I cannot say the same for your knowledge.

AUTHOR: Great Zeus! This one says that the trial was blood sport! That there was gladiatorial music! That it should have been held in the "...Los Angeles Coliseum, where the resemblance to a Roman circus would be unmistakable and the masses could seal..." the defendant's "...fate with a simple thumbs up or thumbs down"!

CHORUS: We are stirred to moral outrage!

PROTAGORAS: This one stirred his archetypes with a spoon. The Coliseum was not a Roman circus, and the Roman circus—though it could be bloody—was not a place of blood sport.

CHORUS: These persons did not know what they were talking about, nor do we. You have failed us, Author.

AUTHOR: Had you not brought these back to me, we would yet live in an orderly and predictable universe, a universe without ducks.

PROTAGORAS: It follows—as does cause follow effect! If we were to examine what these persons said, perhaps we could discover what we do not know.

AUTHOR: Here! This one speaks of a three-ring circus. Surely that is a circus of my own time. This one says the same. Three rings.

PROTAGORAS: If not of your time then it never was.

CHORUS: It follows—as does a duck follow a turtle.

AUTHOR: If we were to examine the circus of my time, perhaps we would discover what it was that these persons did not know they were talking about.

CHORUS: Wonderful! Let us go to the circus! There is one but a short flight away.

PROTAGORAS: A short flight? Do you mean that I must fly? How do I do that?

CHORUS: You simply extend your wings and do this.

AUTHOR: Come back! We have not finished here!

PROTAGORAS: I have no wings.

CHORUS: Then extend your...

AUTHOR: ...imagination! We shall go to the circus in our imaginations! I shall lead you.

PROTAGORAS: The circus in my imagination is not the one you want to see.

AUTHOR: I shall tell you what to see. Here! The great tent rises where yesterday was nothing. We go in. The smell of sawdust is perfume. Here in rising rows are the boards on which the spectators sit. Let us sit. Up there are the great swings from which men and women fly through the air. The band plays a rousing march. Sellers walk amongst the people hawking sweet nothings. "Get your hot dogs." "Get your popcorn." The ringmaster cries for our attention. "Ladieeees and gentlemeeeeeen!" It is all magic and wonderful!

CHORUS: We smell popcorn. May we have some? We have not so much as a penny among us.

PROTAGORAS: Here is a drachma. Buy what you will. What about the rings? I see no rings.

CHORUS: These seats were not made for ducks. We cannot see over the heads of those in front. What is the pink stuff that man is selling?

AUTHOR: It is cotton candy. You would not like it. The rings are before us, those circles on the ground. One is to the front, one to the left, and one to the right.

PROTAGORAS: How do we watch all three at once? We shall be overwhelmed.

AUTHOR: That may well be the purpose of three rings. Here in the center ring the lion tamer snaps his whip at the big cats. In the ring to the left an elephant puts his foot on the head of a beautiful girl. To the right the seals balance huge balls on their noses. Behind them is a canon that will shoot a man into that net over there.

CHORUS: Point the canon at the seals! Point the canon at the seals!

AUTHOR: And here come the clowns! All we are missing is dancing ducks.

CHORUS: A little waddling music, if you please. Sha-boom. Sha-boom.

AUTHOR: Look! That man has put his head into the mouth of a lion!

PROTAGORAS: He shall not take it out again. I have seen this all before.

AUTHOR: But he has taken it out again! He waves at us! Listen to the applause!

PROTAGORAS: Those clowns are clumsy.

AUTHOR: Of course the clowns are clumsy. Etymology tells us so. But listen! The applause has died. The people withdraw. The band falls silent. Let us go. Look! The huge tent falls and is rolled into a ball. The field is dark and empty once again. Was it not enchanting?

CHORUS: We wanted to buy more popcorn.

PROTAGORAS: Yes, enchanting. But there is something in that sheaf of papers in your hand that was not in your remarkable illusion.

AUTHOR: You mean the shadow of the Coliseum.

PROTAGORAS: Yes. I think that I should take you there.

CHORUS: We are fearful. Who knows what lurks in the...

AUTHOR: Do not dare! Then take us to the Coliseum, Protagoras. We are ready.

PROTAGORAS: Behold! The great amphitheater of Rome that was called the Coliseum! An ovate mountain of concrete and stone that was the pride of emperors. The sun is high and hot; it casts but a small shadow here.

AUTHOR: It is monstrous! I can imagine how it loomed in the minds of ancient Romans—and all who followed.

PROTAGORAS: Listen! The tumult of the mob! Something has pleased them greatly. We shall go in. Through these dark portals we pass and then rise up again into the sun. We breathe in the fragrance of blood newly spilled.

AUTHOR: Have you been here before, Protagoras?

PROTAGORAS: Yes. Many times. Zeus thought Hades insufficient. We sit here on these hard stones.

AUTHOR: Tell me what we see.

PROTAGORAS: We have arrived too late for the animal hunts, but we see that this day the lions have won. Dead men are dragged away and proud lions walk slowly back to their dens.

CHORUS: Surely they will not be given ducks. We are but a pitiful mouthful.

AUTHOR: And who are these?

PROTAGORAS: In march the gladiators! These are the famous swordsmen of Rome! They face the emperor and upraise their swords. "We who are about to die salute you!" Listen to the commotion of the crowd. In unison they shout their thirst for blood! The trumpet sounds! Now in the center the combat begins. Sword against shield, sword against armor, sword against sword. How mightily they strive! Uh! A sword bites deep! The vanquished falls. "He is wounded," the mob shouts, rising up in deadly rapture. The victor upward points his sword as he looks to the mob while the vanquished raises a finger to implore mercy of it. But look! They turn their thumbs downward! Obediently the victor downward thrusts his sword, and the conquered now lies still. Author, I am horrified, for you turned down your thumb!

AUTHOR: I am sorry. I was helpless. The frenzy caught me and I simply mirrored what was all about.

PROTAGORAS: These Romans might also plead so.

AUTHOR: Let us leave this place. I can bear no more.

PROTAGORAS: You can bear no more? Look at these Romans. They cannot bear the lull. The combat begins anew as we withdraw.

AUTHOR: Look! The Coliseum crumbles and becomes smaller and smaller. The roar of the mob diminishes to silence. The ages roll in like the tide over sand castles on the beach. It is gone and we are home again.

CHORUS: Our lovely pond is still here!

PROTAGORAS: Perhaps we should now revisit the sayings of the people.

AUTHOR: Yes. We are prepared. Here. This one spoke but four words: "It is a circus."

PROTAGORAS: With these four words he said all? What was it that he saw? You have said that archetypes in our unconscious minds tell us what to say, but what archetype is this? What is the image? Are we now prepared to say?

AUTHOR: You yourself have suggested that the archetypes might be scrambled.

PROTAGORAS: Do you mean mixed? Did he see clowns stumbling about in merry farce and trained lions that would not remove their master's head. Did he at the same time see a jolly gladiator a sword's length from barren death? I think not! It is one error to call the Coliseum a circus and quite another to find farce there. This speaker saw a farcical trial, and for him it evoked the image of the droll diversion that you took us to.

AUTHOR: What of another speaker who said this trial was a Roman circus that should have been held in our own amphitheater, the one we call the Coliseum?

PROTAGORAS: That one made only the first error. He saw the darkness of it, not raillery but depravity. And for him the image of the Roman Coliseum was properly evoked.

AUTHOR: We do not control our archetypes. They are in us all, unconscious, and come forth as they are called by what we see, and say, and hear, and do. Some looked at this trial and clowns came forth; for others bloody combat was evoked.

PROTAGORAS: Yes. Of course. But, tell me, why have you named your own amphitheater the Coliseum?

AUTHOR: Perhaps because it is a grand edifice much like the amphitheater of ancient Rome. Perhaps for darker reasons.

PROTAGORAS: Are bodies wasted there for the amusement of the masses?

AUTHOR: Yes. We call it football. It is played on a great field in the center, what the Romans called the arena, though this field is covered with grass, not sand. And there is also a racetrack—for foot races, after the fashion of you ancient Greeks.

PROTAGORAS: Ah! How well commixed these ancient images are! There were trained animals in the Roman Coliseum and far grander spectacles as well, but the gladiator was its only reason for being. Death was emperor and blood the only absolver. The Circus Maximus was an imitation of the Greek hippodrome and was thus for horse racing, though there were events of other kinds. Athletes often contended and sometimes there were games of a baser sort, but the spilling of blood was not the essence of it. Truly when you speak of circuses you do not know what you are talking about.

AUTHOR: You have asked me what we see in trials that evokes the circus. I cannot say for I have never felt compelled to call a trial a circus, no matter how ridiculous. For me it is another image that arises. But, as for these whose observations have called forth the circus, we might examine one or two trials of my time to discover what the motives might have been.

PROTAGORAS: What is the image that arises when you behold a trial such as this famous one we have discussed?

AUTHOR: I will tell you in a moment, but let me tell you now about what might be the circus elements in these trials. You will recall that when we went to the circus of my time just now, we were surrounded by a festive and noisy crowd. Outside the tent they jostled one another as they hawked their wares, as they bought mindless trifles, as they advertised themselves, as they proclaimed to all the universal truth, and simply gawked in open-mouthed astonishment. Outside the courthouse where the famous trial took place there was such a crowd, jostling, shouting, vying, decrying, exhorting, clowning. Cameras were everywhere, and the self-advertising as well as the journalists leered into every one, projecting themselves around the globe like canon shots. Many held up signs proclaiming this outcome or that. Improbable rubbish was proffered as treasure.

PROTAGORAS: Thus rose up from the unconscious the circus that you say you love. Strange! Do you then love the circus trial?

AUTHOR: Not so strange. We love the circus because it is profane— gaudy, worldly, without consequence. But when what is held to be sacred becomes profane, we are troubled.

PROTAGORAS: Trials are instruments of law. Why do you speak of the sacred and profane?

AUTHOR: I will tell you in a moment, Protagoras. Do you remember the ring master at my circus? He was the one who spoke to us and told us what we saw. "And now!" A drum roll. "In the center ring!" Trumpets sound. "Marvin the Magnificent, tamer of ferocious beasts!" Never mind that most of us know that these beasts are well-fed pets. We watch in awe, for the ring master by his magic has given this encounter cosmic signification. For one whole earth year, as every day for much of the day we watched our television screens transfixed by this famous trial of which we have been speaking, we saw not one ring master but at least two, usually several, and often many. These were the television commentators and the phalanx of experts they brought to bear against our ignorance. "Well, Greta, how many points did Ronnie Crankcase score on this one?" "He scored well, Rodney, and I have would have to say that he is well ahead at this point." "Thank you, Greta. And now Judge Iteration has entered the courtroom and we are about to begin. But first we pause to sell something."

PROTAGORAS: And all this recalled the circus ring master?

AUTHOR: Perhaps. I simply speculate. Do you remember the clowns? You said that clowns are clumsy, but in my time they also have oversized shoes, bulbous noses, painted faces, and funny hats. These are circus clowns, a special breed. We see another kind when lawyers play to bored jurors. In the trial of which we have been speaking, the clownish antics of certain lawyers was a daily cause of amusement or irritation. I merely speculate, but irritation could have evoked the circus.

PROTAGORAS: I also remember feats of daring. A device you called a cannon was to fling a man the length of the great tent. Was there such in this trial? I am prepared for any revelation because my mind is now as dead as my flesh.

CHORUS: Were there dancing ducks? We are prepared for mortification.

AUTHOR: We call them stunts. Yes. The accused was asked to try on in court the gloves that prosecutors said he wore to commit murder.[2] It was said that he first put on cotton gloves to protect the gloves that he was asked to try on. This was necessary, it was said, because the gloves were important evidence. Moreover the gloves had shrunk, it was said, because they had been covered with blood but had dried. The gloves of course did not fit, and a lawyer for the defense was able to make of this an appealing aphorism for the jury. If there was a turning point in this trial, that was it, and if there was anything in this trial that might have called forth the circus from my unconscious mind, that was it.

PROTAGORAS: Thus the prosecutors, as did the cannon man, risked all and lost all.

CHORUS: The cannon was misused—as were the gloves.

AUTHOR: For some of these speakers it was what we of this time call show business rather than the circus. If you knew the theater of Aristophanes, Protagoras, then you know what our show business is. One of the prosecuting lawyers was a woman, and when she changed the style of her hair the whole world knew at once. Some charged her with being too mindful of the television camera. I thought her new hair looked rather Greek. Nice. A lawyer for the defense was fond of colorful neck ties, and when he wore in court one especially ornate, the world was at once informed. A neck tie, Protagoras, is a narrow strip of cloth one wears about the neck.

PROTAGORAS: In this time, then, one goes about ready to be hanged. I do not wonder that you do. If murder is now a circus event, you would all do well to be prepared.

AUTHOR: You know well, Protagoras, the method of arguing a case in court that we of our time employ. We call it *adversarial*, and you, I believe, invented it. Perhaps you should wear a tie. I have one here you might...

PROTAGORAS: I would wear nothing so gaudy, nor do I deserve to do so! Behold my white himation! Would you defile this stately robe?

CHORUS: Nor would we! These white rings about our necks denote a noble race—and they are of no use for hanging.

AUTHOR: They look like the axman's marks to me.

CHORUS: Abomination!

PROTAGORAS: I will be held accountable for the adversarial method of seeking justice, perhaps, but not for the gladiatorial combat you of your time see in court. That what you see should evoke the ancient Coliseum is altogether fitting!

AUTHOR: The judge himself spoke of battle. He expected it, so he said, but still was not prepared. As it was in Rome, the mob was rapt and did not know—or did not care—that the swords slashed first at justice.

PROTAGORAS: The mob, the ring master, the clowns, feats of daring, the theater of Aristophanes—all these have you found in your modern circus and in your circus trials. Memory fails me. Have you yet found animal acts?

AUTHOR: I have found them but decency forbids me to recount.

CHORUS: Would that decency forbade him to count the starving ducks.

PROTAGORAS: The gladiatorial battles of the Roman Coliseum you find in the clash of lawyers. What else so dark as that?

AUTHOR: Perhaps the thumbs of the jurors. Perhaps the barrenness.

PROTAGORAS: You grow weary. But, tell me, what are the dangers in these circus trials?

AUTHOR: Participants and spectators are affected by matters not judicial and justice is lost sight of.

PROTAGORAS: I agree. Most damning.

AUTHOR: Lawyers and witnesses, mindful of the camera, attend to conceit, not to truth.

PROTAGORAS: Again I must agree. Most unjudicial. Without truth there can be no justice.

AUTHOR: A defendant could be convicted to please the mob.

PROTAGORAS: I am certain that has happened.

AUTHOR: Vicarious experience in a fearful realm that few would dare. I saw this corruption of moral being in the mob of the Roman Coliseum.

PROTAGORAS: You overreach but I will consider your conception.

AUTHOR: Corruption of the means of information, what we of this time call the media.

159

PROTAGORAS: Please explain. My antiquity clouds our discourse once again.

AUTHOR: Imagine this, Protagoras. A person of my time goes to the market to buy food. To pay for the food she must stand in line, that is, in a queue. As she stands, her gaze wanders about until it falls—luckless—upon a sort of small newspaper, very deftly placed to catch her restless eyes. There upon the first page are lurid and possibly ghastly pictures. The headlines leave her breathless. She cannot resist. She buys it, takes it home, and spellbound reads every word. What she finds is somewhat less than the apocalyptic revelations proclaimed by the pictures and headlines; it is, rather, sensational fantasy ever so slightly seasoned with factual pepper. We call these little papers tabloids, and you may be confident that she will buy another. This same woman turns on her television set. Ah! A news program, she thinks. Intently she watches. My word! All is confirmed! Again the racy scenes. Witnesses—of course unimpeachable—speak directly into the camera. We also call such as these tabloids, and you may be sure that she will watch again.

PROTAGORAS: I do not understand. What have these tabloids to do with circus trials. What is your concern?

AUTHOR: They are an inevitable part of the circus trial. I will explain my concern. The newspapers and television news programs, upon which we depend for much of the information we live by, envy the success of these tabloids. It seems that no standard of veracity is ever held up to them. Thus envy is soon followed by emulation. What then happens to the information we live by?

PROTAGORAS: May Zeus protect you from shadows! Have you any true concerns?

AUTHOR: Yes. Fear of television cameras in court. Recently—especially since the famous trial of which we have spoken—judges have been loath to allow them in. They say that they fear the cameras will cause their trials to be like circuses. Monstrous criminals have thus avoided the public scrutiny they deserve. The absurd behavior of this thing we call the criminal justice system is also hidden.

PROTAGORAS: You argue both sides so well I fear I will forget which you take. Any others?

AUTHOR: Where large numbers of boisterous persons gather, the atmosphere cannot be judicial. Where at the circus would you carry on the cool and rational search for truth that the trial is supposed to be?

PROTAGORAS: In my time the courts were in the agora and justice was not harmed. You cannot blame your television and tabloid newspapers for loss of judicial virtue. Tell me, did you have circus trials before you invented television?

AUTHOR: Yes. I believe I have told you how men have learned to fly as these graceful ducks do.

CHORUS: Graceful? Waddling is graceful?

PROTAGORAS: I think he was referring to the way you fly. I wait in wonderment to hear how he shall make of this an answer to my question.

AUTHOR: Before the machines in which we fly had become the marvels they now are, a dauntless aviator flew alone across a vast ocean. He became a great hero, but soon afterwards he suffered a grievous loss: his infant son was murdered. A suspect was captured and brought to trial, but—as you have already guessed—that trial became an outrageous circus, and some have always thought that the defendant was convicted and put to death to satisfy the public craving for vengeance. It was as if the mob in the Roman Coliseum had turned down their thumbs before the first judicial blow had been struck.[3]

PROTAGORAS: Grievous! And there was no television to blame.

AUTHOR: No. Newspapers did that ferocious work.

PROTAGORAS: And the lawyers were not censured?

AUTHOR: I do not recall. But long after television was appended to our eyes and ears, but before the cameras were admitted to court, newspapers, radio—radio, Protagoras, is television without the pictures and perhaps worse than television because it allows the listener to make his own pictures—radio, television, and lawyers, even the judge himself, made a circus trial and participated in it. The highest court in the land ruled that the judge was responsible for preventing the circus and thus overturned the conviction.[4]

PROTAGORAS: It seems that these circus trials put trials themselves on trial.

AUTHOR: During the recent trial of the famous athlete, the judge—as he spoke at the beginning of the trial to the assembled lawyers about their behavior—reminded all that some thought the criminal justice system would be on trial.[5]

PROTAGORAS: He was a prophet and the prophecy was fulfilled.

AUTHOR: Yes. And the judge of the most recent of our famous trials was so fearful he seemed not to want even a special form of television intended only for the victims and their families.[6] Now there are judges who do not love a circus.

PROTAGORAS: If your criminal justice system has been convicted, will it be imprisoned or put to death?

AUTHOR: I am shocked by your levity, Protagoras! My civilization tumbles down about us and you find in that a cause for jest.

PROTAGORAS: My civilization tumbled down and the world hardly noticed.

CHORUS: We have a wonderful idea! After the criminal justice system has been put to death, we shall have trials by television only. The victim, or someone who speaks for the victim, shall look into camera and tell the whole world what the criminal has done. The world will then call in its thumbs, and the execution shall be done on camera—with close-ups and re-runs. Only the ratings will tell us how well we have done.

AUTHOR: That has already been tried, not very successfully. Everyone seemed rather to prefer the circus.

PROTAGORAS: Which circus? Surely you do not mean the Roman Coliseum, which some of your time have called a circus.

AUTHOR: We have seen that some do mean the Roman Coliseum when they speak of a circus trial.

PROTAGORAS: These are, of course, your educated citizens, the intellectuals of your time, those who have studied history.

AUTHOR: I do not think so. Lawyers should surely be accounted among the educated, if not the intellectual, but they—

even judges, even judges of the Supreme Court—seem always to mean the modern circus when they speak that word. It is only the rare person who sees the darker images of the distant past.

PROTAGORAS: Which do you see, Author?

AUTHOR: Something altogether different.

PROTAGORAS: Of which you shall no doubt soon tell me. But it is good that you have so well condemned the circus trial.

AUTHOR: Have I condemned the circus trial? A trial that is a circus is at least not merely nonsense—it is entertainment. All others have even less virtue to rest on.

10

Trials Are Rituals, Courts Are Temples

PROTAGORAS: Do you mean to say that everything that goes on in court is meaningless?

AUTHOR: Of course not. What goes on in court is no more meaningless than any other ritual.

PROTAGORAS: You mean to say that what goes on in court is ritual!

AUTHOR: If it looks like ritual and sounds like ritual then it is...

PROTAGORAS: ...a duck. Great Zeus! Have I not yet atoned?

CHORUS: Perhaps Protagoras has atoned, but obviously we haven't. We don't even have any corn. Is a ritual required?

AUTHOR: Here is your corn! No ritual is necessary! But I will thank you to take this matter of crime seriously! I see mutilated ducks lying around here occasionally.

PROTAGORAS: Are you capable of pity? Why do you think justice is ritual?

AUTHOR: Tell me, Protagoras, have you ever noticed that courthouses often look very much like temples? Greek temples, at least. And I think you might admit that Greek temples look a little like Egyptian temples.

PROTAGORAS: Very well! For the sake of getting me back to the comforts of Hades before the end of time, I grant that courthouses look like temples.

AUTHOR: Good. Let us once again go in and watch the services. You will note at once the ambiance. The high priest—I mean the judge—wears a black robe. The seats are hard. There is no color. We await the invocations, the incantations of the swearing in, the supplications for the victims, the processions, the drama of the lawyers. Note that the functionaries of this place claim to represent the people—a very vague entity—or the state—every bit as vague. They say, "The people versus Everyman" or "The State of Blank versus Everyman." Does not all this seem sacred and magical to you, Protagoras? Is not all this what ritual is? And if this is ritual, can myth be far away?

PROTAGORAS: Enter Themis with scales and sword. Enter the Furies. Enter all! None shall be omitted! If the trial is ritual, is it sacred or profane? I know of no other kind.

AUTHOR: The judge should speak this invocation: "We do this because in the beginning we did this to preserve order in our society." Listen to the functionary. He says, "All rise." Note the manner of his speech. He does not simply say, he intones. Is this not the sacred sound of ritual?

PROTAGORAS: If the trial is ritual, then we must hope that it is sacred. But surely you consider these proceedings to be rational.

AUTHOR: Most definitely I do not! There is no intended outcome except the completion of the ritual, certainly not the protection of society from its human predators. These means accomplish no end except what is in the ritual itself.

PROTAGORAS: But what is in the ritual itself *is* sacred, consecrated to the gods?

AUTHOR: In what way, Protagoras, is this ritual different from the ritual that attends the burial of the dead?

PROTAGORAS: If the dead are sacred, then the burial of the dead is ritual. But what is sacred in this place?

AUTHOR: In what way, Protagoras, is this ritual different from the ritual that attends the taking of a spouse?

PROTAGORAS: If such a union is sacred, then a wedding is ritual. But what is sacred here?

AUTHOR: The sacred here is our belief about what we may do and may not do, about what we must do and may not avoid.

PROTAGORAS: But that is law!

AUTHOR: Yes. That which is laid down. By whom we do not know, but we do not question. By what authority we cannot learn, but we do not doubt.

PROTAGORAS: What goes on here is sacred then, for it is as inscrutable as the gods themselves!

AUTHOR: It surely is meant to be.

PROTAGORAS: Nay! It is occult, for it is beyond our understanding!

165

AUTHOR: It has always seemed so to me.

PROTAGORAS: And magical? Behold the sorcerers! They who have power! Mystical? You have said that this is religion, not law!

AUTHOR: It certainly seems to be. Which functionary have you seen here who does not passionately believe? On the other hand, which of these have you seen laboriously, meticulously setting up hypotheses and testing them?

PROTAGORAS: Ohhhhhhhhh! Here stands Protagoras: sorcerer, mystic, priest. Great Zeus, am I beyond pity?

CHORUS: Ommmmmmmmmmmmmmmmm.

PROTAGORAS: What is that?

CHORUS: A sacred sound. We are making a sacred sound. Is that not appropriate? Must we remind you that you said, "All rise"?

AUTHOR: It was not appropriate for ducks.

PROTAGORAS: Nothing said here this past hour is appropriate for rational men. Could you describe what you believe is going on here without indulging in your fantasies?

AUTHOR: What is going on here? It is not manufacturing for there is no product. It is not science for there is no knowledge coming into the light. It is not sport for no lust is being satisfied. Like all ritual, it serves primitive needs but does not extend into the practical world. When it concludes, we may step into the sunshine again and see that nothing has changed. Perhaps it is the reverse of the initiation rite: by initiation a new member of a society comes in, by this ritual an evildoer goes out or comes back in, ritually purified. Society thus learns how it is to regard the individual, whether initiated, expunged, or redeemed. Perhaps we should see this as simply the religious rite of purification brought to a wondrous state of elaboration. Perhaps then we should also see lawyers as a priesthood; they do obtain riches without actually doing anything—except gathering up the offerings the pious bring.[1]

PROTAGORAS: Nonsense! I gathered up nothing but you have gathered up the clouds of Socrates!

CHORUS: Nonsense! We have eaten up the corn and now we must dine on clouds.

AUTHOR: It is the nature of my time—a very scientific and technological and materialistic and pragmatic time—to expect the courts to actually do something, that is, to protect society from criminals. That is why, I think, that we speak of a criminal justice system. A man-made system, you see, has input and process and output; it actually takes in something, does something to what it takes in, and thus produces something. Perhaps by endowing it with this name we thought we could make it produce justice, but that it will never do. This institution, as it has amply and always demonstrated, does not, cannot, produce justice or protect society from criminals. It certainly does protect criminals from society, for no longer may the vigilante, or even the victim or threatened citizen, attack the criminal.

PROTAGORAS: Do you mean to say that the victim may not defend himself?

CHORUS: Do not ever expect a duck to go gently!

AUTHOR: The victim may at times defend himself, but only under such rules of engagement as give the advantage to the criminal. The lawyers—the priests—must have their ritual, and surely they would not unless the criminals were brought to the courthouse alive.

PROTAGORAS: This is madness! The public trial is the means by which the violence of personal vengeance was mitigated. How should we preserve the peace and tranquillity of civilization if every aggrieved person exacted his own punishment?

AUTHOR: I would say that the public trial *was* the means by which the violence of vengeance was mitigated. This ritual no longer satisfies the need for vengeance, and that surely is what it was always meant to do.

PROTAGORAS: It was meant to bring order to the world by rational means!

AUTHOR: Rational indeed! It is primitive doing, doing, doing, just to help us cope with, to make us feel better about, the darkness of human nature that we feel helpless before.

167

PROTAGORAS: The trial is a foundation stone of civilization. It must take its place alongside all else that makes us civilized.

AUTHOR: The trial must take its place alongside the rituals of birth, coming of age, marriage, and death; it is the ritual of transgression, a life-crisis ritual that not everyone requires.

PROTAGORAS: The trial is essentially procedure forged over many years on the hard anvil of experience. But that the hammer of necessity has struck many times at primitive means of vengeance heated in the searing fires of barbarism, we should have not this but bloody tumult.

AUTHOR: Behold, my world! Here stands Protagoras, the smithy of justice! And for a fee he will shoe your horse!

PROTAGORAS: I speak of the means of justice! We can do nothing without means!

AUTHOR: What is the difference, Protagoras, between ritual and other procedures? A procedure of technology has a desired result or it is abandoned at once. Only a ritual can be performed over and over again without the desired result and still survive.

PROTAGORAS: You have, then, made the miracles of your time by such means as grant immediate success? Such means in my time were magical.

AUTHOR: By means of procedure followed by success, eventual success. We proceduralize things we do so that we do not have to constantly reinvent. Ritual has surely also hit upon this mental strategy but only to insure that things are done as the gods may wish. The result—being the will of the gods—is assumed, is not questioned, is not measured, and perhaps does not matter. In my time the marriage ritual has the desired result only about half the time, but still we have the marriage ritual. So it is with this ritual we now observe. No matter what the result, the priests will say that it is right. And as the will of the gods, of course it is. But there is no useful, practical outcome. Something is said about order in human affairs but little or nothing is done to actually achieve that order. How, Protagoras, is this place different from that Hall of Justice of ancient Egypt where the dead were judged, a magical place where magical spells had effect? Those who died in sin were purified by magical incantations and then tested on the balance scales.[3] Here as there the scales are at the center, and transgressors are purified by magical means, by ritually killing them, by casting them into prison and thus out of society, by endless incantations that please the lawyers and mystify all others.

PROTAGORAS: There is certainly an effort to exert control.

AUTHOR: The effort is all symbolic. Yes, one may infer from the icons here that society condemns, that society punishes, but all that society condemns and punishes continues unabated. Yes, something is said about human evil but nothing is actually done about it.

PROTAGORAS: I must ask you what you mean by *symbolic effort.*

AUTHOR: I suppose I mean the attention given to the symbols of this place. The black robes of the judge to mark him as sacred, as the force of society. The sacred book upon which hands are laid. The sword that lops off the heads of the condemned. The balance scales, which are the centerpiece of all this magic. Those who are brought into this chamber as defendants are polluted, unclean, defiled. Thus we see that they are subjected to symbolic acts of cleansing, some by death, some by payments of life-time spent in prison, others by payments of money.

PROTAGORAS: The old man endlessly repeats himself! The balance scales are the means of fairness. Surely there is fairness.

AUTHOR: You mean to say that the balance scales are the means of weighing, which is supposed to result in what we call fairness, but fairness is never truly the point of this ritual, correctness is, the following of rules. All behavior must be as has been prescribed. The words must ring of mystery and timelessness. *De jure, turpis causa, ex post facto, duces tecum, de bene esse.*

CHORUS: *Venire de novo, animus furandi, capias ad respondendum, mala prohibita, quantum meruit.*

PROTAGORAS: Sensus verborum est spiritus legis. If you wish we shall henceforth speak only Latin.

AUTHOR: That will not be necessary. What goes on here is ritual but my argument is not. I merely wanted to show that much of the language of this place is Latin, now a dead language—or at least it has fallen into disuse. I should note, however, that not long ago it was widely used in the rituals of the Catholic Church, still a strong institution in my time.

CHORUS: That will not be necessary. We do not know the word for corn.

PROTAGORAS: It is *frumentum*. In my time agriculture was thought to be sacred work. Was it therefore also sacred ritual? One could wonder thus, but we were speaking of justice not religion!

AUTHOR: Has the judiciary grown in power as the power of religious authority has diminished? Has my civilization become more legalistic as it has become less religious? The sun sets in the west. I must conclude my argument.

PROTAGORAS: You must conclude that what we see here is justice.

AUTHOR: I fear that *justice* has become a shibboleth of lawyers.

PROTAGORAS: Shibboleth! What language now? I dread what is to come.

AUTHOR: We are told that we must dread the law. Is not dread a part of ritual? Tell me, Protagoras, when the first trial occurred. How many years ago?

PROTAGORAS: You know I do not know.

AUTHOR: Would you say that it was at least one million years ago?

PROTAGORAS: There were no beings such as us one million years ago. And certainly there were no Greeks.

AUTHOR: Then the first trial occurred somewhat less than one million years ago?

PROTAGORAS: Of course! Much less. There were on that occasion men such as we are, and there surely was a civilization. Do you annoy me with purpose, or are you merely uncouth?

AUTHOR: Then there was a first trial on some particular day in the past of our common civilization, and on the day before that particular day, or any day before that, there was no trial.

PROTAGORAS: Agreed. I trust you know where this is leading us.

CHORUS: We trust you know what you are talking about.

AUTHOR: A foolish trust indeed. Then tell me how those who held that first trial decided what they were to do. What was their model? What had they seen or done that could guide them?

PROTAGORAS: I do not know nor do you. Men have always invented; to be a man is to invent.

AUTHOR: Men have always made their inventions out of familiar things; the old, transformed, becomes the new. But what might have been the old and familiar thing that, transformed, became the trial?

PROTAGORAS: Very well! A ritual!

AUTHOR: And could that ritual have been the same that, transformed, became the tragedy, as many have thought? I mean of course the ritual of the year-demon, the vegetation god, who in your time was Dionysius.[2]

PROTAGORAS: You overreach. The irrational impulses of my time cannot be taken as an explanation of anything so formal as the effort to examine the facts of a misdeed.

AUTHOR: Perhaps the trial evolved in parallel with tragedy and also thus preserves the forms of earlier rituals: the *agon*—the contest, as between lawyers, which in your language has the sense *to weigh*, as well as *to struggle; pathos*—suffering, ritual death; the messenger—that is, the witness; *threnos*—lamentation; *peripeteia*—reversal, sudden change of fortune; *anagnôrisis*—recognition, at last, of truth.[5]

PROTAGORAS: I do not need this lesson on my own culture. Why must you explain everything by looking backward?

AUTHOR: The law looks ever backward, and it is loath to do what has not been done before. It looks back to judgments already made and not undone in hope of avoiding a brave new judgment. Its proceedings constantly refer to the balance scales, an ancient model indeed. It looks ever back to the beginning of time to find its reason for being, to the original roles and models, to the ancestors who wrote the Constitution constantly referred to in this place, that is, to the sacred beginnings, the original sacred act. And as it was in the beginning, its modus operandi is *prohibeo* not *annuo*.

PROTAGORAS: Is that not as it should be? Would you have us abandon our humanity? Should we, as if we were beasts, prohibit nothing and approve of all?

AUTHOR: I merely meant that we could say *Thou shalt* instead of *Thou shalt not*. The list of things we can do is certainly shorter than that of things we cannot.

PROTAGORAS: The good of mankind is greater than the evil or we should not be.

AUTHOR: In the church, Protagoras, there is the ritual of confession. He who confesses his sins is expected to show honest contrition and determination to amend his ways. Is this same sacrament not to found here? He who confesses his crimes must be contrite and transformed or he surely will not win the sympathy of the judge and possible decrease of punishment.

PROTAGORAS: And of course all criminals are expected to confess. Is this not the purpose of torture?

AUTHOR: Your reasoning is tortured—unless torture results in contrition, and I suppose it might.

PROTAGORAS: And if even the most heinous criminal confesses and is contrite then we shall forgive him and he shall go free. Nemesis shall be banished instead!

AUTHOR: No. The required purification may require extreme means, for water alone will not do. The enormous sacrament may be necessary.

PROTAGORAS: I believe that you are saying that the execution of a criminal is a sacrament.

AUTHOR: Consider, Protagoras, the ritual of execution. As I shall show you, it is not enough for this institution of which we speak that the condemned be dead; rather it demands that death be sacramental. It preserves still the forms of the past. Think of the headsman of medieval times, how he was dressed—a hood to make him faceless; of the place of execution—a sort of alter; of the beholders—symbolically society, as gathered for any other sacrament. How much has changed from that time to my own?

172

Not very much. We still have faceless executioners, tables or chairs to serve as alters, and somber witnesses.

PROTAGORAS: You said you would show me that an execution must be a sacramental death.

AUTHOR: In this land, not long ago, a man was to be executed for murder. His executioners found him in his cell apparently dying of an overdose of drugs. They rushed him to a hospital to have his stomach purged of these vile substances. Once he was revived and no longer in danger of dying, he was taken back to the prison, strapped to a table, and given drugs that killed him.[4]

PROTAGORAS: And how was this sacramental?

AUTHOR: Surely you understand. A simple death would not satisfy the requirement of the judge that the criminal die for his sins. The ritual of execution must be performed.

CHORUS: True! The criminal could not be both executioner and executionee.

PROTAGORAS: Nonsense! What law says such a thing?

AUTHOR: The highest court of this land has said so. The executionee must know that he is being executed and why he is being executed. The inexorable logic of sacrament would lead it to this conclusion.

PROTAGORAS: Absurd! What did the people say of this?

AUTHOR: One said, speaking of the condemned, that it was not "his job" to be executioner. Another spoke of absurdity, as you did. One of the executioners said they were bound by law to do as they did.

CHORUS: The executioners were bound by law, and the executionee was bound by straps to the table. All was as laid down. The executionee was laid down...

PROTAGORAS: You are suggesting that execution is sacrifice!

AUTHOR: Is any criminal entirely alone in his guilt? One must ask this: How did the criminal become a criminal? Was there anything about his birth, his rearing, his daily life, that others made and controlled? Do I see these shadowy others hovering behind this defendant in this hall of justice?...You do not answer, Protagoras. Is such a notion alien to you?

CHORUS: We will answer. Ducks make their own feathers.

PROTAGORAS: You are questioning free will.

AUTHOR: Such a death is for the good of all society, is it not? Then execution as sacrifice does not seem so strange. Nor does the last supper of which all who must die partake.

PROTAGORAS: Stop! I will hear no more of this!

AUTHOR: Do you mean that you will hear no more of my argument or no more of trials as ritual?

PROTAGORAS: I shall hear no more nonsense! The command I received from the great Zeus did not require participation in farce!

AUTHOR: Do you reject all of what I have said about trials as ritual or only part of it?

PROTAGORAS: Perhaps we might say that trials are ceremonial.

AUTHOR: But none of it is ritual?

PROTAGORAS: The purpose of such ritual as may be found in a trial is to stress matters of great importance, such as swearing to tell the truth. In your land, I believe, the witness places his hand on a book believed to have magical powers. Plato would have some witnesses swear by three divinities all at once: Zeus, Apollo, and Themis.[6]

AUTHOR: To see a ritual within a ritual changes nothing for me. The whole of the trial is ritual, for the reason that you have suggested: to stress a matter of great importance. Trials have always been rituals, and when they are performed the feelings that were always there are refreshed. Vengeance, redemption, purification, restoration—the emotions evoked by these all come back anew.[7] And if this institution has failed—as I believe it has—it has failed because it is no longer capable of achieving this end.

PROTAGORAS: Trials are about justice, not feelings!

AUTHOR: I make this proposal, Protagoras. We will watch this trial and you shall note such minor rituals as come to light and perhaps comment upon them. If you find nothing to engage your intellect, we shall leave this place and go back to the idylls of the pond.

PROTAGORAS: Great Zeus, still I endure. A sharp rap! What is that?

AUTHOR: The judge has struck his gavel upon the bench. A symbolic ritual act indeed!

PROTAGORAS: And what is a gavel? What does it signify?

AUTHOR: It is a hammer, the maul of the stone mason, the very mallet you see in the hand of the judge. It signifies his authority. Surely the etymology of this word parallels the history of this institution.

CHORUS: Nay! Not so! The origin of this word is unknown. And there is surely no mallard in the hand of the judge. Mallards have green heads.

PROTAGORAS: How would you ducks know that? And I said *mallet*, not *mallard*.

CHORUS: It says so right here in this dictionary. We are mallards and we surely know the color of our heads!

AUTHOR: Do ducks have dictionaries?

CHORUS: One of us went to the library and got it.

PROTAGORAS: I asked about the gavel only a moment ago!

CHORUS: He was a very fast duck, refreshed as he was by the recent but now exhausted offering of corn.

AUTHOR: Protagoras is right! My sanity is gone! Let me see that book! Yes! Yes! I see! Homonyms, they would have us believe. First, the hammer I mentioned. Second, a form of tribute in medieval times, but this second is traced to a Proto-Indo-European root. Let me see! Let me see! Yes! The root is *ghabh-*, to give or receive. We shall give the judge our honor and respect and he shall receive it. And through the Latin *habere* we shall *behave* ourselves. It is clear to me that the source of this word is not at all unknown. Unattested perhaps but not unknown. It is a clear case of confusing what is done with what it is done with. The gavel commands the tribute of honor and respect.

PROTAGORAS: Impeccable scholarship. Aristotle himself would be shamed. But perhaps we are now free to otherwise engage ourselves. I have recently noted, as you have commanded me to do, that the judge said, "Strike that remark from the record." This struck me, I must admit, as ritualistic or at least symbolic. What has been said cannot be unsaid, as the purpose of this command would seem to be. Words once spoken will have their way.

AUTHOR: Listen! A witness is being sworn in. Did you hear: "...so help you God?" The myth behind the ritual act is made explicit.

PROTAGORAS: You yourself have said that where there is ritual there must be myth. This is certainly only to stress a matter of great importance, but here is an expression of another kind. A lawyer said, "May it please the Court ..." What majesty is here that he should plead so? What model is this?

AUTHOR: Perhaps we are in the court of an English king. Perhaps this is the same majesty who, as he opened court, said, "The people are here." I suppose he meant the lawyers at the table to the right.

PROTAGORAS: Hear this! The crime was "...outrageously and wantonly vile, horrible and inhuman." It "...involved the depravity of the mind." Is this the language of cool and rational jurisprudence? What model is this? What monsters does this lawyer call forth? Great Zeus, he vies with Homer himself!

AUTHOR: Were there not monsters in the world when this ritual began? You must forgive him for looking backward to that time. All lawyers look backward.

PROTAGORAS: This lawyer looked not back but forward! The law is rational!

AUTHOR: Mere pretense! It has wrapped itself in fine Aristotelian logic. "The greater contains the less." "For every wrong there is a remedy." "That is certain which can be made certain." "The law respects form less than substance." By these maxims the truth of this ritual is to be hidden from us.[9]

PROTAGORAS: Listen! The judge has said, "Approach the bench." The lawyers go to stand before the judge. They speak in whispers. Is this conspiracy? Why may we not hear?

AUTHOR: The bench is the judge, symbolic of the judge. Interesting! According to this dictionary, the Proto-Indo-European source of this word is the root *bheg-*, which means *to break*. In Old Norse it means *a hammering*.

CHORUS: May we then say, "Hello bench"?

PROTAGORAS: I think not. Should you speak so, there would be no doubt about what is to be broken.

AUTHOR: In Old High German this bench could be a money-changer's table.

CHORUS: The judge is at the money-changer's table and the jury is in a box.

AUTHOR: This root also seems to be the source of *bungle*. *Bench* and *bungle* seem to be distant cousins.

PROTAGORAS: Will you cease your private musings and answer my question? What is this discussion at the bench?

AUTHOR: Something has gone wrong with the ritual and the judge is trying to fix it. You see, the lawyers are the Kouretes and the judge is the chief of these. Surely you remember that the Kouretes were the elite of their society, metal-workers and thus very like magicians. It is the most ancient of your rituals, Protagoras.[10]

PROTAGORAS: I see no dancing here. I hear no singing. No swords clash on burnished shields.

AUTHOR: The dancing and the singing and the clashing here are of another kind.

PROTAGORAS: This is not ritual. Ritual is an experience of the body, expression of the body.[11]

AUTHOR: The body is much involved in this ritual. See the jury sitting in a row, raptly attending to the proceedings, or at least expected to, the judge marching grandly to his high bench, the bailiffs escorting persons about, the court recorder sitting silently with fingers tapping—note that this person is now wholly obsolete—the lawyers strutting, gesticulating, making obeisance to the judge. The *body* of the defendant must be placed *here*. The *body* of the witness must be placed *here*. Why? Because *pain* of the *body* is central here. The *body* must be therefore be emphasized. In my time, Protagoras, the most brutish and savage criminal is brought to court immaculately clean and well dressed. Would you, judge or jury, inflict *pain* upon this *body*?

PROTAGORAS: And of course that is the emblem of Dionysius on yonder wall!

AUTHOR: No. That is a seal of this institution.

CHORUS: A seal!

AUTHOR: Not that kind of seal. This is an image that confirms

177

the doings of this place. You see there in the center the figure of Themis, or perhaps her daughter Dike, who was also called Astraea, I think. Whoever she is, there she sits above this court, the balance scales in her left hand, a sword in her right. You know this goddess well, Protagoras.

PROTAGORAS: By so many ways you know her, and by so many names, but I knew her only as Themis. Hers was the bright face of justice and order, and she had neither scales nor sword. Zeus it was who held the golden scales; so said Homer. Athena it was who held the sword, protector of our liberties. Once I saw Themis hold a sceptre and perhaps a spear or staff as well, but she is not the subject of this seal.

AUTHOR: How then explain this seal with balance scales and sword?

PROTAGORAS: It is your myth, not mine. You may explain it as you wish.

AUTHOR: My myth? And are such goddesses as this the creation of my own time? Or perhaps this one is Roman, Astraea or Carmenta. How very like the Romans to give their goddesses such practical tools as scales and sword!

PROTAGORAS: Themis has no part in this ritual that we observe. In your time—as in mine—she is revered but not obeyed, and she would grieve again to see that supplicants must accept such justice as may be had here.

AUTHOR: Ah! You have then concluded that this is a ritual!

PROTAGORAS: I have concluded only that it is time to return to our sacred pond.

AUTHOR: You have perhaps concluded that our institution of justice is not Greek, that we have somehow lost our way.

CHORUS: Listen! This very moment a lawyer said, "The prosecution rests." If he were a Proto-Indo-European, he would have said that he stands—and yet he sits.

PROTAGORAS: Hush! Let us go to our pond.

11

Change: What Models Do We Have?

AUTHOR: Tell me, Protagoras, what changes in this institution would make us Greek again.

PROTAGORAS: Such change is not possible.

AUTHOR: Perhaps you yourself have changed, Protagoras. At least you are not the cynic I thought you were.

PROTAGORAS: You are the Cynic; I am a Sophist. I thought we had agreed.

CHORUS: And whether we have agreed or not, we are mallets.

AUTHOR: That's *mallards!*

CHORUS: Forgive us! You unnerved us when you said *seal*. It was wishful thinking.

PROTAGORAS: Such change is not possible because your system leaves nothing behind. Everything ever done has been duly recorded, and everything that has been recorded must be argued again and again. You have thus thwarted logic and wisdom and given yourselves over to timid orthodoxy. Such is not the search for truth, nor is it Greek.

AUTHOR: What is truth?

PROTAGORAS: Zeus spare me! Truth is certain knowledge.

AUTHOR: But have you not said that there is no certain knowledge?

PROTAGORAS: I have not. What I see and hear and touch is true. Your system looks forever back to that which others of times long past have seen and heard and touched and done, and thus it does not find truth but rather artifact.

AUTHOR: We would say that it is a rule-bound system. It has so many rules that it simply cannot move. But why is change not possible? Could we not discard some rules?

PROTAGORAS: How many rules have you? How many books of rules have you, and how many books to elucidate the rules? How many to justify? Where would you begin? Which part of your vast library of law would you first turn to rubbish?

AUTHOR: Let us see where we might begin. Suggest a rule that we might discard.

CHORUS: The duck rule! It is demeaning.

PROTAGORAS: When a judge may say that you did not see what you saw, or did not hear what you heard, or do not know what you knew, then there must be a rule on which he stands—or sits.

AUTHOR: Very well! That rule is discarded. Henceforth you did see what you saw, you did hear what you heard, and you do know what you knew. What progress have we made?

PROTAGORAS: How many other rules thus must fall? How many others stood on this one?

AUTHOR: I do not know. I am innocent.

PROTAGORAS: How would you discover?

AUTHOR: I do not know. I am not a lawyer.

PROTAGORAS: There would be yet another library, vaster than the one before. You cannot change. What you have made in a thousand years you will not unmake in ten thousand.

AUTHOR: Unless... Unless...

PROTAGORAS: Yes! We await enlightenment! Let us breathe again.

CHORUS: Yes. Let it fly. If it looks like a duck, and flies like a duck...

AUTHOR: Unless... Unless we abandon it altogether! We could send it to the great landfill of antiquity and let it rot with other discarded institutions! It should be good company for monarchy and aristocracy and colonialism and empire and slavery. For magic and alchemy and philosophy. Have I said this before?

PROTAGORAS: Then you shall have no justice. Yes, I think you have.

AUTHOR: We shall have justice! We shall make a new beginning.

PROTAGORAS: You may make a new beginning, but you shall still have balance scales. You yourself have said that justice is achieved by weighing and that weighing is done with balance scales. How then would you have justice without the scales? Even the etymology of the word requires the scales.

AUTHOR: Then we shall have not justice but rather good behavior. We shall have what we deserve.

PROTAGORAS: You shall all be hanged.[1]

AUTHOR: I mean that we shall have our lives and limbs, our freedom and our rights, our wealth and property. Surely these are all secured by good behavior. How gain, then, good behavior?

PROTAGORAS: How then, indeed! Philosophy shall go begging! Teachers will wear rags! Let me hear you. You have said that good behavior is that which injures neither lives nor limbs, neither your freedom nor your rights, neither wealth nor property. All else is bad behavior. That is your problem and that problem is the business of this institution of justice that you despair of.

AUTHOR: This system that we have was made in the marketplace. It has balance scales, prices, payments, because the marketplace was the model. We could choose another model. We have already done this once—with the door. Do you remember?

PROTAGORAS: I remember unsatisfactory results.

AUTHOR: We examined the ax, the bow and arrow, the knife, the adz, the drill, and the sickle.

PROTAGORAS: And would you make your good behavior with these tools?

AUTHOR: I was thinking that we should go to where these tools are used, as once we went to the marketplace. There we could consider how good behavior should be made. Or—if you wish—how bad behavior may be banished.

PROTAGORAS: Then we should go to war.

CHORUS: To war! To war! Where is the cannon?

PROTAGORAS: If weapons could make good behavior we should have had it long ago.

AUTHOR: Yes. We should go to warfare, to agriculture, to animal husbandry, to fishing, to construction, to hunting. The people by their metaphors reveal they know these models well. We shall yet find a model.

PROTAGORAS: All of these are ancient. Is there nothing new?

AUTHOR: We talk much these days of management. We now know how to manage almost everything. We have new medicine and soon shall be immortal. We have new science more powerful than sorcery. We have espionage and surveillance from which no one may hide.

PROTAGORAS: Wonderful! Perhaps we should visit the ancient activities.

AUTHOR: Warfare then. The people speak incessantly of war— war on crime, war on drugs, war on illness, war on this, war on that. They just say *war on* and then fill in the blank with whatever they see as the enemy.

PROTAGORAS: And because they thus speak metaphorically, they are prepared to find good behavior in the warfare model.

AUTHOR: Yes. Here we stand arrayed for battle. Over there the enemy awaits. How bright our armor is, how sharp our swords! The sun glistens on our shields and the breeze unfurls our banners!

PROTAGORAS: How do we know that those over there are the enemy?

AUTHOR: They have attacked us. They have killed, raped, pillaged, and plundered.

CHORUS: Would it not be better to rape and then kill? To plunder the pillage or pillage the plunder? The models you have evoked in us are queer ducks indeed.

PROTAGORAS: This is merely slogan. He provokes in us a noble fury to power us to battle. Think of dead ducks in the mouths of seals.

CHORUS: To war! To war! We shall impale them on our bills!

AUTHOR: Excellent! Now that we have captured the essence of this human activity, perhaps we should examine that essence as model. To be brief, that which harms us, or threatens to do so, must be destroyed. What shall be the central image, Protagoras, the symbol of this new institution in the affairs of men?

PROTAGORAS: The sword of course.

CHORUS: No! The cannon! The seals shall be blown from their pelts!

AUTHOR: A new edifice shall be erected—a new temple—and above the door shall hang the sword. Inside we shall find the war room. In the war room sit the generals. They send soldiers on patrol. The soldiers find the enemy and destroy them. This is the way it would have been save for a wrinkle in the fabric of civilization.

CHORUS: Search and destroy!

PROTAGORAS: Shall you have any rules for this bloody enterprise?

AUTHOR: I shall leave that to these ducks, for they float on water.

CHORUS: You mean *swim* on water!

AUTHOR: Yes. A Freudian slip. You shall write the rules. We will call them rules of engagement.

PROTAGORAS: If you have as many criminals as you say you do, this war must be terrible indeed.

AUTHOR: War is hell. But soon we shall have peace. Henceforth when we speak of war on crime, we shall mean what we say.

PROTAGORAS: You will need many more soldiers. How will you pay them?

AUTHOR: We shall pay them with the money we now pay lawyers—with much left over.

PROTAGORAS: You shall kill millions in the cause of good behavior.

AUTHOR: We have already killed millions for lesser causes. Our justification is clear. Many volumes shall these ducks write. Their scholarship will be ponderous and cited endlessly through the ages. Whole new schools shall arise, specialties shall proliferate, technology shall provide new means. We shall at last be safe from crime. We shall no longer fear the criminal.

PROTAGORAS: I fear soldiers more than criminals. Perhaps we could examine a more gentle ancient occupation.

AUTHOR: Very well. If you wish. Let us go to agriculture. Here on this fertile plain we stand with plow, hoe, and sickle. With the first we turn the soil to ready it for seed, with the second we chop the weeds that menace and imperil the nascent crop, and with the third we harvest what we have sown. Which of these shall be our symbol and our guide?

PROTAGORAS: Surely not the first, for it does violence to earth. Neither should we choose the third, or we should cut down the good.

AUTHOR: Then our symbol shall be the hoe, and with it we remove the weeds. The evil weeds shall look on it with fear.

PROTAGORAS: And criminals are of course the weeds.

AUTHOR: Yes. We plant our seeds in fertile soil, and we nurture them with water when there is no rain. But what is good for nutritious onions is also good for noxious weeds. The weeds must be destroyed; we will chop them up with hoes.

PROTAGORAS: Who shall say which green thing is weed? A weed is but a plant that no one loves.

AUTHOR: Perhaps we should say that the unloved are weeds— and therefore must be removed. To be unloved is to be unnurtured, and the behavior of the unnurtured must be bad.

PROTAGORAS: To be unloved and die for that is heartless punishment.

AUTHOR: You are thinking of the scales, Protagoras. This is a different system, a new age. There is no punishment here, no payments to be made for crimes committed. Those who are removed are not punished; they are simply removed.

PROTAGORAS: If they are chopped down by the hoe, they are killed. Death is painful. Pain is punishment. You may examine your etymology.

AUTHOR: We are reinventing, and soon etymology will take account. The ducks shall write and the hoe shall chop. When bad behavior is discovered, it becomes another reason for chopping with the hoe. It will be effective. Soon there will be no bad behavior.

CHORUS: We shall write and soon there will be no bad behavior. These green heads shall henceforth be protected.

PROTAGORAS: Zeus himself shall frown! Themis shall rebel! Weeds are not weeds by aspiration. It is mishap of descent. They must not be answerable for ill fortune.

184

AUTHOR: Still you fondle your scales. You caress them and try to make them balance, but in this place there are no scales for judicial weighing. This is a different system. The scales here are used only for weighing goods, for deciding what you must pay for goods. If the death of weeds is so objectionable, then their seeds should not be planted. Our new system could see to that. The ducks shall write. Weeds shall not be at all rather than be harmful and thus be chopped down by the hoe.

CHORUS: The ducks shall write. The ducks shall write. The ducks shall write.

PROTAGORAS: The ducks shall write and the hoe shall chop.

AUTHOR: We have all agreed then. Agriculture is our model! The people know it well. They say, "They have sown the wind, and they shall reap the whirlwind."[2] They say, "Whatsoever a man soweth, that shall he also reap."[3]

PROTAGORAS: Perhaps before we undertake this change we could examine animal husbandry and fishing and construction. Even hunting may offer a useful model.

AUTHOR: Very well! We shall take a quick look at these, though I am eager to proceed. Here we are where animals live. Look at these fine oxen. They are enormous, broad at the shoulders, and very good for plowing. But they were not such when first we domesticated them. No. We had to breed them very carefully and, having bred them, train them so that their behavior would be good and useful. So it was with horses, and with sheep, and ducks, and all the other animals that man has taken as his own.

CHORUS: Tyrant! We shall write you into oblivion!

AUTHOR: We are now in another system. You shall write as I tell you.

PROTAGORAS: You have quite lost your head, Author. Was it your breeding or your training that we should blame?

AUTHOR: Yes. Forgive me. The shadows now are long and I am weary. I must not hurry so. Tell me what our central symbol is.

PROTAGORAS: It shall be the shepherd's crook. It is both the staff of authority and the means of sorting out the good and the bad. You shall wield it with righteous vengeance.

AUTHOR: I—we—shall wield it only for the good. The wolves shall bow down before it. It shall evoke in all the image of good behavior, and by this model shall the people make good behavior. They speak endlessly of the value of good breeding—which of course makes good behavior.

PROTAGORAS: And, of course, they shall all rise up as sheep. Virtue shall be made of fear. There shall be no good in good behavior. Perhaps in fishing we could find a model more temperate than this.

AUTHOR: Here by this pond we see these fishermen. They cast out their lines with baited hooks. Look! That one has a bite. He tugs on his line and soon will bring his catch to land. What lesson do we find in this? Will this pond now be safer for the dwellers here?

PROTAGORAS: It will only have less life.

AUTHOR: This fish was more voracious than others or else would not have taken the bait. It lived by prey and no others were safe in its presence. Could we thus tempt evil out of the pond of life?

CHORUS: Would that you could tempt out the turtles!

PROTAGORAS: More likely would you tempt out all vigor and appetite. The price of safety shall be emptiness.

AUTHOR: With hook and net and harpoon we will go a fishing. We shall catch the bad with bait of greed. This one we throw back because it is too small. This one we keep to throw upon the fire. Soon we shall have a tranquil sea. There shall be nothing but good behavior, for we shall make it by hook or crook. The criminal will take the bait. The people certainly understand this model, for when a lawyer looks too far for evidence they say he is on a fishing expedition.

PROTAGORAS: A dead sea is tranquil but has no behavior at all! Eat lustily while you can for soon you will catch nothing.

AUTHOR: Shall our symbol be the hook, the net, or the harpoon? Let it be the harpoon! With dread the shark beholds the poised harpoon!

PROTAGORAS: With dread Protagoras awaits the models yet to come!

AUTHOR: Behold our planet, Protagoras! Plains, forests, jungles, deserts, mountains. Rivers, creeks, lakes, seas, oceans. The canopy of sky above with sun, moon, planets, stars. Where in all of this is man?

PROTAGORAS: It is he who makes catalogs.

CHORUS: It is he who sees plains, forests, jungles, deserts, mountains, rivers, creeks, lakes, seas, oceans, sun, moon, planets, stars. He is indeed a marvelous beast.

AUTHOR: No! Man is no beast for he is a builder, and he constructs of all this his own designs. These stones lying in the fields are but rubbish, but they rise as temples from the mind and hands of man.

CHORUS: Beavers build dams. Birds make nests. Ants erect hills. This list goes on and on. Do we have time to hear it all?

PROTAGORAS: We do not have time to build a pyramid, but if pyramids are built of rubbish we have all that we will need.

AUTHOR: I mean that man designs and then builds what he has designed. With hammer, drill, chisel, saw, adz, man builds his concrete world. By the model of this grand edifice of stone, we could design and build a world community without a place for bad behavior. Such a world would be a monument to the good of man. Bad behavior simply would not be possible. "Build thee more stately mansions, O my soul, ..."[4]

CHORUS: You have hit the nail upon the head.

PROTAGORAS: I see the hammer both as symbol and as chief conceptual tool. Blunt force will make us good. If the grand edifice of which you speak is a pyramid, you have perhaps discovered that a pharaoh sits alone on top. You are thus assured that this monument has no place for Greeks.

AUTHOR: It should also have no place for criminals.

PROTAGORAS: Your world would not be if both Greeks and criminals were excluded.

AUTHOR: I mean that, in such a world as we could design and build, only good behavior prospers. The bad should simply be inappropriate and useless. Every crime attests a flaw—in design or in construction. These ducks must therefore labor until they get it right. After a few revisions the scales will be put away for good, along with the rack, the strappado, the thumbscrew, and other instruments of torture.

PROTAGORAS: Revisions and revisions—and revisions of revisions. You shall put away the scales when doom has cracked the beam, when the pans are sieves and the weights have turned to earth.

AUTHOR: Let us go hunting. Presently we shall dine on the red flesh of our prey.

CHORUS: Ghastly!

PROTAGORAS: You have not begun to know the horror!

AUTHOR: I shall take my bow and arrows and mount my chariot. Drawn by this eager steed I shall quickly catch the quarry. You, Protagoras, shall go around that clump of woods and sound your hunting horn. Frighten the hapless beasts into the open where I may strike them with my arrows. You ducks will take your spears and go to the other side. There you shall cut off all escape and take them down with savage thrusts. Ah! Organization! It calls to mind the days of yore! Man is king of all the earth!

CHORUS: May we remind you that we are ducks, not men? We are much more likely to be the prey. And we trust it is not ducks who are hiding in those woods.

PROTAGORAS: Dare I ask? Who is hunter here and who the prey?

AUTHOR: A striking query, Protagoras. Is it the criminal who hunts—or he of good behavior? Are we the prey? All too often, I believe, you lawyers make game of good behavior.

PROTAGORAS: Our symbol is an arrow crossed upon a bow. Splendid! Justice is now a blood sport!

AUTHOR: I mean that this model should teach us to be heedful of who is hunter and who the prey. Whose flesh is to be upon the table? The better order and the greater power belong to those of good behavior, but it is the criminal who by nature hunts. We of good behavior must be stung into the field to track the wicked down. And when we catch him in our gentle nets, your system is wont to set him free again.

CHORUS: We agree. Shoot the bad and spare the ducks.

AUTHOR: I agree. I would have a gun in every house of good behavior and make every honest man a hunter.

PROTAGORAS: You shall have blood upon the hearth.

AUTHOR: Let it be bathed in blood until the fire goes out!

PROTAGORAS: Blood sport satisfies blood lust. I would have my good behavior made of cool reason, not hot blood.

AUTHOR: You have rejected all these ancient models, Protagoras. Do you propose that only the marketplace can guide us to good behavior?

PROTAGORAS: I have not rejected your ancient models, nor do I dispute the worth of good behavior. My time for all its calamities and wars was not so barbarous as yours, and thus I am unable to accept your ruthless solutions. You have said that you would replace justice with good behavior, but you have thus far proposed to achieve this revolution only by deadly means. Your good behavior is therefore inherently bad.

AUTHOR: The change that I propose can be achieved only at deadly cost. The bad must be crushed or surely the good will perish.

PROTAGORAS: There are no men perfectly good nor any completely bad. Protagoras is both good and bad; so too Author and all these elegant ducks. Tell me if I am to die because I am bad or live because I am good. The world is much changed if I may do both at once.

AUTHOR: Philosopher!

PROTAGORAS: Philosopher, yes. Your history tells you so.

AUTHOR: Then philosophize! Show me how to get good behavior out of these models that you do not reject!

PROTAGORAS: Shall we begin with agriculture? As I labor in my ancient field of corn, I meditate upon the little pains of being. My hoe points to a novel thought. This weed—I say to myself—is like the greed that steals my gold. It shall therefore not flourish with the corn, for it diminishes both the corn and me. Behold! I chop it down, and when it grows again I will chop it down again.

AUTHOR: You chop only at bad behavior. The thief will come back again.

PROTAGORAS: Perhaps. My civil soul detests the violence of positive restraint. Let the hoe of justice do that work.

AUTHOR: Justice! The scales again! You have learned nothing!

PROTAGORAS: I have learned this: the work of the hoe must never cease, for the ground where justice thrives is also good for crime. I must forever tend my field with vigilance. Watch my hoe. Even as I chop these weeds with careful vigor, so would I prosecute all crimes both large and small.

AUTHOR: You have skipped over warfare. Is this because warfare is not careful, not the child of quiet deliberation?

PROTAGORAS: No. Because I do not wish to be at war with myself. I have found nothing in that model that does not propose attack upon the civil body. Justice proceeds by exacting steps, not by marching to the drum. And you have said that war is the root of pious bombast.

AUTHOR: Justice proceeds by weighing with the scales.

CHORUS: Author proceeds by pious bombast. Let Protagoras proceed to animal husbandry—and elegant ducks.

PROTAGORAS: When I behold a splendid horse, I see the hand of man. I know that such an animal could not be except that man has bred and nurtured him.

CHORUS: And when you behold a duck?

AUTHOR: He sees a splendid roast.

CHORUS: Abomination!

PROTAGORAS: I know too that such a man as Alexander could not be except that he was bred to conquer, that he was nurtured by the wisdom of philosophy. Alexander, the man and god, Bucephalus, the great steed on which he rode in battle, both came forth by human plan. It was Aristotle who made of him the creator of a world, the trainer who made Bucephalus a worthy mount. Breeding and learning. I cannot meditate on these without reflecting on the stunted state of man.

AUTHOR: How do you differ from me in this matter of good breeding?

PROTAGORAS: You would breed servile sheep and I great horses.

AUTHOR: Great war-horses, then?

PROTAGORAS: No. Great of stature, great of dignity, great of deed. Greatness is not wrought all of good or all of bad. The alloy is as manifest by trial.

CHORUS: Yes. A great duck is as a great duck does.

AUTHOR: We should see who would make the best behavior!

PROTAGORAS: We should but shall not. The man who overreaches is humbled by the gods.

AUTHOR: The man who underreaches is condemned by fate. You have seen that in my time the line of Agamemnon falters.

PROTAGORAS: I have seen too little wisdom—and too much disdain of justice.

AUTHOR: Cast your hook into this pond, Protagoras, and tell me what you catch.

CHORUS: Catch the turtles and rid the world of demons!

PROTAGORAS: Fishing is good for contemplation, for under this bright surface dark mysteries abide. I cast my line for secrets, not for perils to exterminate. A turtle could indeed outplay my hook, but I may catch a pearl. What I say, Author, is that this model that leads you to murderous intent guides me to quiet search for knowledge. If there is any hope for your institution of justice, it will be found in knowledge, not in revolution. If when man first sought the means to regulate behavior he had been fishing by this pond rather than, as you have proposed, trading in the marketplace, he would have thought that somewhere in there was the prize of wisdom had he but the fortitude to fish it out.

AUTHOR: I now despair of reformation. Tell me what model you find in building, the creation of the new by deliberate design.

PROTAGORAS: My hammer would not fall to make a prison of the world nor to bend the glowing steel of human will. Rather would I open ceilings to the sky and doors to wide horizons.

AUTHOR: Poet!

PROTAGORAS: No! Poet I am not, though I have sought the virtues sung by the poets of my time. You have asked me how I would design and build a better world; I would embrace great poetry as design and thus by teaching make moral men.

AUTHOR: You did so in your own time and yet your Greece has vanished—as my own civilization surely will.

PROTAGORAS: I did all I could, and fate has done the rest.

AUTHOR: Only one of the ancient models remains for your examination. What do you find in hunting?

PROTAGORAS: Hunger is a hunter and so is lust for blood. One comes home with food, the other with bloody hands. I have no more to say.

AUTHOR: Then no ancient model will serve the need for change. You have dismissed them all.

PROTAGORAS: None have I dismissed and none dismisses justice.

AUTHOR: You, Protagoras, are but another justice tinker!

PROTAGORAS: A tinker?

AUTHOR: Yes. A fixer. A mender. You will affix another patch to this collapsing edifice. You have indeed destroyed my argument and left me standing here alone!

PROTAGORAS: If only I could say that petulance never wins an argument —or that truth always does.

AUTHOR: You must be kin to a legal scholar of my time who knows of values more consequential than truth.[5]

PROTAGORAS: Amazing! Surely you will tell me what these values are?

AUTHOR: Well, if I read him aright, liberty is one.[6]

PROTAGORAS: Then we may have liberty without truth?

AUTHOR: You must ask our legal scholar. Such a question wears the habit of philosophy and is therefore taboo for me.

PROTAGORAS: What others?

AUTHOR: Equality. And privacy is yet another.[7]

PROTAGORAS: These rank higher than truth?

AUTHOR: So I think he said.

PROTAGORAS: I am too spent to undo such admixture.

AUTHOR: He also said that if truth were our principal concern, science would provide the means of justice.[8] What do you think of that?

PROTAGORAS: An interesting proposal. The balance scales are also an instrument of science.

AUTHOR: Yes. Instead of bringing charges, we would state hypotheses instead. The evidence—which would now be data—would be examined, and the hypotheses would be accepted or rejected by a truthful test. Such vague standards as *reasonable doubt* and *preponderance of evidence* would be ceded to the past. Instead of rules of evidence, we would have criteria for the acceptance of data.

PROTAGORAS: Could you clarify for me the *vague* standards of which you speak? I fear that you mean standards not precise enough for you.

AUTHOR: If the kind of standard I am thinking of were a jumping bar for horses, your horse would never win and mine would never lose.

PROTAGORAS: You would, then, replace these with a *truthful* test of science. Oh, happy modern world!

AUTHOR: Yes! With probability. With a test that is compatible with our probabilistic universe. Would you be satisfied to know that we could test the hypotheses of guilt with abundant certainty?

PROTAGORAS: Again I must ask you to define your terms. What do you mean by *abundant* certainty?

AUTHOR: I mean almost as much as you like.

PROTAGORAS: Then I would like almost *absolute* certainty.

AUTHOR: Neither you nor Zeus shall ever have that, but you will be pleased to know that we can say just how certain we will be. We can say before we apply our test that the results are likely to be wrong no more than one time in twenty, or one time in fifty, or even one time in a hundred.

PROTAGORAS: I would prefer one time in a thousand, or even one time in a hundred thousand.

AUTHOR: Should you make the criterion so onerous, you would almost never convict the guilty. Should you make it much weaker than one time in twenty, you would often convict the innocent.

PROTAGORAS: Then I would prefer one time in a hundred thousand if I were guilty or one time in ten if my adversary were innocent.

AUTHOR: You would do very well in the modern practice of law, Protagoras. The science model is remarkable indeed. The management of human behavior could thus take its place among such human achievements as the blowing up of cities and travel to the planets.

PROTAGORAS: Marvelous indeed! The sun seems to roll along that mountain top.

AUTHOR: Wonderful that you think so! I see the approaching darkness as an omen.

CHORUS: The combatants have worn each other out. No one is left to build the new tomorrow. Alas!

PROTAGORAS: What could be worse than cynical ducks?

AUTHOR: Candid ducks.

12

A Concluding Dialog

AUTHOR: The sun has set, Protagoras, and you have grown very faint.

PROTAGORAS: I have not grown at all; I have wasted away.

AUTHOR: Ah! These models are so troublesome. I sometimes wonder if anyone has heard what I think I said.

PROTAGORAS: If you would tell me what model you intend to evoke, perhaps I would hear what you mean to say. Take some pains to know what you are talking about.

CHORUS: We wonder if either of you hear what you say. If Author is correct, neither you nor we have any hope of knowing what we are talking about. For reasons we do not know we came to listen to this nonsense, and none of us know what we have heard. Perhaps it is only dreaming and we shall soon awaken.

AUTHOR: If this is a dream, only one of you is having it. Do you know which? Only that one is a duck and all the others are thus figments.

CHORUS: Verily, we thought we were all ducks. Please go on with your discussion while we talk this over. We fear we are deceived.

AUTHOR: Take care! Dreaming is done with images and so too will your talking be. And dreaming or not, you are deceived.

PROTAGORAS: It was my hope that I would never hear this argument again!

AUTHOR: Have I answered all your questions, Protagoras? About the collective unconscious? The neural networks of our brains? Other facts you need to refute my argument?

PROTAGORAS: The day was long and my memory fails. Could you very briefly summarize for me the principal points of the argument I am to refute?

CHORUS: Beware! Author does nothing briefly.

AUTHOR: Certainly not as briefly as ducks talk over a philosophical question more unyielding than any I have posed, but I shall be as pithy as I can be and yet leave out nothing of the essence.

CHORUS: Oh, if corn could be as pithy as this Author is!

AUTHOR: Thank you. At the beginning of this day, Protagoras, I read to you some common expressions the people of this land employ as they talk about crime, such utterances as, "He must pay for this crime," "Society does not charge a high enough price for crime," "We must increase the criminal's cost of doing business," "I have paid my debt to society."

CHORUS: Has Author truly paid his debt to society? He owes both pith and substance.

PROTAGORAS: Yes, I recall. From these you inferred that the whole of the criminal justice system came out of an ancient marketplace.

AUTHOR: I inferred that the marketplace was much in the minds of those who spoke these words, though quite unconsciously so. And, of course, I wondered about the appropriateness of such words. How could these persons speak of prices and buying and selling as they voiced their fear of crime? Only because they do not know what they are talking about. After thousands of years of such talk, they no longer hear themselves.

PROTAGORAS: I believe you also found justification in these words for human slavery.

AUTHOR: I did. And I also said that our system of justice has made life very cheap. If a human life can be paid for with a few years in jail—or perhaps no more than a fine—then a human life has only a modest monetary value. Murderers buy lives at cut-rate prices every day. So do winebibbers and others of bad behavior. Ask any judge. Ask him also why I may not do the same. Why should it matter that I would keep the life I buy and not spill any blood? In our system of justice—in this marketplace with its balance scales—all human lives are clearly on the block, and I am prepared to offer a fair though petty price.

PROTAGORAS: I cannot answer now. The day is over and I am too far gone. What did you say of metaphor? That wherever one finds a metaphor one also finds an image and thus a model?

196

AUTHOR: Yes. I think I also said that what we do is usually consistent with what we say, that is, what we say and what we do are guided by the same models. Thus when we say that a criminal must pay for his crime we also establish prices for crimes and then extract payment. Since the beginning of recorded time the most common payment has been the fine—money! The ancient *lex talionis*—an eye for an eye and a tooth for a tooth—is the quintessential rule of the judicial marketplace, but we have always been willing to haggle over the price—in money—of any eye or any tooth.

PROTAGORAS: Some models, I think you said, are more appropriate than others as we attempt to unravel new mysteries of our lives.

AUTHOR: Whatever we do not understand, what is new to us, we attempt to comprehend by means of models that we already have. As our knowledge increases we may find our first model inappropriate, unsatisfactory. Then we may search for a better model. Our conception of the cosmos has grown in such a way. Long ago the universe was a wondrous set of glass spheres, each but the largest suspended within another; now it is the swirling debris of a grand explosion.

PROTAGORAS: You have said that our models are largely unconscious, and for this reason you say that we do not know what we are talking about. Thus when we speak of paying for a crime— or cause a criminal to pay a price—we do not know that what we say and do is inappropriate because we do not know that we are talking about commerce.

AUTHOR: That is what I think I said.

CHORUS: Does he mean that he is not certain that he recalls what he said or that he is certain that he did not know what he was talking about?

PROTAGORAS: How did you explain that the cosmos got a new model but justice did not?

CHORUS: We explained nothing.

AUTHOR: I think I did not, but if you must have an explanation consider that the study of the cosmos led to evidence that destroyed the old model.

PROTAGORAS: And now you claim to have found evidence that has—for you—destroyed the old model of justice, that is, the marketplace with its balance scales.

AUTHOR: Yes. I think I said that the evidence shows that our system of justice is hopelessly flawed.

PROTAGORAS: Then much of our common culture is likewise flawed, for we found these metaphorical balance scales in ancient Egypt, at the very beginning of civilization. We found judgment of the dead by means of these balance scales.

AUTHOR: Yes. And we have found such judgment in civilizations that followed after Egypt, all that we have examined.

PROTAGORAS: But now you are speaking of religion, not justice.

AUTHOR: I am speaking of both, and the essence of both is ritual. Judgment essentially in the form of the weighing of the soul that we found in ancient Egypt has become our system of justice. When demons come upon us, we must have our ritual, and we are unable to do anything else. If we can somehow find someone to punish, all will be well again, the balance scales will be satisfied, justice will be served. But—alas—crime continues unabated.

CHORUS: How many other ill fitting models do these humans have? It is to wonder.

PROTAGORAS: Justice deals with reality. Surely there is a difference between reality and myth.

AUTHOR: Of course there is. Reality is never made as well as myth.

PROTAGORAS: Reality is what we see and hear and touch! We do not make it!

AUTHOR: If justice is reality, then reality is made by magic.

PROTAGORAS: Bah! Please go on with your summary. You spoke of archetypes and replaced them with prototypes. Archetypes, you said, underlie metaphor and thus are fundamental.

AUTHOR: Yes. Archetypes are inherited ideas—fundamental models—that arose from distant human experience. They are the common content of all human psyches. But new knowledge from neuroscience brings this concept—this model—into question, and I think it may be better now to speak of prototypes of our neural networks. These are stored in some physical fashion in the material of our brains.[1]

PROTAGORAS: And are of course inherited.

AUTHOR: The structure of the brain certainly is inherited, but I can say no more. I can only tell you what I have read, Protagoras, and you know very well that I do not know what I am talking about.

CHORUS: We have listened this whole long day to someone who does not know what he is talking about! Refute this madness, Protagoras, and let us huddle for the night. The rats will soon be prowling.

PROTAGORAS: Let Author continue his summary. The rats must wait. They shall have a late dinner.

CHORUS: Abomination! Loathing! Abhorrence! Make him pay, Author!

AUTHOR: Make him pay what? What is a duck worth? Let us see. There are about a dozen ducks here. At ten dollars a head that would be about one hundred twenty dollars. That is what you must pay, Protagoras, should your procrastination cause the death of these ducks.

PROTAGORAS: Zeus defend me! I do your bidding!

AUTHOR: Not my bidding.

CHORUS: Nor ours.

PROTAGORAS: I do the bidding of Zeus, and he would have me refute this argument by means of intellect and logic. I must have a summary that I may carefully deliberate.

AUTHOR: It is not that you must have a summary! I have won you over! You cannot refute my argument and I am lost!

CHORUS: We are lost! The rats shall strip our bones!

PROTAGORAS: And then shall eat the bones! I shall refute this argument with a single stroke of logic.

AUTHOR: Come, my good ducks, let us stand shoulder to shoulder—wing to wing. Our defense shall be our solidarity.

PROTAGORAS: That is what justice has always been, yet you despair of it.

AUTHOR: As do many others of this land. You have heard what they have said. They look at the sacred rituals of justice and see a circus. If this is our defense from darkness and the horrible creatures in it, then we are doomed. Your balance scales have made for us a plague.

PROTAGORAS: The balance scales are but a tool. They do the bidding of him who makes them. They cannot be the cause of the failure of your system of justice.

AUTHOR: He who makes them bids them do magic. Weighing evidence is weighing that which has no weight.

PROTAGORAS: Weighing evidence is judgment! It is a human faculty upon which all civilization depends. The scales are a helpful metaphor, but they are no more than that. In judgment the balance is my servant.

AUTHOR: This servant has betrayed you. Tell me what it has told you. What is the first step in weighing facts? The second? The third? How do I know when I have finished weighing? How do I know when judgment is complete?

PROTAGORAS: You have asked me this before and still I have no answer. Except this: when I tell you that I have a talent of silver I tell you only what the balance has told me. Without it I do not know how much silver I have. Likewise with judgment; without it I do not know which fact outweighs another. When I must choose among dissenting facts, I cannot be without it.

AUTHOR: Why not? Lawyers of my time almost never speak of the scales, and I think that they would never miss them. They have utterly forgotten what they do their weighing with.

PROTAGORAS: I was speaking of judgment, not of the scales.

AUTHOR: When you say that one fact outweighs another, you are speaking of weighing and thus of the scales. We examined other tools: the ax, the bow and arrow, the knife, the adz, the drill. None of these would serve you in making choices?

PROTAGORAS: Of course not! What could any of these tell me of weightiness?

AUTHOR: Nothing. But they might tell you of strength or hardness or truth if you were to consult them as you consult the scales. If you were not the prisoner of your balance scales, you would not think weightiness so crucial. What else can we know about facts as we make our choices?

PROTAGORAS: We know what we see and hear and feel. We make judgments about that which we cannot know with certitude.

CHORUS: Oh weariness! Protagoras is reduced to thoughtless recitation!

AUTHOR: This very day in court we saw and heard—and felt—the failings of judgment. Criminals were freed and victims were invisible. Wealth had great value but human life had little.

PROTAGORAS: I saw only the failings of this judge or that. The institution itself is sound but needs good judges and lawyers.

AUTHOR: Where do propose to get *good* judges and lawyers? Are not *good* judges and lawyers those who have made this institution what it is? Why is it that in a civil action a human life is worth so much more than it is in a criminal action? In a civil action lawyers get a large percentage of the take.

PROTAGORAS: You have lost your amateur standing, cynic!

AUTHOR: You were shocked by what we saw and heard in court. You saw as I did that the priesthood of the law seeks not justice but the preservation and profits of its rites.

PROTAGORAS: I would say that I was annoyed. Shock does not come easily to one who has seen what I have seen.

AUTHOR: I have seen the ruin of justice in my own land and many another desecration as well, but shock still comes easily to me.

PROTAGORAS: What is true and what is false shock you equally. You have deprived yourself of the means of judgment.

AUTHOR: Is it true or false that I have seen the ruin of the means of justice?

PROTAGORAS: Whether true or false I cannot say, but that you say that you have seen it I could not deny.

AUTHOR: Do you by the words you use—that is, the metaphors—reveal what you think is true? At sentencing time, the judge says that he will *weigh* the crime against the punishment. Can you doubt that somewhere in his psyche there is the image of the balance scales, the beam teetering as he puts into a pan first this punishment and then that? He will *deliberate*—weigh with the scales—and perhaps consult sentencing guidelines, which are in fact tables of prices for various crimes.

PROTAGORAS: Yes. I believe that Aristotle himself has said that the measure is always compatible with the thing measured.[2]

AUTHOR: And thus is a crime to be measured by a crime, a punishment by a punishment, a fact—that is, the evidence—by a fact. But how will the judge weigh the crime against the punishment? How will he measure the crime by means of the punishment or the punishment by means of the crime? I think that I have shown you that in this land the severity of the punishment is not a measure of the evil of the crime and that the evil of the crime does not forecast the severity of the punishment. If crime and punishment ever were compatible they are not now.

PROTAGORAS: How would you measure a crime by a crime? A punishment by a punishment or a fact by a fact?

AUTHOR: If I put two crimes side by side, can you tell me which is worst? Here is a murder on this side, on this side a robbery. How do you judge this comparison?

PROTAGORAS: Very well! And, of course, of these two punishments, this one is the more to be feared. Of these two facts, this one is the more persuasive. By this alone you cannot make the punishment fit the crime, but do not crime and punishment both weigh something in the scales? Is it not logical to fit the most feared punishment on the most evil crime?

AUTHOR: I have shown you that in this land that does not happen with any persuasive regularity. No! Making a punishment fit the crime is mischief of the scales. Crime and punishment are not the same sorts of things, and you cannot compare them. If you think you can, then you are thinking of the scales, putting the crime in this pan and the punishment in the other and waiting for the beam to balance.

PROTAGORAS: Then a judge may not judge, for you have deprived him of all means.

AUTHOR: I would deprive him only of magic, for the use of the metaphorical balance scales is magical.

PROTAGORAS: How is a judge to judge if he cannot weigh?

AUTHOR: That is a question I have asked myself, and my answer was that he cannot. We have no recourse but to focus on truth, and truth is not discovered by magical means.

PROTAGORAS: Judicial processes focus narrowly on the facts of matters of law.

AUTHOR: Judicial processes focus too narrowly because the balance scales are at the center. All attention is on that which is in the scale pans. A broader view would certainly include other ways to solutions for this problem of crime.

PROTAGORAS: We attempted to find other ways and we failed.

AUTHOR: We searched in the past.

PROTAGORAS: The past, then, is a poor guide and is to be ignored. Why then do you boast of being Greek?

AUTHOR: Any progress we make is a result of overcoming the past. When we are in jeopardy we throw the baggage of the past overboard in an effort to save ourselves, and thus are we liberated.

PROTAGORAS: Please! I beg you. Complete your summary. It is dark and I must be gone to Hades.

AUTHOR: Do you recall that we examined trials as ritual and speculated a bit about where the form of such ritual came from?

PROTAGORAS: I do, and I wondered at such a novel conception.

AUTHOR: It was by no means novel. It is far too obvious to be novel. I have read or heard this notion elsewhere, but I do not recall a serious scholarly treatment, only fanciful characterization, as in calling a trial a circus.

PROTAGORAS: Your treatment was, however, serious and scholarly.

AUTHOR: I made no such claim, but now I am able to see a trial in no other way. Perhaps when you refute this argument of mine, I will be able once again to see the proceedings of the law in all their majesty.

PROTAGORAS: Finish your summary and I shall refute it.

AUTHOR: I have finished my summary.

CHORUS: And a marvelous summary it was, too! All the major points, most concisely. An unfailing recapitulation, wonderfully brief. Would that our feathers covered our bodies as well.

AUTHOR: So, now, Protagoras, refute! Prove me wrong. You could—if it were your whim—prove me right, but I beg you to prove me wrong. Why do you hesitate?

PROTAGORAS: This that I thought could never be has come to pass! Where is justice now? Great Zeus send me back to Hades!

AUTHOR: She is where you left her, in the dust!

PROTAGORAS: This was not my doing. I followed rules.

AUTHOR: No! You made the rules.

PROTAGORAS: Great Zeus, now take my hated tongue and with mercy make it into dung!

CHORUS: A couplet! Exit ducks!

AUTHOR: No! Wait! He is not to blame. I retract my charge. We have naught to blame but archetypes. They are the villains of this piece.

CHORUS: We thought you had decided on prototypes.

AUTHOR: Whatever they are, they have done us in. What do you say to that, Protagoras?

PROTAGORAS: A moment, please. I must compose myself... I am recovered. You know, Author, that I am not here by choice. I was sent by powers that may not be denied.

AUTHOR: Yes, I know. Because of the importance of this matter, I decided to go right to the primeval summit.

PROTAGORAS: What I do not understand is why I was chosen. When you made your request, or prayer, or whatever it was, what did you say? Do you happen to remember your exact words?

AUTHOR: Of course I remember. I said, "Get me a good lawyer."

NOTES

Foreword

1. I put this note here so that I would not forget where the word came from: *metaphor* + *enuresis* (involuntary urination). If you mistake this scatological metaphor for scatology, please remember that it is your mistake, not mine.

2. This is not a new idea, of course. Noam Chomsky thinks that such efforts as mine have tended to characterize the study of language. Noam Chomsky, *Knowledge of Language*, p. 1. Since I have focused narrowly on metaphor and its related concepts, I will not consider myself the target of any criticism of old-fashioned language study.

3. One scholar has already done for certain aspects of social policy what I have attempted to do for criminal justice. See Donald A. Schön, "Generative metaphor: A perspective on problem-setting in social policy," in *Metaphor and Thought*, ed. Andrew Ortony.

Chapter 1

1. All of these comments are from ordinary media sources. Because there is nothing unusual about them, I have not identified the sources individually.

2. An average sentence of seven years for murder appears to be well established in common knowledge if not in fact. I have read and heard this average many times but cannot cite a particular source.

3. Summaries of experimental studies of the effects of punishment are to be found in most general textbooks on psychology. At the moment I am looking at Ernest R. Hilgard and Gordon H. Bower, *Theories of Learning* (3rd edition), an old textbook still on my shelves. Once again I note the questionable effectiveness of punishment delayed (p. 139), which is the only punishment in our criminal justice system.

Chapter 2

1. This quotation is from an electronic text version of Aristotle's *Poetics, XXII*, as translated by S. H. Butcher. A page number is not

given because page numbers have little relevance for electronic text. I have a hardcopy version, of course, on aging yellow paper, but I prefer Butcher's translation. The interested reader may laboriously consult a hardcopy version of this text for the given quotation or get an electronic text version - which should be readily available whatever the year now is - and search it easily with a word processor. For more on Aristotle being wrong about metaphor see also Colin Murray Turbayne, *The Myth of Metaphor*, pp. 21-27. Turbayne has Aristotle saying that metaphor is ". . .the one thing that cannot be learned from another. It is the mark of genius." (top of p. 21) To this I say that mastery of metaphor need not be learned from another, for all humans with normal linguistic ability are inherently masters, not literary masters, of course, but masters nevertheless else they would be speechless. As for this trait being "the mark of genius" I say that it is the mark only of a living, functioning human brain. It is interesting to me that Turbayne cites Aristotle in a passage in which he shows how such as Newton and Einstein changed our attitudes through their skillful use of metaphor; it is my conviction that Newton and Einstein, while they certainly changed our attitudes, did not know what they were talking about any more than the rest of us do. Turbayne makes this point very well about the middle of p. 22 but apparently does not think that it applies to Newton and Einstein.

2. See Walter A. Shelburne, *Mythos and Logos in the Thought of Carl Jung: The Theory of the Collective Unconscious in Scientific Perspective*, especially pp. 28-33, for what I regard as an excellent treatment of Jung's concept of the collective unconscious. I have read much of Jung without getting what I think I understand into any sort of coherent order. Shelburne's understanding of Jung, on the other hand, appears to me to be not only coherent but also confident, and for this reason I cite him rather than Jung himself. For the particular point of the origin of archetypes, see p. 54.

3. See Paul M. Churchland, *The Engine of Reason, the Seat of the Soul*. See especially pp. 319-324 for a quick handle on Author's transition from the archetypes of the collective unconscious to prototypes of the neural networks, but keep in mind that these pages are summary. This book, an essentially non-technical examination of current knowledge of the human brain, is required reading for all who long for self-understanding.

4. "A newly-coined word is one which has never been even in local

use, but is adopted by the poet himself. Some such words there appear to be: as ernyges, 'sprouters,' for kerata, 'horns'; and areter, 'supplicator', for hiereus, 'priest.'" Aristotle, *Poetics, XXI*, translated by S. H. Butcher. Though he speaks of "newly-coined" words, he says that the poet "adopted" them. His examples, furthermore, only "appear to be." Butcher's translation could be at fault, of course.

5. Weller Embler, *Metaphor and Meaning*, p. 37, near the bottom, and p. 41, second paragraph. If you read on to p. 38, you may think, as I did, that Embler, like Turbayne, anticipated my assertion that we do not know what we are talking about.

6. See Note 5 above, again.

7. Sir Alan Gardiner, *Egyptian Grammar*, p. 442 ff.

8. See Shelburne, pp. 38, 39. I find myself substituting model for pattern as I read these pages.

9. See Churchland, pp. 27-34. There are other passages that will do as well, but I find Churchland's discussion of how the brain may reduce a vast sea of unique human faces to a few that are prototypical very illuminating as regards this notion of neural prototypes.

10. Shelburne, pp. 76, 77.

11. Ibid., pp. 6, 7, but especially bottom of p. 6.

12. Owen Thomas, *Metaphor and Related Subjects*, Chap. 2, but especially p. 42.

13. Otto Jespersen, *Language: Its Nature, Development and Origin, XXI-11* (pp. 431, 432).

14. See in second paragraph of passage cited in Note 13 above. See also Turbayne, *The Myth of Metaphor*, about the middle of p. 76. I take this passage to mean that Turbayne understands that the original meaning, and thus the model also, remains alive in what we call dead metaphors.

15. For example see Ernst Cassirer, *Language and Myth*, Chap. 6, "The Power of Metaphor," but especially p. 89. This little book, in the clear English of an appreciative colleague, is not easy reading, and I cannot but think that in the original German it must be nearly incomprehensible, but by reference to my own experiences I think I have gotten the gist of it. I recall one such experience that addled my brain and left me struggling (if not gasping) for words that would symbolically capture the experience. The memory of that moment still evokes in me a mystical thrill, and I am by no means given to the mystical.

16. Ibid., pp. 92, 93.

17. This seems to me to be the gist of what Embler has to say in the chapter titled "Metaphor in Everyday Speech" (*Metaphor and Meaning*).

18. See for example Shelbourne, p.7, near the bottom, and Turbayne, p. 22, about the middle of the page. To these implied warnings against confusing the model with the thing itself, I will add this simple guidance: if you always recognize your metaphors for what they are, you will always know what you are talking about.

Chapter 3

1. This is the whole point of Shelburne's *Mythos and Logos in the Thought of Carl Jung: The Theory of the Collective Unconscious in Scientific Perspective.*

2. Shelburne, pp. 138, 139. See also Turbayne, p. 48 ff. Here, except for his apparent restriction to the individual in the present, Turbayne could be describing the development of an archetype. Of course, the archetype he might have described would make this endlessly repetitive series of inferences by every human on the planet unnecessary.

3. Shelburne, p. 41.

4. Recall the title of Churchland's examination of current knowledge of the human brain.

5. Author's statement is perhaps overreaching but for general support see Shelburne, pp. 55-61.

6. Shelburne, p. 41.

7. Carl G. Jung, *Psychology of the Unconscious*, p. 86. Jung cites Steinthal in stating the importance of analogy in the development of human thought. Steinthal thought that the phrase "even as" (as used in stating an analogy) was vastly important. Consider the frequency with which Homer used this phrase!

8. John Searle, Chomsky's Revolution in Linguistics, pp. 20-23, in *On Noam Chomsky: Critical Essays*, Gilbert Harman, editor.

9. See Churchland, pp. 134 and 260.

10. See Churchland, pp. 134 - 139. Note that the conflict between Chomsky's theory of language and current knowledge of the human brain arises essentially from the rules proposed by Chomsky, rules innate to brain structure; according to Churchland, however, neural

networks do not typically contain rules or function by reference to them (p. 135 ff.).

11. See Peter Davies, *Roots: Family Histories of Familiar Words*, pp. 206, 207. See also Note 1, Chapter 6, below.

12. Bruno Kisch, *Scales and Weights: A Historical Outline*, p. 26.

13. See Embler, p. 27 ff.

14. I have no source for this except my own memory of a television production concerning the theory of relativity. Einstein was shown sitting in a rail coach watching a receding clock tower. Imagining how this clock tower would look if he were receding at the speed of light, according to this production, led Einstein to the discovery of relativity.

15. Author has been flirting with the psychology of James Hillman, which extends "... Jung's notion that archetypes underlie and structure all of our conceptions.... From Hillman's perspective, everything must be experienced as an image of the psyche in order to be experienced at all." Shelburne, p. 85. See also James Hillman, *Archetypal Psychology: A Brief Account*, especially pp. 6-15.

Chapter 4

1. That is, a device placed on the shoulders for carrying two balanced loads. See Kisch, p. 26. The root word is Indo-European *wegh-*. See Note 1, Chapter 6.

2. Adolf Erman, *Life in Ancient Egypt*, pp. 92-95, especially illustration on p. 95.

3. *The Cambridge Ancient History*, Third Edition, Vol. I, Part 2, Early History of the Middle East, p. 38.

4. Ibid., p. 36 ff.

5. Erman, pp. 108-109.

6. E. A. Wallis Budge, *The Gods of the Egyptians*, Vol. 1, pp. 24-25.

7. A. E. Berriman, *Historical Metrology*, pp. 85-90.

8. Sir Flinders Petrie, "Weights and Measures," *Encyclopaedia Britannica*, 9th Edition, Vol. XXIV, pp. 478-91.

9. Kisch, p. 30, Figure 4.

10. R. O. Faulkner, translator, *The Ancient Egyptian Book of the Dead*, pp. 56, 57.

11. Thomas George Allen, translator, *The Book of the Dead or Going Forth by Day*, p. 1.

12. Erman, pp. 269-272.

13. Ibid., pp. 44, 45.

14. Faulkner, *The Ancient Egyptian Book of the Dead*, p. 27.

15. R. O. Faulkner, *The Ancient Egyptian Coffin Texts*, Vol. 2, p. 84, Spell 452.

16. Apparently no earlier than about 1310 BC, according to R. O. Faulkner's dating.

17. As regards this contention, it is interesting to note such ancient Egyptian words as *Sw* (the air god Shu), *sw* (ascend), and *sw* (sun, which also rises). Each includes the feather hieroglyph. It is also interesting to note certain ancient Egyptian expressions — or rather translations of them — that support the notion that the desire was to see the truth rise. Among these are "May he not be found to be light in the balance..." (E. A. Wallace Budge, *The Book of the Dead*, p. 362), for if he were light the truth would not rise. In *The Book of the Dead* as translated by Thomas George Allen, p. 84, "... may truth rise to the nose of Re..." likewise supports this notion. S. G. F. Brandon saw the Egyptian conception of the weighing of the heart, as described in Spell 30 in *The Book of the Dead*, as representing a test of the truthfulness of the declaration of innocence, the so-called negative confession in Spell 125 (*The Judgment of the Dead*, p. 40). Thus, the weighing of the heart may be seen as a proceeding in a judicial trial. It may be that the "truth rising" idea may yet survive in a formulation that modern lawyers and judges employ: "(something) does not rise to the level of (something)."

18. Alan H. Gardiner, "The Eloquent Peasant," p. 13, *Journal of Egyptian Archeology*, 9 (1923).

19. Ibid., pp. 11-14.

20. Ibid., p. 10, Note 4. Gardiner cites Pierre Lacau, *Textes Religieux Egyptiens*, 37, 3, for the "balance of Re"; this is equivalent to Spell 452 (Vol. 2, p. 84) in Faulkner, *The Ancient Egyptian Coffin Texts*.

21. Ibid., p. 6. Gardiner notes that this tale seemed to be popular during the twelfth and following Egyptian dynasties; thus it probably should not be dated earlier than about the 20th century BC.

22. Faulkner, *The Ancient Egyptian Coffin Texts*, Vol. 1, p. 265 (Spell 335, Part II). This same metaphor is to be found in *The Book of the Dead*, Spell 17 (as translated by Faulkner, p. 48, and by Allen, p. 30).

23. That this was the beginning of the judicial metaphor is only conjecture, of course, but it seems to me to be as good a candidate as the one Gardiner offered. See Note 20 above. The metaphorical use of

scales in the judicial context of *The Eloquent Peasant*, however, would seem to be roughly contemporary with the coffin texts from which these two candidates came, and if there is any way to make them clearly antecedent to *The Eloquent Peasant* I have not found it. See Note 21 above. It would therefore be just as defensible to consider the scales of *The Eloquent Peasant* as the beginning of the judicial metaphor.

24. Denis Grivot and George Zarnecki, *Gislebertus Sculptor of Autun*, between pages 32 and 57. For similar judgment scenes see S.G.F. Brandon, *The Judgment of the Dead*, plates between pages 130 and 131.

25. From an electronic text version of the *Iliad* as translated by Samuel Butler.

26. Retrieved online from the Perseus Project of the Classics Department at Tufts University. Homer, *Iliad*, 7.1, Lines 25-30.

27. Author exaggerates. Using the online resources of the Perseus Project, he has laboriously translated some passages, word by word.

28. See *Liddel & Scott Intermediate Lexicon*, Perseus Project, Classics Dept., Tufts University. (http://medusa.perseus.tufts.edu)

29. Kisch, p. 32. See *Encyclopedia Britanicca* (balance) for dating of first use of balance scales as early as 5,000 BC.

30. Ibid., p. 33.

31. Ibid., Fig. 4, p. 30.

32. Electronic text version of the *Iliad* as translated by Samuel Butler, Book 8.

33. Retrieved online from the Perseus Project of the Classics Department at Tufts University. Homer, *Iliad*, 8, Lines 65-75.

34. See, for examples, James B. Pritchard, editor, *Ancient Near Eastern Texts*, pp. 51, 208, 218, 219, 223, 423, and 439. For an example of metaphorical use of the balance in this region in late (c. 900 AD) times see S. G. F. Brandon, *The Judgment of the Dead*, p. 158.

35. Retrieved online from the Perseus Project of the Classics Department at Tufts University. Homer, *Iliad*, 22, Lines 205-215.

36. Ibid., Aeschylus, *Agamemnon*, Line 250.

37. Psychostasia is the weighing of the soul. The term, apparently first used in a modern context by S. G. F. Brandon, has been applied by modern scholars to instances of religious ritual in which the scales are employed in judgment. Gilbert Murray, in *Ritual Forms Preserved in Greek Tragedy*, which is included in Jane Harrison, *Themis*, pp. 341-363, lists Psychostasia among the lost or fragmentary plays of Aeschylus. By reference to Julius Pollux, a 2nd century AD Greek

writer, Murray describes the weighing of souls thought to have been shown in this lost play (p. 350).

38. Retrieved online from the Perseus Project of the Classics Department at Tufts University. Demosthenes, *Olynthiac*, 2, 22.

39. Ibid., Aeschylus, *Libation Bearers*, Line 60.

40. Ibid., Plato, *Protagoras*, 356b.

41. See *Liddel & Scott Intermediate Lexicon*, Perseus Project, Classics Dept., Tufts University. (http://medusa.perseus.tufts.edu)

42. From an online text of the Old Testament, presumably the King James version.

43. John Lemprière, *Classical Dictionary*, p. 670 (Themis); Harrison, Themis, p. 480 ff.; Thomas Bulfinch, *Bulfinch's Mythology*, p. 15 Note.

44. Harrison, *Themis*, p. 528.

45. From an online text of *Pericles* by Plutarch, as translated by John Dryden.

46. From an online text of *Histories*, Book I, by P. Cornelius Tacitus, translated by Alfred John Church and William Jackson Brodribb.

47. From an online text of *The Discourses*, by Epictetus, Book 1, Chapter 11. Translator not given.

48. Ibid., Book 2, Chapter 26.

49. G. D. G. Hall, *The treatise on the laws and customs of the realm of England commonly called Glanvill*, p. xi.

50. Ibid., p. 28.

51. Ibid., p. xxv.

52. Epictetus, *The Discourses*, Book 1, Chapter 11.

53. From an online text of *The Decameron*, by Giovanni Boccaccio.

54. From an online text of *All's Well That Ends Well*, by William Shakespeare, Act II, Scene III.

55. From an online text of *Richard II*, by William Shakespeare, Act III, Scene IV.

56. John Milton, *Paradise Lost*, Book IV, Lines 993-1005.

57. From an online text of *Measure for Measure*, by William Shakespeare, Act IV, Scene II.

58. Voltaire, *Candide*; Rousseau, *Confessions*; Nietzsche, *Thus Spake Zarathustra*.

59. Ralph Waldo Emerson, *Essays*, IV. Spiritual Laws; Nathaniel Hawthorne, *The House of the Seven Gables*; Herman Melville, *Moby Dick*, Chap. 1.

Chapter 5

1. From an online text of *The Code of Hammurabi*, translated by L. W. King, items 206 and 207. Protagoras is of course a free-born man, and if Author were to murder him, rather than, as he swore, unintentionally injure him, he would pay with his life. The conversion of one half mina to $160 accomplished as follows: According to *Encyclopaedia Britannica*, Ninth Edition, Vol. XXIV, Weights and Measures (Sir Flinders Petrie), p. 486, the weight of a mina in the so-called "light" Assyrian system was 7,750 grains [about 1 lb. English]. The current price of silver is assumed to be $20 per ounce, thus yielding $160 for 8 ounces or about one half mina.

2. Alan H. Gardiner, *The Eloquent Peasant*, p. 13. (at line B1, 148 or 149), *Journal of Egyptian Archeology*, 9 (1923).

3. W. K. Simpson, *The Literature of Ancient Egypt*, p.39, as translated by R. O. Faulkner: "Deal punishment to him who ought to be punished."

4. R. O. Faulkner, *A Concise Dictionary of Middle Egyptian*, p. 16.

5. Gerald E. Kadish, Professor of History and Near Eastern Studies, Department of History, Binghamton University (SUNY), Binghamton, NY, by e-mail, Jan 31,1996. Professor Kadish considers Faulkner's rendering of the Egyptian word as pay, in his *Dictionary of Middle Egyptian*, "a bit mysterious" because Faulkner cited the passage from *The Eloquent Peasant* in support of this rendering even though he himself rendered it as deal in his translation of the same passage. Nevertheless, Professor Kadish accepts the meaning pay in this passage as translated by Faulkner, though with a restriction. In a subsequent e-mail communication (Feb. 5, 1996) Professor Kadish said this: "I'm a bit uneasy about this use of 'pay'. Clearly it is intended in the sense of the criminal having punishment meted out to him, but it is less clear that you have an instance in the sense of paying for one's crime. I do not think it is much of a jump from one to the other, but I am not quite clear that we have the latter case here. We have here 'pay out to', but not, I think, to pay in this sort of intransitive sense." This restriction, however, does not harm the point Author wants to make; he wants only to show that there was an instance of a metaphorical use of a pay word in ancient Egyptian.

6. E-mail consultation with Andrew Gross and Daniel Oden, New York University, 12 thru 21 February 1996. Andrew Gross cautioned

me to "be careful about retrojecting modern metaphors into ancient contexts..." and suggested that I study other biblical passages that contain this idiom, such as 1 Kings 2:35, 21:2, 6, and Isaiah 43:4, 61:3. This I did, with the help of Daniel Oden and Richard Goerwitz's Bible Browser at Oriental Institute, University of Chicago. Note that the Hebrew verb *natan* is often transliterated *ntn* since in Hebrew, as in ancient Egyptian, the vowels are not given. Daniel found that *nadanu* (presumeably *ndn*), the Babylonian equivalent of the Hebrew *ntn*, is used in the *Code of Hammurabi* (laws 217, 221-225, 242, 243, 247, 251, and others) to mean "pay". He added this cautionary but encouraging note: "Since you are very aware that this is not a linguistic theory, but simply noticing a shared concept between cultures, it seems your conclusions regarding the use of [*ntn*] in the Exodus "...and you shall give/pay [*ntn*] life for life..." is, with qualifiers, appropriate. The idea of "paying" extending from monetary fines or bills to that of "paying" an eye, foot, or spleen, what have you, is what seems to be documented. I'm sure Andrew has warned about the dangers of seeing semantic parallels between languages. But that does not appear to me to be what you are after." (20 February 1996)

7. Ibid., Exodus 21, 22-25 and 1 Kings 20, 39.

8. See Note 1 above. According to this source a talent is 60 mina and thus about $20,000.

9. Retrieved online from the Perseus Project of the Classics Department at Tufts University. Aeschylus, *Agamemnon*, Line 1562.

10. See *Liddel & Scott Intermediate Lexicon*, Perseus Project, Classics Department, Tufts University.

11. Retrieved online from the Perseus Project of the Classics Department at Tufts University. Euripides, *Andromache*, Line 1029.

12. See *Liddel & Scott Intermediate Lexicon*.

13. Perseus Project, Aeschylus, *Eumenides*, Line 267.

14. See *Liddel & Scott Intermediate Lexicon*.

15. From an online text of *The Code of Hammurabi*, translated by L. W. King, item 209.

16. Rev. Claude Hermann Walter Johns, article on the Code of Hammurabi, *Encyclopaedia Britannica*, Eleventh Edition. This material is included with the text identified in Note 15 above.

17. This is speculation, of course, but it is supported somewhat by Kisch's belief that the first balances were no more than sticks, with pans attached to the ends, resting at their middle on the tip of a finger.

The weighing done with such a device was only approximate but certainly adequate for many kinds of exchange. See Kisch, pp. 27-9.

18. See pay, atone, and expiate in *The Oxford Dictionary of English Etymology*.

19. It is interesting to note that the Code of Hammurabi includes the prices both of commodities and crimes. If you want to know the price of an ass for a day of threshing, consult the code. If you want to know the price of stealing the ass, consult the code.

20. For example, see the *Guidelines Manual* of the United States Sentencing Commission. The sentencing guidelines provided by this manual apply only to the federal criminal justice system, but the individual states use similar guidelines. The manual referred to by Author was retrieved online from the WWW page of the United States Sentencing Commission on 15 March 1996 (on this date the URL was http://www.ussc.gov.).

21. From an online text of *Laws* by Plato, as translated by Benjamin Jowett, Book IX.

22. Gerald Simons, *Barbarian Europe*, p. 84 ff.

23. *Grolier's Encyclopedia*, (online version) punishment (article by Patrick D. McAnany).

24. Chapter 1.4 (h) The Sentencing Table, and Chapter 5, Part A, Sentencing Table, in the *Guidelines Manual* of the United States Sentencing Commission.

25. Ibid., Chapter 2, Part D.

26. Ibid., Chapter 1.4 (e) Multi-Count Convictions.

27. Ibid.

28. Ibid., Chapter 3, Part A.1.2. Official Victim.

29. Gerald Simons, op. cit., p. 84.

Chapter 6

1. From *The American Heritage Dictionary*, the Indo-European root words are: *agwesi* (ax), *arkw-* (bow and arrow), *swer-* (knife), *ter-* (drill), *sek-* (sickle), *aukwh-* (cooking pot), and *dhwer-* (door). The Indo-European language is described at the beginning of the appendix that contains these words.

2. S. A. Semenov, *Prehistoric Technology, an Experimental Study of the oldest Tools and Artefacts from traces of Manufacture and Wear*, p. 173.

3. A search of texts available thru the Perseus Project of the Classics Department at Tufts University turned up no ax metaphors in the works of these Greek writers.

4. James Joyce, *Ulysses* (quoted material from an online text).

5. Ibid.

6. Nathaniel Hawthorne, *The Scarlet Letter* (quoted material from an online text).

7. Semenov, p.203.

8. From texts of Perseus Project: Aeschylus, *Libation Bearers*, line 379; Euripides, *Orestes* , line 274.

9. Sir Francis Bacon, *The Essays*, "Of Revenge."

10. Proverbs 25:18.

11. George Byron, *Don Juan*, Canto the Fifteenth.

12. Ben Franklin, a letter to a friend about water spouts.

13. Semenov, p.101.

14. Brewer's *Dictionary of Phrase and Fable*, p. 292.

15. Ibid.

16. Homer, *Iliad*, 16.394. (text at Perseus Project, Tufts University)

17. Ibid. 15.467.

18. Semenov, p. 179.

19. Sir Alan Gardiner, *Egyptian Grammar*, p. 518.

20. Semenov, p. 78.

21. Homer, Odyssey, 9.375. (text at Perseus Project, Tufts University)

22. Semenov, p.115.

Chapter 7

1. It has been reported that, nationally, the average cost to execute a prisoner is $2.6 million. See "Death-row rolls likely to grow," The Frederick (Maryland) *Post*, October 18, 1995, p. A-10.

2. Jonathan Swift, *Gulliver's Travels* (quoted material from an online text).

3. Plato, *Laws*, Book IX (quoted material from an online text).

4. "Judicial failures," The Frederick (Maryland) *Post*, December 23, 1995, p. A-6.

5. "Never any justice for the victims," The Frederick (Maryland) *Post*, April 11, 1996, p. A-8; and "Driver gets jail term in fatal crash," Ibid., May 15, 1996, p. A-1.

6. Plato, *Laws*, Book XI (quoted material from an online text).

7. Ibid., Book X (quoted material from an online text).

8. Ibid., Book IX (quoted material from an online text).

9. *Encyclopedia Britannica* (see trial by combat and jury).

10. *Manual of Model Civil Jury Instructions*, Ninth Federal Circuit (California), section 1.06 - Ruling on Objections.

11. Ibid., section 1.08 - Conduct of the Jury.

12. Ibid., section 1.09 - No Transcript Available to Jury.

13. Author has no particular source for this claim, but see "Keating conviction thrown out," The Frederick (Maryland) *Post*, December 3, 1996, p. A-1.

14. This was actually a quite severe sentence. In an actual case the sentence was even more severe. A drunken driver got eighteen months for killing a woman and seriously injuring another although the relevant sentencing guidelines allowed as little as probation. See "Driver gets jail term in fatal crash," The Frederick (Maryland) *Post*, May 15, 1996, p. A-1.

15. Author recalls that another judge in another (actual) trial made such a remark, but he cannot recall the details.

Chapter 8

1. Ninety percent according to *Encyclopedia Britanicca*.

2. "Area experts say system worked in O.J. trial," The Frederick (Maryland) *Post*, October 4, 1995, p. A-1.

3. "'Trial of the Century' highlighted system's flaws," The Frederick (Maryland) *Post*, October 25, 1995, p. A-11.

4. "Judicial failures," The Frederick (Maryland) *Post*, December 23, 1995, p. A-6.

5. "Hearing weighs judge's manslaughter sentence," The Frederick (Maryland) *Post*, February 20, 1996, p. A-2.

6. Jack Anderson and Michael Binstein, "Burger predicted circus-type trials," The Frederick (Maryland) *Post*, June 29, 1995, p. A-6.

7. "O.J. urged to return blacks' support," The Frederick (Maryland) *Post*, October 6, 1995, p. A-6.

8. "CNN O.J. Simpson Trial - Feedback," http://www.cnn.com, October 5, 1995, p. NA.

9. Ibid.

10. A Titan of Greek mythology regarded as goddess of justice.

11. A goddess of ancient Egyptian mythology who was the personification of law and justice. See Note 10, Chapter 4, above.

12. "Jurors would send system to slammer," The Frederick (Maryland) *Post*, June 3, 1996, p. A-8.

13. "Assaults continue on Bill of Rights," The Frederick (Maryland) *Post*, February 12, 1996, p. A-6.

14. "POLITICIANS SPEAK OUT ON SIMPSON VERDICT," http://www.cnn.com, October 3, 1995, p. NA.

15. Certain judicial scholars hold that man-made law must be in accord with natural law in order to be valid. Natural law is inferred by man from nature, especially the nature of man and his societies.

16. "Simpson trial draws jeers 'round the world," www.cnn.com, October 3, 1995, p. NA.

17. "Prosecutors decry sentencing guidelines," The Frederick (Maryland) *Post*, January 16, 1995, p. A-8.

18. "Leniency," The Frederick (Maryland) *Post*, January 25, 1995, p. B-8.

Chapter 9

1. This comment and others that follow were obtained through a more or less random sampling of those to be found on the Internet.

2. A reference to the O.J. Simpson murder trial.

3. A reference to the trial of Bruno Richard Hauptmann in 1935 for the kidnapping and murder of the infant son of Charles Lindbergh in 1932.

4. A reference to the trial of Sam Sheppard for the murder of his wife.

5. "Lawyers put on show as Simpson trial opens," The Frederick (Maryland) *Post*, January 24, 1995, p. A-4.

6. "Judge weighs coverage of bombing trial," The Frederick (Maryland) *Post*, May 13, 1996.

7. "O.J. lawyers decry family's 'media blitz'," The Frederick (Maryland) *Post*, December 1, 1994, p. A-2.

Chapter 10

1. See Ritual, *The Encyclopedia of Religion*, Vol. 12, Mircea Eliade (ed.)

2. See Note 37, Chapter 4, above.

3. See notes 10 and 11, Chapter 4, above.

4. "Inmate revived, then executed," The Frederick (Maryland) *Post*, August 12, 1995, p. A-3.

5. See Gilbert Murray, "Ritual Forms Preserved in Greek Tragedy," in Jane Harrison, *Themis*.

6. From an online text of *Laws* by Plato, as translated by Benjamin Jowett, Book XI.

7. See Note 1 above. See especially p. 405, right hand column, near the bottom. This discussion concerns religion in particular but Author has generalized to the ritual of the trial.

8. See Note 1, Chapter 6.

9. The maxims are said to be from Part 4 of the California Civil Code: §3536, §3523, §3538, and §3528, respectively.

10. Figures in an ancient Greek rite. See Harrison, *Themis*, p. 25 ff.

11. *The Encyclopedia of Religion*, Vol. 12, p. 406, left hand column.

Chapter 11

1. Apologies to Thomas Carlyle. Protagoras never read him.

2. Biblical: Old Testament

3. Biblical: New Testament

4. Oliver Wendell Holmes.

5. Alan Dershowitz, "Crime and Truth," *Slate* (an online magazine), posted Tuesday, March 25, 1997.

6. Ibid.

7. Ibid.

8. Ibid.

Chapter 12

1. See Note 3, Chapter 2, above.

2. Aristotle, *Metaphysics*.

REFERENCES

Aeschylus, *Agamemnon*. An online text of the Perseus Project of the Classics Department at Tufts University.

Aeschylus, *Eumenides*. An online text of the Perseus Project of the Classics Department at Tufts University.

Aeschylus, *Libation Bearers*. An online text of the Perseus Project of the Classics Department at Tufts University.

Allen, Thomas George, translator, *The Book of the Dead or Going Forth by Day*. Chicago: The University of Chicago Press, 1974.

Aristotle, *Metaphysics*. (An electronic text version)

Aristotle, *Poetics*. Translated by S. H. Butcher.

Bacon, Sir Francis, *The Essays*. (An electronic text version)

Berriman, A. E., *Historical Metrology*. New York: E. P. Dutton & Co. Inc.

Boccaccio, Giovanni, *The Decameron* . (An electronic text version)

Brandon, S. G. F., *The Judgment of the Dead*. London: Weidenfeld and Nicolson, 1967.

Brewer's *Dictionary of Phrase and Fable*. Revised by Ivor H. Evans. New York: Harper & Row, Publishers, 1970.

Budge, E. A. Wallis, *The Gods of the Egyptians,* Vol. 1. New York: Dover Publications, Inc., 1969.

Bulfinch, Thomas, *Bulfinch's Mythology*. New York: Thomas Y. Crowell, Publishers, 1970.

Byron, George, *Don Juan*. (An electronic text version)

Cambridge Ancient History, The, Third Edition, Vol. I, Part 2, *Early History of the Middle East*. Cambridge, The University Press, 1971.

Cassirer, Ernst, *Language and Myth*. Translated by Susanne K. Langer. New York: Dover Publications Inc., 1953.

Chomsky, Noam, *Knowledge of Language, in Convergence*, A Series Founded, Planned, and Edited by Ruth Nanda Anshen. New York: Praeger Publishers, 1986.

Churchland, Paul M., *The Engine of Reason, the Seat of the Soul*. Cambridge, Massachusetts: The MIT Press, 1995.

Davies, Peter, *Roots: Family Histories of Familiar Words*. New York: The McGraw-Hill Book Company, 1981.

Demosthenes, *Olynthiac*. An online text of the Perseus Project of the Classics Department at Tufts University.

Eliade, Mircea, editor, *The Encyclopedia of Religion*, Vol. 12. New York: Macmillan Publishing Company.

Embler, Weller, *Metaphor and Meaning*. DeLand, Florida: Everett/Edwards, Inc., 1966.

Emerson, Ralph Waldo, *Essays*. (An electronic text version)

Encyclopedia Britannica. (Online version)

Epictetus, *The Discourses*. (An electronic text version)

Erman, Adolf, *Life in Ancient Egypt*. Translated by H. M. Tirard. New York: Dover Publications, Inc., 1971.

Euripides, *Andromache*. An online text of the Perseus Project of the Classics Department at Tufts University.

Euripides, *Orestes* . An online text of the Perseus Project of the Classics Department at Tufts University.

Faulkner, R. O., *A Concise Dictionary of Middle Egyptian*. Oxford: University Press, 1991.

Faulkner, R. O., *The Ancient Egyptian Coffin Texts*, Vol. 2. Warminster, England: Aris & Phillips, Inc., 1978.

Faulkner, R. O., translator, The Ancient Egyptian Book of the Dead. New York: Macmillan Publishing Company, 1985.

Gardiner, Alan H., "The Eloquent Peasant," *Journal of Egyptian Archeology*, 9 (1923).

Gardiner, Sir Alan, *Egyptian Grammar*. Oxford: The University Press, 1957.

Grivot, Denis and George Zarnecki, *Gislebertus Sculptor of Autun*. New York: The Orion Press, 1961.

Guidelines Manual of the United States Sentencing Commission, as it was on 15 March 1996 at the URL http://www.ussc.gov.

Hall, G. D. G., editor. *The treatise on the laws and customs of the realm of England commonly called Glanvill*. London: Thomas Nelson and Sons, 1965.

Hanford, James Holly, editor, *The Poems of John Milton*. New York: The Ronald Press Company, 1953.

Harman, Gilbert, editor. *On Noam Chomsky: Critical Essays*. Garden City, New York: Anchor Press/Doubleday, 1974.

Harrison, Jane, *Themis: A Study of the Social Origins of Greek Religion*. London: Merlin Press, 1977.

Hawthorne, Nathaniel, *The House of the Seven Gables*. (An electronic text version)

Hawthorne, Nathaniel, *The Scarlet Letter*. (An electronic text version)

Hilgard, Ernest R., and Gordon H. Bower, *Theories of Learning* (third edition). New York: Appleton-Century-Crofts, 1966.

Hillman, James, *Archetypal Psychology: A Brief Account*. Dallas, Texas: Spring Publications, Inc., 1988.

Homer, *Iliad*. An online text of the Perseus Project of the Classics Department at Tufts University.

Homer, *Iliad*. Translated by Samuel Butler. (An electronic text version)

Homer, *Odyssey*. An online text of the Perseus Project of the Classics Department at Tufts University.

Jespersen, Otto, *Language: Its Nature, Development and Origin*. New York: W. W. Norton & Company, Inc., 1964.

Joyce, James, *Ulysses* . (An electronic text version)

Jung, C. G., *Psychology of the Unconscious*. London: Kegan, Paul, Trench, Trubner and Co. Ltd. 1922.

King, L. W., translator, *The Code of Hammurabi*. (An electronic text version)

Kisch, Bruno, *Scales and Weights: A Historical Outline*, New Haven and London: Yale University Press, 1965.

Lemprière, John, *Lemprière's Classical Dictionary*. London: Bracken Books, 1994.

Manual of Model Civil Jury Instructions, Ninth Federal Circuit, (California). Retrieved online but no longer available.

McAnany, Patrick, article on punishment, *Grolier's Encyclopedia* (online version).

Melville, Herman, *Moby Dick*. (An electronic text version)

Nietzsche, *Thus Spake Zarathustra*. (An electronic text version)

Ortony, Andrew, editor. *Metaphor and Thought*. New York: Cambridge University Press, 1993.

Oxford Dictionary of English Etymology, The. C. T. Onions, editor. New York: Oxford University Press, 1966.

Oxford Dictionary of Quotations, second edition, Oxford University Press, London, 1955.

Petrie, Sir William Matthew Flinders, "Weights and Measures," *Encyclopaedia Britannica*, 9th Edition, Vol. XXIV. New York: Charles Scribner's Sons, 1888.

Plato, *Laws*. Translated by Benjamin Jowett. (An electronic text version)

Plato, *Protagoras*. An online text of the Perseus Project of the Classics Department at Tufts University.

Pritchard, James B., editor. *Ancient Near Eastern Texts*. Princeton, New Jersey: Princeton University Press, 1969.

Rousseau, *Confessions*. (An electronic text version)

Semenov, S. A., *Prehistoric Technology, an Experimental Study of the oldest Tools and Artefacts from traces of Manufacture and Wear*, New York: Barnes & Noble, 1973.

Shelburne, Walter A., *Mythos and Logos in the Thought of Carl Jung: The Theory of the Collective Unconscious in Scientific Perspective*. Albany: State University of New York Press, 1988.

Simons, Gerald, *Barbarian Europe*. New York: Time-Life Books, 1968.

Simpson, W. K., *The Literature of Ancient Egypt*. New Haven: Yale University Press, 1972.

Swift, Jonathan, *Gulliver's Travels*. (An electronic text version)

Thomas, Owen, *Metaphor and Related Subjects*. New York: Random House, 1969.

Turbayne, Colin Murray, *The Myth of Metaphor*. New Haven: Yale University Press, 1962.

Voltaire, *Candide*. (An electronic text version)